Female Rule in Chinese and English Literary Utopias

Utopianism and Communitarianism
Gregory Claeys and Lyman Tower Sargent
Series Editors

Female Rule in Chinese and English Literary Utopias

Qingyun Wu

SYRACUSE UNIVERSITY PRESS

Library of Congress Cataloging-in-Publication Data
Wu, Qingyun, 1950–
        Female rule in Chinese and English literary utopias / Qingyun Wu.
            p. cm.—(Utopianism and communitarianism)
        Includes bibliographical references and index.
        ISBN 0-8156-2623-1
        1. Women in literature.   2. Utopias in literature.   I. Title.
    II. Series.
    PN56.W6F46   1995
    820.9′352042—dc20   94-24666

To Lin Jin
My daughter and friend

QINGYUN WU received her M.A. in English from Southern Illinois University at Carbondale and Ph.D. in Comparative Literature from the Pennsylvania State University. She is an assistant professor of Chinese and the director of Chinese Studies Center at California State University, Los Angeles. She had published three translated novels from English to Chinese before she came to America in August 1985. Her translation of Bai Hua's novel, *The Remote Country of Women*, with Thomas Beebee, is published by University of Hawaii Press. Her research interests lie in Chinese women's writing both in classical and modern Chinese literature, and she has begun a book-length study on *tanci* as a genre for women.

Contents

Acknowledgments

I would like to thank Caroline D. Eckhardt, Daniel Walden, Thomas Beebee, Carol Farley Kessler, Charles Mann, Patrick Cheney, Arthur Lewis, and other professors at Penn State, as well as A. Owen Aldridge, for their support of this study as a dissertation. I am grateful to Nan Bowman Albinski for her generous share of writings and information on Lady Florence Dixie and to Paul S. Ropp for his suggestions for revision.

I appreciate the insightful criticism of my readers, Ellen Widmer and Frances Bartkowski, and of the series editor, Lyman Tower Sargent. Without my colleague Ruben Quintero's careful editorial assistance, it would have been difficult for me to complete revision of the manuscript. I am also grateful to California State University, Los Angeles, for giving me a research grant.

Many critics and scholars from the East and the West have influenced this work. My notes as well as extensive references in the text reflect my admiration for those whose works made this book possible.

Permission granted by the author or the publisher to quote from the following sources is also gratefully acknowledged:

Bai Hua, *Yuanfang Youge Nu'er Guo* (The remote country of women). Beijing: Renmin Wenxue, 1988.

Bai Hua, Introduction to *Yuanfang Youge Nu'er Guo* (The remote country of women). Taibei: Sanmin Shuju, 1988.

Ursula K. Le Guin, *The Dispossessed: An Ambiguous Utopia*. New York: Avon Books, 1974.

Ursula K. Le Guin, *The Language of the Night*. New York: Harper Collins Publishers, 1992.

Edmund Spenser, *The Faerie Queene*. New York: Longman, 1977.

ix

Female Rule in Chinese and English Literary Utopias

1

Feminism in Literary Utopias

Utopian writing, according to one definition, expresses "impulses and aspirations which have been blocked by the existing society."[1] A feminist utopia, like any utopia, is inherently both critical and prophetic. But it differs from other utopias by offering a focused critique of patriarchal oppression and by basing its projected futures for women or for humanity on female values. In *Power/Knowledge*, Michel Foucault says: "The history which bears and determines us has the form of a war rather than that of a language: relations of power, not relations of meaning."[2] Maneuvering within the dualistic structure of women and men, most feminist utopias take the form of an imaginary war between the sexes centered on the issue of female rule. The concept of female rule, as used in this book, refers not only to women's controlling influence in government, but also to their power to change sexual or gender relationships in all aspects of life.[3]

My goal in this book is to transcend Eurocentrism in feminist utopian study by examining the structural theme of female rule, including its critiques of patriarchy and its future visions for women, in a range of Anglo-American and Chinese works. I begin by comparing a pair of sixteenth-century texts, which can be called prefeminist utopias: Edmund Spenser's *Faerie Queene* (1596) and Luo Maodeng's *Sanbao's Expedition to the Western Ocean* (1597).[4] I then analyze three pairs of feminist utopias: Florence Caroline Dixie's *Gloriana; Or, the Revolution of 1900* (1890) and Chen Duansheng's *Destiny of the Next Life* (1796); Charlotte Perkins Gilman's *Herland* (1915) and Li Ruzhen's *Destiny of the Flowers in the Mirror* (1828); and Bai Hua's *Remote Country of Women* (1988) and Ursula K. Le Guin's *Dispossessed* (1974). Each of the four pairs represents a phase in the development of

1

feminist utopian thinking with its unique characteristics. Their mutual illumination supports my hypothesis that the politics of female rule, as expressed in the utopian literatures of both the East and the West, undergo three significant transformations: first, from the negation of rule by women to rule by the female who impersonates the male; second, from rule by an individual female to collective female rule; and third, from ideal matrilineality to anarchism by the female principle.

Feminist utopias can be seen on two levels: as the expression of timeless, universal dreams of the impulse for women to escape and transcend patriarchy, or as the manifestation of the goals of specific women's movements. Because the feminism visible in Chinese utopian writings has not been directly influenced by women's movements, it is on the first level that my comparisons rest. And although they show a clear historical milieu and a thematic progress, they are not confined by temporal and spacial history and cultural boundaries. This cross-cultural juxtaposition will demonstrate the universality of the feminist utopian impulse and of the development of human attitudes toward women and women's political power.

Feminist utopias in English and American literature have emerged in three distinctive epochs: premodern feminist utopias grew under the circumstances of the bourgeois revolution for human rights; modern feminist utopias resulted from the women's movement of the late nineteenth century and the feminist movement of the twentieth century; and contemporary feminist utopias since the 1970s have developed in harmony with feminist criticism and theorization. Although a few male scholars, such as Krishan Kumar, still exclude feminist utopias from mainstream utopian study,[5] the Western feminist utopia has become a prominent political and literary fact: "Utopian society-at-large becomes woman's arena at last."[6]

Conversely, the oriental feminist utopian study remains unexplored.[7] The underlying questions addressed, therefore, are whether feminist utopias exist in the Chinese literary tradition, and if so, whether they are similar in their ideology and devices of literary representation to those of Western feminist utopias. These questions pose enormous difficulties: first, notions of feminist utopia and of feminist utopian criticism have not yet been established in China; second, as we shall see, Chinese literary feminist utopias are not only scarce but also have no direct link with Chinese women's movements.

What does feminist utopia mean to the Chinese? *Feminist*, a term imported from the West, emerged at the end of the nineteenth century. It has several translations: *Nüxing* (women or feminine); *Xinnü-xing*(new + women); and *Nüquan* (women's rights or women's power). *Nüquan* not only catches the essence and spirit of militant feminism, but also allows for the inclusion of men who fight for women's rights. *Utopia* is also an imported term. To convey its double meaning in Greek of *eutopia* (a good place) and *outopia* (nowhere), the Chinese call the former *Lixiangguo* (ideal + state or land) and the latter *Wutuobang* (imitation of the sound "utopia" in Chinese). Plato's *Republic* is called a *Lixiangguo*, whereas Thomas More's *Utopia* is translated as *Wutuobang*. Although in More's case, *Wutuobang* does not contain truly negative connotations, in modern Chinese the term becomes the equivalent of fantasy or wishful thinking (kongxiang).[8] After criticism of utopian socialisms in Marx and Engels's *Communist Manifesto* was introduced to China, the term *utopia* was equated with naïve, bourgeois daydreams. In the early nineteenth century, some Westernized utopian novels appeared in Chinese. They are disparagingly called "political fiction" *(zhengzhi xiaoshuo)* and have been criticized for their fantasy and abstract didacticism:

> Political novels written either by Chen Tianhua, Cai Yuanpei or by Liang Qichao suffer from a common disease: the giant wings of political ideals carry the descriptive pen to dance in the empty air, either drawing fantastic pictures of what would occur in sixty years or arresting illusions of the dream, or portraying faraway wonder islands. All this is but abstract didacticism which, though full of poetic gusto, does not touch the real ground. This kind of novel came into being with the trends of Enlightenment and Revolutionary Thought and vanished like smoke when the modern novel matured.[9]

Consequently, utopian literature and its criticism have been ignored in contemporary China, and the feminist utopia is still perhaps an unheard-of notion. Yet, the question of whether feminist utopias exist in Chinese literature should be answered in the affirmative, because China has two essential conditions for the feminist utopian impulse: patriarchal oppression and a feminist tradition.

Patriarchy is universal in the civilized world. But Chinese feudalistic patriarchy, with its convention of polygamy, was much crueler to women than Western bourgeois patriarchy of the monogamous tradition.[10] Historically, Chinese women were among the most oppressed in the world for three reasons: Chinese patriarchy was the most complete in theory and practice; China had a foot-binding custom that disfigured women psychologically and physically; and China maintained a tradition of female suicide to emphasize the honor of chastity.[11]

Over two thousand years ago, Confucius ranked women with inferior men *(xiaoren)* and yoked them to the Three Obediences and Four Virtues: Before marriage, a woman was obedient to the wishes of her father; when married, to her husband; and in widowhood, to her son; also, a woman was confined to feminine decorum in moral virtue, speech, demeanor, and work. Politically, the Confucian order of *yang* (male) over *yin* (female), which resembles the Western convention of culture over nature, barred women from power in state as well as domestic affairs. In education, Confucianism proclaimed that "ignorance is a woman's virtue." Women were allowed to read only those books considered appropriate for them, such as *The Four Books for Women*,[12] which instilled the Three Obediences and Four Virtues into their minds from childhood. In marriage, China practiced polygamy until 1949. The most sensible advice for a woman was that she suit herself to the character of her husband, or, metaphorically speaking, "married to a rooster you follow a rooster; married to a dog you follow a dog." Foot-binding originated by the Emperor of South Tang (907–960) and popularized in the Song Dynasty (960–1279), externalized man's desire for woman to be a sexual object in seclusion. This cruel practice produced psychological suffering that exceeded even the physical torture.[13]

Both Chen Duansheng and Li Ruzhen wrote their feminist utopias in the Qing Dynasty (1616–1911), the darkest age for women in Chinese history.[14] With the rise of neo-Confucianism during this period, female subordination became most demanding, foot-binding most popular, and the requirement for female chastity most extreme. According to the custom of Lienü, a long tradition centered on female chastity,[15] widows were not allowed to remarry but were encouraged to follow their husbands into the grave. At the slightest sexual provocation, a woman was supposed to commit suicide to defend her reputation or chastity. Female suicide, in fact, was often imposed by the male-dominated family to defend the family honor. Cheng Yi, a Confucian theorist of the Song dynasty, says: "To die of starvation is a trifling matter, to lose chastity is a grave matter." Encouraged by the authorities, Cheng Yi's words became the maxim for women in the Qing Dynasty, and chastity became practically a synonym for female self-annihilation. Yet, paradoxically, although Chinese patriarchal oppression has been among the cruelest in the world, China also has a strong feminist tradition, as revealed by its prehistorical matrilineality, double-track creation myth, legends of women warriors, and female rulers.

Before further discussion, I must clarify the term *matrilineality*. In feminist scholarship before the end of the 1980s, matriarchal and pseudomatriarchal were often used to describe a type of society ruled by women or inhabited by women only, such as Gilman's Herland. But Riane Eisler's epoch-making book *The Chalice and the Blade* (1987) started a conceptual revolution; Eisler argues against the use of matriarchy for societies or communities ruled by women, because in those societies the position of men is not in any sense "comparable to the subordination and suppression of women characteristic of the male-dominant system."[16] Moreover, matriarchy, as the counterpart of patriarchy, suggests domination hierarchies—"the ranking of one humanity over the other."[17] Eisler proposes the new term *gylany* to describe the improved alternative to a system based on such a dichotomous ranking. She explains:

> *Gy* derives from the Greek root word *gyne*, or "woman." *An* derives from *andros*, or "man." The letter *l* between the two has a double meaning. In English, it stands for the *linking* of both halves of humanity, rather than, as in androcracy, their ranking. In Greek, it derives from the verb *lyein* or *lyo*, which in turn has a double meaning: to solve or resolve (as in *analysis*) and to dissolve or set free (as in *catalysis*). In this sense, the letter *l* stands for the resolution of our problems through the freeing of both halves of humanity from the stultifying and distorting rigidity of roles imposed by the domination hierarchies inherent in androcratic systems.[18]

Employing Eisler's distinction, I will use matrilineality to describe pre-patriarchal societies and gylany to describe anarchist feminist utopias like Le Guin's Anarres.

Anne K. Mellor, as late as 1982, still insisted that "no substantiated anthropological or archeological evidence has been found to support the historical existence of a matriarchal society."[19] By matriarchal, however, Mellor means the same as Eisler's matrilineal, and there is evidence that prehistorical matrilineal societies existed in China.[20] Yongning Naxi, a matrilineal model in remote antiquity, for example, has powerfully survived the pressures of civilization to the present day.[21] These historical facts are significant because they suggest that the whole civilized or male-dominated social system is a usurpation. If it were possible to install an egalitarian matrilineality in contemporary China, it would not be a revision but a re-revision or a revolution (turning back to the origin).

Prehistorical matrilineality made female rule very powerful in Chinese mythology, as identified in goddesses such as the "Eastern Mother," the "Western Mother," the "Queen Earth," and, later, the Buddhist Goddess of Mercy.[22] The Chinese creation myth underscores the difference between male power and female power. Before the beginning of the world there was *Hundun* (non-differentiated substance). Pangu, creator of the world, lay inside the egg of *Hundun*. Being nurtured in a state of sound sleep, he grew over eighteen thousand years there. One day he woke up and hacked away at *Hundun*, whose pure, lighter elements gradually rose up to become heaven, and whose impure, heavier parts sank down to form the earth. Then Pangu grew taller and taller into a great giant. He stood alone like a pillar between heaven and earth to keep them from merging together. Pangu eventually sacrificed himself to bring all things (except human beings) into the world. Human beings on earth were made from mud by the Goddess Nüwa.[23]

That Confucius called the matrilineal stage Dark Chaos (another name for *Hundun*) was not an accident. According to his *Spring and Autumn Annals*, at that original time no differentiation was made between man and woman, husband and wife, brother and sister, low class and high class, and young and old. People recognized only their mothers. They were nurtured and grew like children in their mother's dark womb. This picture of egalitarian matrilineality is indeed analogous to that of the time of *Hundun* in the myth of Pangu. Pangu, the man, created the clearly differentiated world, which means patriarchal civilization. Then a power structure was constructed and wars started. In a fit of martial anger, Gonggong broke the pillar of Heaven with his head; the sky collapsed, flames spat up in the forests, and fierce animals fled the fire to terrorize people's lives. The Goddess Nüwa was distressed to see her own creatures suffer and finally mended the sky with molten, colorful rocks. Human beings again began to enjoy a happy, peaceful life, and the universe returned to its original order. The myth of Nüwa gives Chinese women a continuous sense of responsibility in family or national crisis, cushioning the moments of patriarchal collapse. In *Retold Stories*, Lu Xun wrote a new version of "Nüwa Mending the Sky," in which he added a male dwarf who stood between Nüwa's legs, pecking her with Confucian morals. This double-track creation myth implies that the male represents differentiation, production, and destruction through violence, whereas the female represents nondifferentiation, reproduction, and reconstruction.

Apart from this feminist vein in mythology, there is also a tradition of women warriors corresponding to that of the Western Amazons. Kleinbaum says the Amazon was a product of the male imagination: "a dream that men created, an image of a superlative female that men constructed to flatter themselves. Although men never invoked the Amazon to praise women, they described her as strong, competent, brave, fierce, and lovely—and desirable too."[24] Similarly, the Chinese "woman warrior" is a product of patriarchy. But instead of being opponents to the male sex, like the Amazons, Chinese woman warriors are utilized to aid men in their wars in honor of father, family, and nation. During the period of the Warring States (475–211 B.C.), Sunzi, the Chief Military Commander of Duke Wu, trained 180 court women to help expand their military power and conquer surrounding states. In a popular legendary tale, Hua Mulan ceases her womanly work and puts on war dress to defend the country on the frontiers, taking the place of her aged father.[25] Collective groups of women warriors— including daughters, mothers, and widows—known as the Women Warriors of the Yang Family of the Song Dynasty,[26] frequently appear in Chinese fiction, drama, and poetry.

Hua Mulan and the Women Warriors of the Yang Family have been encouraging examples for Chinese women breaking into a masculine world. Apart from these paragons, however, several strong female rulers in Chinese history also have demonstrated women's capacity to govern. Empress Lü, the first empress of the Han dynasty, was in actual control of the country for fifteen years after the death of her husband, Emperor Gaozu. While in power, she reduced taxes, lessened corporal punishment, and established good relations with neighboring countries. Liu Ziqing praised her as "an unusual woman who, with minimum learning, was able to rule a country which had to be rebuilt after Chin suppression and destruction."[27]

The most powerful female ruler was Wu Zetian, the only female emperor in Chinese history. Born in A.D. 624, Wu Zetian was called to court at the age of fourteen as an imperial concubine of the lowest rank. When the old emperor Tang Taizong died, she was sent to a nunnery along with other maids in the palace. Because of her intimate relationship with the emperor she returned to court at the age of 28 and became the empress at 32—that position being generally regarded as the highest one a woman could reach. But, Wu Zetian's ambition was to run state affairs. To pave a way for her political career, she revised the *Book of Clans* into the *Book of Names*, a fatal blow to the old forces of "hereditary aristocrats and warlords". In religion, she conducted the prayer to the Heaven on Mount Tai as the emperor had, and in social reform, she made Twelve Proposals to promote agricultural production and democratic politics. During the years of natural disasters, Wu Zetian put on worn-out skirts to encourage thrift. Because of her exceptional capability in statecraft, Tang Gaozong tried to give his throne to her but met resistance from his prime minister and court on the principle: "The emperor governs the Way of *yang*, while the empress manages the virtues of *yin*." After Tang Gaozong's death, Wu Zetian dethroned her son, Li Xian, and governed the state as dowager. The resistance from Tang loyalists and patriarchal forces was extremely fierce, and she was denounced as Daji and Baosi, the beauties who had ruined the state and caused the downfall of a dynasty in Chinese history. But she successfully suppressed the rebellions of Tang loyalists, along with arguments against female rule, and proclaimed herself the "Holy Mother–Providential Emperor" *(Shengmu Shenhuang).*

Through hard struggle, Wu Zetian won complete political and feminist success. Several provinces reported the transexual change of hens into roosters to urge Wu Zetian to assume the crown according to providential will. Eight hundred common people and six thousand monks, priests, officials, and imperial relatives petitioned for her to become emperor. Even the figurehead emperor, pressed by the situation, asked to be renamed Wu along the maternal line. In 690, Wu Zetian inaugurated her own dynasty (690–705) as Zhou. To consolidate her power, she found a theoretical basis in Buddhism for a woman to rule the world and deified her image as the incarnation of Maitreya. Her reign laid the foundation for the coming Golden Age of the Tang Dynasty.

Wu Zetian was a unique female ruler not only because of her success as a declared emperor but because of her struggle as a woman for women. During her rule, she gave attention to women's religious status, welfare, education, and access to public offices.[28] Naturally, this historical figure has inspired the literary feminist imagination. When Cheng Duansheng's prime minister, in *The Destiny of the Next Life*, fails to run state affairs after the discovering of her sexual identity, Hou Zhi (?–1830) wrote a sequel, *Re-creation of the Heaven*, which calls on the spirit of Wu Zetian. Hou Zhi's feminist voice, however, is still muffled. Li Ruzhen, in *The Flowers in the Mirror*, more successfully realizes the potential of Wu Zetian's feminism.

Because of severe patriarchal oppression, and occasional examples of assertive feminism in Chinese history, feminist utopias might be expected to be abundant in the nation's literary tradition. On the contrary, they are quite scarce. In the eighteenth century, a woman called Chen Duansheng wrote *The Destiny of the Next Life*, a monumental feminist utopian dream in *tanci* form.[29] Because of its popularity, the plot of female transvestism became the norm of women's *tanci* fiction. Hou Zhi's *Re-creation of the Heaven* and Qiu Xinru's *Flowers from the Brush* (c. 1845) both claimed themselves as sequels to *The Destiny of the Next Life*; and as Zhao Jingshen observes, "such works are produced by women who cannot seize political power as women but express their desire by imagining themselves as disguised men."[30] In the nineteenth century, Li Ruzhen wrote *The Flowers in the Mirror*, which is now well known in the West. At the turn of the twentieth century, the famous feminist revolutionary Qiu Jin, in her utopian novel *Pebbles that Fill up the Sea* (1907) used Chen Duansheng's *tanci* form and combined Li Ruzhen's mythical design with Western feminist thought. Unfortunately, Qiu Jin only completed six chapters out of twenty. Bai Hua's *Remote Country of Women*, published in 1988, may be the only feminist utopia in twentieth-century Chinese literature. (Although other contemporary feminist utopian writings influenced by Western models may exist, none have appeared in book form.) The scarcity of Chinese feminist utopias, particularly their absence as the product of modern women's movements, needs some explanation. Two reasons are briefly suggested: first, due to the sustaining power of Confucian patriarchal ideology, "traditional China has been notable among the major civilizations for its lack of feminist protest and of overt sexual conflict."[31] Second, China has never had a strong utopian literary tradition in general.

Four concepts and factors may explain why traditional Chinese women were extremely inarticulate about their sufferings: (1) as a woman's tongue is confined to obedience and virtue, it lacks a subversive vocabulary; (2) "wife accompanies when husband sings; wife follows when husband walks"—a woman cannot have her own head but must become her husband's extended tongue and legs; (3) older women, particularly mothers-in-law, participate in persecuting younger women, partly because of Confucian ideas and partly in vengeance for their own earlier misery, so that women persecute women in a vicious circle; (4) men hear and record only those female voices that defend patriarchy. As in the example of Ban Zhao, a Confucian woman scholar who wrote the *Commandments for Women*—the oppositional voice has been drowned simply by burying or ignoring it.[32]

The war between the sexes is thus fought rather one-sidedly throughout Chinese history. Unlike the Western tradition of battling against Amazons, Chinese patriarchy does not reject women warriors as long as they fight as allies and do not rule. When the war is over, women warriors voluntarily retreat to their feminine abodes.

The issue of women holding actual political power leads to confrontation or open war of the sexes in China. All female rulers, either good or bad, have been regarded as usurpers of state power by men, condemned for reversing the order of *yin* and *yang*, and vilified down through the centuries simply because of their gender. The last empress dowager, Ci Xi (1835–1908), heightened the historical denunciation of women by her abuse of state power in modern history.[33] In contemporary politics, Jiang Qing, the late Mao Zedong's wife, has been particularly excoriated for her wolfish ambition in publicizing the "matriarchal society."[34] She was accused of insisting on a longstanding historical precedent for a matriarchal society and for the exercise of power by women as preparation for seizing state power after Mao's death.

Although English feminist utopias have obviously benefited from the Western literary utopian tradition, China unfortunately does not have such a tradition upon which feminists may build. In the 1920s, Gerard Budok even doubted the existence of oriental utopias. In *Sir Thomas More and His Utopia*, he remarks:

> History provides us with many instances of despotism of oriental monarchs, of a state of deplorable bondage of their subjects of extravagant luxury and fabulous riches, of stringent poverty and dire want, but, although allusions to these evils are made in oriental and Arabic tales, we do not hear of writers who, moved with compassion at the hard fate of their fellowmen, felt called upon to act as social reformers and to embody their ideas on social improvements in a kind of state-romance.[35]

Since the 1970s, however, numerous articles and several dissertations have been written on the subject of Chinese utopias and utopianism.[36] Scholars generally agree that China has three major schools of utopian thought: Daoist (Taoist) Utopianism, Confucian Datong (which has been translated into Grand Union, Great Harmony, or One World, in English), and Buddhist concepts of paradise.[37] In classical utopias embodying any of these notions, Chinese women seldom appear as a separate identity, a single problem, or an independent chapter of history; traditional China did not have a genre of utopian fiction modelled after Plato's *Republic* or Thomas More's *Utopia*.[38] Confucius merely mentions that all women are sisters and that each woman has a home to which she can turn;[39] he has nothing to say about women's share in public affairs. Because he ranks women with inferior men, his Datong is undoubtedly patriarchal.

Not until the rise of modern utopian works influenced by the West at the beginning of the twentieth century did women's equality with men become a part of the utopian scene. In Cai Yuanpei's *New Year's Dream* (1904), a man called "A Chinese Citizen" dreams that he enters a land of freedom, equality, and fraternity where all boundaries and feudal moral codes are abolished and men and women are equal. In Chen Tianhua's *Roar of the Lion* (1905), a village called People's Rights is discovered on an island; its inhabitants practice martial arts, abolish the custom of foot-binding, and adopt Western civilization. The villagers prepare to sow their revolutionary seeds throughout the whole nation of China. Another modern author, Kang Youwei, (Kang Yuwei) can be said to be a radical feminist of modern China. In his *Book of Datong* (1903), he not only advocates the elimination of all boundaries but considers the boundary between men and women the first to be removed, because sexual egalitarianism is the passport for the road to Datong. His feminist concerns include the issues of clothes, childbirth, and education. A worship of motherhood and reproduction, as in Gilman's utopian Herland, can also be found in Datong. *The Book of Datong*, however, is noted more for its ideology than its literary imagination.

The complete version of *The Book of Datong* was published in 1935. Since then, almost no significant utopian work has appeared in China. Several major factors may account for the disappearance of utopia from contemporary Chinese literature: (1) utopias are regarded as bourgeois fantasies; (2) creative writing has been limited to the methods of realism or romantic revolutionary realism; (3) communism, the paradigm of Marxist scientific utopianism, which offers the vision of an affluent society without class, state, family, marriage, or private ownership, has dwarfed all other possible utopian dreams and has become the only permitted legitimate and ultimate Chinese utopia; (4) Chinese leaders, from 1949 to 1972, considered themselves practical founders of an ideal society rather than dreamers. Notwithstanding, the country has engaged itself in a series of utopian experiments, such as the Great Leap Forward and the People's Commune. The Great Cultural Revolution can be said to be Mao's last national utopian movement, which, as is now acknowledged, went wrong.[40]

These four circumstances also help to explain why there are almost no specifically feminist utopias in modern China. We need, however, to understand why Chinese women's movements did not incorporate feminist utopias. From a historical perspective, we may say that the Chinese people have a stronger practical utopian impulse than an imaginary one. In Chinese history, several rebellions have been inspired by Messianic utopianism, intertwined with either Daoism or Buddhism. The Yellow Turbans Rebellion (A.D. 86–216) "marks one of the earliest attempts to actualize a planned utopia in the history of China."[41] In 1851, Hong Xiuquan combined Christianity with Confucian Datong utopianism, roused a nationwide peasant uprising (the Taiping Rebellion) against the Qing Court, and established a utopia, the Heavenly Kingdom of Great Peace. In this kingdom, Chinese women realized their utopian dream for the first time: they walked around in unbound feet, took to battle dress, lived in barracks, and fought and worked as counterparts to men. The Taiping Rebellion also brought successive reforms in marriage and distribution of wealth. Some outstanding women, like Hong Xuanjiao, became officials or army commanders, and exerted considerable influence on the Central Taiping government.[42] After holding onto its utopia for thirteen years, the Heavenly Kingdom of Great Peace was crushed by the combined forces of the Qing Court and foreign forces. Fan Wenlan, a famous Chinese historian, praises the Taiping Rebellion for its "historically unprecedented, glorious, and progressive liberation of women."[43] This premodern women's movement ended, however, with the fall of the Heavenly Kingdom of Great Peace.

The modern Chinese women's movement started at the end of the nineteenth century with the Anti-Footbinding Movement and reached its climax in the 1911 Revolution. Political sparks from the Western women's movement, especially that of Britain, kindled the fire of the Chinese suffrage movement, which "sought gender equality within the structure of parliamentary rules."[44] Chinese women did not win national suffrage, however, until a second women's movement was kindled by the May Fourth Movement.

Following the success of the Chinese revolution in 1949, Chinese women have realized the second stage of their utopian dream. Relatively speaking, they have won economic independence, marital freedom, educational equality, and access to different levels of leadership. This success, on the other hand, has curtailed "the future development of an indigenous feminist ideology and movement."[45] Moreover, according to the analysis of Phyllis Andors, the women's revolution in China is unfinished. The socialist revolution has failed to liberate Chinese women because Marxist ideology lacks "a conceptual framework for an analysis of a relatively autonomous sex-gender system" and because the Chinese socialist mode of production is still structured on a deeply male-supremacist family order.[46] The economic reform movement that has emerged since the end of the 1970s has revived the old patriarchy, weakened women's social status, and even jeopardized some women's economic independence.[47] This socialist collapse, in turn, is conducive to the rise of a new feminist consciousness. The women's movement in China, after the May Fourth Movement, was (to borrow Ernst Bloch's words) "at once outmoded, replaced and postponed."[48] It has been replaced by a class struggle and postponed, in that Chinese women still envision a future of feminist utopias. Bai Hua's *Remote Country of Women* indicates this future.

The theme of female rule in feminist utopian literature, East and West, has four phases. The first phase stretches from the Greek myth of the Amazons in the West, and the ancient legend of women warriors in China, to the women's movements in the nineteenth century. In this period of about three thousand years, female rule, embodied by the Amazonian reign or the Country of Women, represents barbarism, unnatural anarchy, lawless tyranny, and sexual temptation.[49] The fantasized worlds ruled by women often end with the subjugation of women to men's law and a restoration of the "normal order." Such symbolic representation of female rule in traditional literature serves to consolidate patriarchal rule, or to educate gentlemen in humility through experiencing an imaginary alternative power. Edmund Spenser's Amazon State and Luo Maodeng's Country of Women are exemplars.

In the fourteenth century, Christine de Pisan wrote *The Book of the City of Ladies* intentionally to reverse the traditional representation of Amazons and assert the plausibility of female rule. I have left this unique French text out, however, as an exception that did not develop into a historical trend. Although the examples I have chosen, Spenser's *Faerie Queene* and Luo Maodeng's *Sanbao's Expedition to the Western Ocean*, both contain utopian elements for women, they cannot be called feminist utopias because of their final negation of female rule. These two works provide a contrast, as well as a historical turning point, to illuminate the concept of female rule in feminist utopias.

Before the seventeenth century, English utopian literature was strictly men's territory. In 1666, Margaret Cavendish, the Duchess of Newcastle, published her *Description of a New World Called the Blaz-*

ing World, the first utopian fantasy in English by a woman. In 1692, Mary Astell published her feminist utopia, A Serious Proposal to the Ladies for the Advancement of Their True and Greatest Interests.[50] During the eighteenth century, several feminist utopias appeared: Sarah Robinson Scott's A Description of Millenium Hall, and the Country Adjacent (1762); Clara Reeve's Plans of Education; with Remarks on the System of Other Writers (1792); and Charles Brockden Brown's Alcuin (1798).[51] In the nineteenth century there was a steady growth of feminist utopias. Those of the early and mid-nineteenth century, such as Mary Griffith's Three Hundred Years Hence (1836), Jane Sophia Appleton's "Sequel to 'The Vision of Bangor in the Twentieth Century'" (1848), and Elizabeth Cleghorn Gaskell's Cranford (1863),[52] resemble feminist utopias of the previous centuries in their advocacy of women's participation in education, business, and marriage reform, as well as their lack of interest in political power. The women's communities created by those utopias signify no real danger to the patriarchal system, because they merely attempt to influence the society around them through their feminine virtues.

By the end of the nineteenth century, women's movements in Britain and America had stimulated the political consciousness of women utopists, who now entered the second phase. Refusing to use women or women's rule as merely a symbolic instrument, the new utopias radically altered the traditional representation of female rule, refuting the principles of patriarchal ideology, speaking for women's rights, and envisioning a substitution of female rule for patriarchal rule as a means to either better or reestablish human society. Two types of feminist utopias appeared almost simultaneously: one reformist and the other separatist. According to Lyman Tower Sargent and Nan Bowman Albinski, the former are primarily British, the latter are American.[53] Among the British feminist utopias are Elizabeth Burgoyne Corbett's New Amazonia: A Foretaste of the Future (1889), Florence Dixie's Gloriana; Or, The Revolution of 1900, Amelia Garland Mears's Mercia, the Astronomer Royal; A Romance (1895), and Cora Minnett's Day After Tomorrow (1911). These utopias not only advocate women's suffrage and involvement in all aspects of political and social life, but also envision women as legislators, members of Parliament, and prime ministers. Their utopian protagonists generally demonstrate women's superiority over men in public affairs and their confidence and capability in transforming undesirable societies into good ones. Dixie's Gloriana represents "the dominant tone and preoccupations" of the second phase.[54] Chen Duansheng's Destiny of the Next Life shows strong similarities to Dixie's *Gloriana* in that the protagonist in both works reaches the position of prime minister by impersonating a male.[55] Their narrative strategy is characterized by an individual woman striking into the masculine world to compete with men and to realize female rule by means of transvestism.

Women's collective rule and separatism are the hallmark of the third phase. Female collective rule must demonstrate itself by separating women from the existing world. This phase is represented by *Herland* (1915) and develops into the *Herland*-type feminist utopias of the 1970s.[56] By visualizing an ideal world governed by female values, these feminist utopias deconstruct the patriarchal world and fantasize an all-female community. Carol Farley Kessler, in her "Introduction" to *Daring to Dream*, points out that half of the fourteen feminist utopias published during the 1970s in the United States "contain all-female societies."[57] This fact well represents women's desire for an alternative achieved by means of political separation. Li Ruzhen's *Flowers in the Mirror* also plays the politics of female separatism, though not in an all-female world. Written in the early nineteenth century, it shed a rather belated influence on the rising women's movement in twentieth-century China, much as Gilman's *Herland* did on Western modern feminist utopian thinking. Gilman's utopian vision contains similarities to Li's ultimate Daoist utopianism. They both tend to reveal, however, a female superiority over the male, as well as an escapism from contemporary political realities.

Speaking of recent feminist utopias by women, Sally M. Gearhart says: "there is a movement towards collective approaches to action, a strong statement of lesbian separatism, an indictment of men as the source of violence."[58] Emphasizing its communitarian dimension, Kessler observes that female autonomy has been viewed positively "as freedom for the development and expression of potential, especially within the context of a supportive community, occasionally composed of women only."[59] However, "several writers of the 1970s have satirized this separatism."[60] Abhorrence of the totalitarianism inherent in *Herland*-type utopias leads Angela Carter to declare in her *Sadeian Woman*, "Mother goddesses are just as silly a notion as father gods."[61] Marion Zimmer Bradley expresses a wish for power balance in *The Ruins of Isis*. No matter what defects *Herland* and *Herland*-type utopias may have, their operating mechanism is the female principle, as defined by Le Guin: "To me the 'female principle' is or at least historically has been, basically anarchic. It values order without constraint, rule by custom not by force. It has been the male who enforces order, who constructs power-structures, who makes, enforces, and breaks laws."[62]

In order to overcome separatism and the potential for matriarchal totalitarianism, without giving up the female principle, feminist utopias of the fourth phase emphasize the elimination of sexual differences and dualities such as superiority/inferiority and ruler/ruled. Marge Piercy's *Woman On the Edge of Time* envisions the elimination of biological sexual differences by modern technology. Le Guin's *Left Hand of Darkness* also fantasizes a world of biological androgyny. Such an androgynous world is "unfeasible," in Herbert Marcuse's sense, because it "contradicts certain scientifically established laws, biological laws, physical laws."[63] On the one hand, it expresses some women's dream of emancipation from the biological chain; on the other hand, it thwarts their feasible dream of "being equal and woman" through sociopolitical means. Five years after the publication of *The Left Hand of Darkness*, Le Guin wrote *The Dispossessed*, in which she suggests a higher form of anarchism governed by the female principle to cope with postmodern society. I choose to analyze Le Guin's later book to illustrate the fourth phase, not only because it shows a political practicality, but also because it identifies utopia with a dynamic process of infinite transformation. Le Guin is politically mature in lifting the sharp boundary between eutopia and dystopia. To her, utopia is, like science fiction, a "thought experiment." The future in fiction, as well as in science fiction, is a metaphor, whose meaning is multiple and ambiguous.[64] Le Guin is profoundly influenced by Daoist philosophy and its notion of "returning." The future, "as indistinct as an ancient past," is "not something to be judged but something rather that sits in judgement on the present."[65]

Although set in a bisexual society corresponding to the fourth phase, the idealized matrilineal society in Bai Hua's *Remote Country of Women* belongs to the third phase. This fictional land, based on an actual matrilineal community existing today near China's western border, bears striking similarities to Western all-female utopias: it embodies such qualities as an extended family structure, a matrilineal rule, the sharing principle, ritual rather than law, and the equation of dynamic Nature with the female principle. My comparison of *The Remote Country of Women* with *The Dispossessed* will demonstrate that Bai Hua's matrilineal utopian model embodies the Western concept of the female principle, while Le Guin's utopia inherits the basic values of all-female utopias and carries their female principle into her anarchism, a gylanic utopia with neither man nor woman in power.

Le Guin joins Bai Hua in using the idea of "returning" to project a future for humanity, not just women.

With an emphasis on female rule, feminist utopias become metaphors for asserting women's competitive power with men, their female autonomous power, and their "micropower" in changing the relations of men and women in education, production, family, and sexual life.[66] Feminist utopia creates visions for individual women, for women collectively, and for humanity in general; its ultimate purpose is to eliminate the sexual power struggle and to create a gender-free anarchism operated in accordance with the Law of Nature, which is seen as the female principle.

2

Monstrous or Natural

The Faerie Queene and *Sanbao's Expedition to the Western Ocean*

In the West, the traditional war against female rule was long ago depicted as an endless battle against the Amazons. During the mythic war between the Greeks and the Amazons, Heracles invaded the Amazon state, deprived the unyielding Queen Antiope of her armor and sacred girdle, and gave her sister Hippolyta to Theseus, King of Athens, as a captive. The captive eventually married the king, followed him to Athens, and gave birth to Hippolytus, a handsome son. Antiope's armor symbolizes women's political power and the girdle her sexual power. Queen Antiope's freedom, because she is deprived of these, means nothing if not death. Hippolyta, the queen's double, survives through accepting the status of a captive, entering wifehood, following her husband, and bearing sons. Queen Antiope acts as the archetype of the monstrous, while Hippolyta serves as the paradigm of the legitimate. In the Middle Ages, the Amazon was regarded as "almost irredeemably pagan, a violation of God's order," and a transgressor of "the bounds of nature and her sex."[1] The war against the Amazons reached its climax in the Renaissance during Elizabeth I's reign, when the Amazon state became a metaphor for "the Monstrous Regiment of Women," as portrayed in Edmund Spenser's *Faerie Queene*.[2]

In the East, the war against female rule is reflected in the development of the myth of the Country of Women. The Country of Women was first recorded in the *Wonders of the Mountains and Rivers* as an independent female state with no association with men. In *The Jour-*

18

ney to the West (1596), it becomes a land of sexual temptation.[3] Although its women are said to be able to run state affairs and do anything men can do, they appear as powdered and rouged ladies who do not really fight with men. In Luo Maodeng's *Sanbao's Expedition to the Western Ocean* (1597), the Country of Women, with its fierce women warriors and sexual violence, matches the Western notion of a "monstrous regiment."[4]

Edmund Spenser's *Faerie Queene* and Luo Maodeng's *Western Ocean* are both allegorical romances with warriors as their central figures. In spite of the geographical distance between them, the two works share a similar historical transition from feudalism to burgeoning capitalism. It calls for a strong nationalism and a justification of overseas expansion, a powerful impulse towards a world-state utopia,[5] and a symbolic employment of women and female power to serve a general utopian impulse.

Spencer and Luo both employ female sexual power as a force of seduction and corruption and view female reigns as political perversions that emasculate men. Female rulers are distinctively portrayed in two types: the monstrous and the natural, or legitimate. The legitimate type, without an independent female realm, takes service to the country as its ideal and assists patriarchal rule; whereas the monstrous female reign is always subjugated by an idealized woman, who eventually hands power over to the male ruler and retreats into a subordinate position.

The General Utopian Impulse

Referring to the failure of prefeminist literature to treat women as historical beings, Virginia Woolf says: "[Woman] pervades poetry from cover to cover; she is all but absent from history."[6] This is exactly the case with both *The Faerie Queene* and *The Western Ocean*. Although lady knights or women warriors fight in many scenes, as women in actual society, they are merely marginal concerns to Spenser and Luo. What, then, are the primary concerns of these two authors of such monumental works making it necessary for them to marginalize women? It appears that a world-state utopian impulse, essentially patriarchal, directs both authors' political intentions and structural designs.

By the sixteenth century, the successes of Columbus (1492) and Vasco de Gama (1498) had not only spurred European expansionists to explore new territories on land and sea, but had also inspired English utopists to search their imaginary maps for an Earthly Paradise hidden in some unexplored corner of the world. While Thomas More used the device of sea voyages to "discover" his utopia, modelled partly after the newly found societies of America, Spenser adopted the tactic of conquering fallen lands to "establish" a world-state utopia.[7] Spenser's utopian dream entails a world utopia governed by Britain, which would conquer human evils and master newfound territories.[8] This dream leads to Spenser's "generall end" in *The Faerie Queene* to "fashion a gentleman or noble person in vertuous and gentle discipline" and parallels his "generall intention" to establish the "glory" of his utopian Faeryland, even at the risk of sometimes overshadowing "our soueraine the Queene."[9]

The Faerie Queene is more a social and political work with public concerns than a book of individual spiritual regeneration such as the medieval romantic epic. Typical of courtier literature found during the Renaissance, *The Faerie Queene* does idealize the court or the reigning monarch; yet, instead of perpetuating the present, Spenser advocates striving for a better government and a better ruler in his New World, Faeryland. Spenser's idealizing impulse, therefore, gives *The Faerie Queene* a well-designed utopian structure. As stated in his letter to Raleigh, Spenser intends the private moral values in the brave knight Arthur to embody the political virtues of Arthur as king. In Book I, the Red Cross Knight's individual perfection arises from his public mission to deliver the kingdom of Una's parents from the scourging dragon. With the Red Cross Knight becoming the patron saint of England in a vision of the New Jerusalem, Spenser establishes the holiness of the Christian or Protestant world. In Book II, Spenser transfers temperance (the Golden Mean) from the individual to the social level, establishing the ideal temperance of Faeryland through a balance between the graceful temperance of the Elfins and the militant temperance of the Britons. In Book III, Spenser moves sexual chastity gradually to a political chastity that controls all other public virtues.[10] In Book IV, Spenser starts to shape the public virtue of concord through friendship, which works as the underlying virtue of the rest of the books. In Book V, through Artegall and Britomart, Spenser attempts to use "justice" to restore the lost Golden Age. In Book VI, Calidore sees the reflection of the Golden Age in the shepherds' community and its destruction at the intrusion of reality. In Book VII, Spenser recovers his utopian faith in the final realization of the Golden Age and simultaneously justifies battling against evils in Faeryland, because all changes are movements towards perfection.[11]

To bolster his general utopian impulse, Spenser employs three

Western utopian traditions: Cokaygne, the Golden Age, and the Philosophers' Utopia.[12] The "Cokaygne Utopia," described in the fourteenth-century English poem *The Land of Cokaygne*, is a paradise of gluttony, licentiousness, and idleness. "Of all the components of utopia, it contains the strongest element of pure fantasy and wish-fulfillment."[13] Like Circe's isle in the *Odyssey*, such a utopia tempts men to seek private benefits and diverts them from their public pursuits. Spenser uses the myth of Cokaygne in the sections on the House of Pride, the Cave of Mammon, and the Bower of Bliss. These episodes constitute "a panorama of the objects of Appetite."[14]

The concept of the Golden Age, founded by Hesiod and developed by Virgil and Ovid, becomes "a standard Renaissance metaphor for the pre-Lapsarian paradise."[15] In Book V, Spenser describes the Golden Age of Saturn:

> For during *Saturnes* ancient raigne it's sayd,
>> That all the world with goodnesse did abound:
>> All loued vertue, no man was affrayed
>> Of force, ne fraud in wight was to be found:
>> No warre was knowne, no dreadfull trompets sound,
>> Peace vniuersall rayn'd mongst men and beasts,
>> And all things freely grew out of the ground:
>> Iustice sate high ador'd with solemne feasts,
> And to all people did diuide her dred beheasts.[16]

Unfortunately, "For from the golden age, that first was named, / It's now at earst become a stonie one."[17] Facing this corruption of the modern world, Spenser attempts to restore social order by means of justice. Although Calidore, the knight of courtesy, gets a glimpse of this Golden Age, this pastoral paradise is easily destroyed by evil forces.

In opposition to Cokaygne, the Philosophers' Utopia is based on the model of Plato's *Republic*, which requires an ideal government and a philosopher-king and maintains a hierarchical structure. Spenser visualizes Faeryland governed by Gloriana as his Philosophers' Utopia. This Faeryland incorporates different classes into a hierarchical but harmonious society. The Philosophers' Utopia is a world of war and change, whereas the Golden Age is the primal constancy. Titanesse, goddess of Mutability, destroys the pleasant state of life in the Golden Age, while Nature restores the poet's ultimate faith in the Golden Age. No wonder Edwin Greenlaw asserts that "the golden age doctrine is the *Faerie Queene*'s fundamental principle."[18]

In Spenser's utopian scheme, the private world of Cokaygne is to be conquered, and the lawful realm of Faeryland is the world's transitional stage to the Golden Age. In this process of transformation, however, as long as the Blatant Beast is still at large, humanity must be content with the Philosophers' Utopia and must put up with the artificialities of the court. This circumstance explains why the Muse directs Spenser from his route of singing "in lowly Shepheards weeds" to the new task of singing "Knights and Ladies gentle deeds" and "Fierce warres."[19] The utopian dream of Spenser's world appears destroyed by his seeming pessimism at the end of Book VI. Yet, the triumph of the Golden Age in the *Mutability Cantos* restores Spenser's utopian impulse as the main artery in his epic.

In 1597, a year after the appearance of *The Faerie Queene*, Luo Maodeng's *Western Ocean* was published.[20] Although written in vernacular prose,[21] rather than in a courtly poetic form, it shares striking similarities with *The Faerie Queene* in both its narrative strategies and its utopian impulse.[22] Like *The Faerie Queene*, it is a romance of warriors replete with supernatural elements, folklore, and legendary traditions.[23] More than superficial historical fiction, *The Western Ocean* takes on the garments of history. The plot of the sea voyage is based on the historical record of the Chinese explorer Zheng He, popularly known as Sanbao, who led seven expeditions to the western oceans from 1405 to 1433, scores of years before the voyages of Columbus and De Gama.[24] But instead of seven separate sea voyages, Luo recounts a single seven-year voyage stopping at thirty-nine countries. Although Luo culls material from history, popular legends of Zheng He, and books such as *Yingya Shenglan*, *Xingcha Shenglan*, and *Xiyou Ji*, he absorbs the borrowed material skillfully into his own fantastic framework.[25]

Although *The Western Ocean* hardly matches *The Faerie Queene* in aesthetic refinement, Luo Maodeng shares Spenser's interest in national and imperial politics. In the late sixteenth century, China confronted the danger of Japanese expansion. Japan had invaded Korea in the 1590s and had threatened to intrude into Chinese territory. Luo Maodeng declares that the purpose of writing *The Western Ocean* is to use the story of Zheng He to revive the Chinese national spirit. Just as Spenser opposes Spanish expansion and attempts to establish a world-state utopia headed by Britain, Luo, responding to the peril from Japan, wants to reestablish the harmonious suzerain order centered in China. Disappointed in military officers' fear of death and ministers' love of money, Luo also intends to educate the gentlemen at court using the form of courtier literature. Although Spenser praises the glory of his present "Queen" and government, Luo celebrates China's past glory and Ming Emperor Zhu's courage in seeking to recover that glory. Both writers design adventurous quests as missions ordered by the ideal court. Luo's story begins with a myth: China's State Seal is carried away to the West by Yuan Emperor Shun on a white elephant.[26] Emperor Zhu Di is determined to find the lost seal and dispatches Sanbao on his expedition. The lost State Seal obviously embodies China's glory and hegemony. Their expedition is dedicated towards searching for the State Seal, subjugating barbarous countries, helping lands in distress, and executing Celestial (Confucian) law and justice. These goals epitomize Luo's utopian desire to reestablish China's glorious position at the center of the world. The quest for an ideal ruler and ideal government constitutes Luo's utopian impulse, just as it does Spenser's.

The Western Ocean, like *The Faerie Queene,* has a utopian plot. The novel contains one hundred chapters; the first seven establish the holiness of Jin Bifeng and his divine mission to rescue the suffering East. Chapters 8–20 praise Emperor Zhu Di for entrusting the expedition to Sanbao and portray the training of Sanbao in temperance and humanity, through incidents such as the building of ships and the sacrifice of sick soldiers to pacify the angry sea. Chapters 21–85 depict Sanbao's and his warriors' administration of justice by punishing state usurpers, subjugating barbarous forces, correcting lascivious customs, and giving charity to poor and weak countries. In chapter 86, Sanbao reaches the Country of Heavenly Paradise and relates a utopian vision. In chapters 87–97, he learns of his own "injustice" through the rebellion in Hell of the innocently killed; by practicing ritual "clemency," Jin Bifeng lets all the innocent dead ascend from Hell to Heaven and saves Sanbao's expeditionary ships from sinking into the sea as a heavenly punishment. The book ends with a scene of the Confucian Utopia at the Ming court.

Luo Maodeng draws his ideas from three major utopian traditions in China: the Daoist natural harmony, the Confucian Datong, and the Buddhist paradise. Daoist utopianism is derived from Lao Zi's *Dao De Jing.* It takes Dao, the law of nature, as the model for perfect individuals and an ideal society and rejects civilization as the root of evil. Its utopia, located either in a remote country or a hidden mountain valley with a small population, has an extended family structure and a scanty but sufficient sustenance. The Daoist utopia is vividly portrayed in Tao Yuanming's prose narrative, "The Peach Blossom

Spring."[27] The utopians come to settle in a secluded place to escape the war and tyranny of the Qing Dynasty. They till the land and live in harmony with nature without any concept of time or evil. This pastoral society resembles the Western Arcadia or the Golden Age.

Daoism is a dual philosophy. The pastoral utopia can be said to embody the *yin* side of Lao Zi's utopianism. The *yang* side is shown in Lao Zi's political concern with a sage ruler and a good government. A this-worldly social vision, later combined with Messianism, becomes a political utopianism most subversive to the existing system. According to certain Daoist texts, once every several hundred years the world is purged by natural disasters, and "the Taoist messiah Li Hung, believed to be a reincarnation of Lao Tzu, will descend to the earth. He will, with the assistance of some divine beings who have already disguised themselves as human beings on earth, give a final judgement to the people in the world . . . transfer the dying universe into an ideal state —a eutopia" ruled through nonaction.[28]

The Buddhist utopian vision is conceived in the antithetical images of Heavenly Paradise and Hell. The former is a place of reward for good people; the latter serves to punish evildoers and sinners. Like Daoist messianism, Buddhist messianism invents a subversive, this-worldly myth of utopia that pronounces the end of the world and the salvation of humanity by Maitreya: "The time of Metteya [Maitreya] is described as a Golden Age in which kings, ministers and people will vie one with another in maintaining the reign of righteousness and the victory of truth."[29]

According to the description in the *Book of Rites*, the Confucian vision of Datong resembles the Western Golden Age, as well as Plato's egalitarian city-state utopia. Datong is said to have existed in the past but was lost because of social disorder. Order, justice, and virtue are essential to this society in which everyone has a place: officials are chosen according to their merits; men and women, old and young, love each other, and widows, orphans, and the disabled are well taken care of. Due to its social practicality, Confucius' Datong has been the most influential current of utopian thought in China.[30]

In Luo Maodeng's call for Daoism, Confucianism, and Buddhism to strengthen China, he blends these three Chinese utopian traditions. Luo secularizes the Buddhist Heavenly Paradise and locates it on the edge of the Western Ocean, which adds Buddhist worship to the utopian characteristics of the Daoist Peach Blossom Spring. He uses Hell not merely as a place of punishment, but also as a utopia where the wronged can rebel against the Judge of Hell and cry for justice. By portraying Jin Bifeng, the incarnation of an Ancient Bronze Buddhist Statue, as a Messiah trying to rescue the suffering Eastern world, however, Luo eventually combines Buddhist messianism with Confucian government and establishes a utopia resembling Maitreya's Golden Age and the Western Philosophers' Utopia.

In Luo's novel, there are no paradises of Cokaygne like those in Spenser's *Faerie Queene*,[31] yet temptations are found in lands with promiscuous women and in the Country of Women. Material temptations, such as the riches of Mammon's subterranean palace in *The Faerie Queene*, seldom occur along the western ocean—as China then was a more affluent country. Luo, however, makes it a point to guard against corruption. On a seashore where poverty gives rise to robbery, Sanbao teaches the robbers a lesson: "Rather hungry with pure water than sated with dirty food."[32]

The Country of Heavenly Paradise, discovered at the end of their voyage, parallels Calidore's discovery of the Golden Age in Book VI of *The Faerie Queene*. This earthly paradise is described by its king:

> My humble country is named the Heavenly Paradise, also called Xiyu. Ever since the Master of the Hui introduced Islam into this country, the whole nation has observed its religious principles. We neither raise pigs nor distil wine. The land is well cultivated and bears good harvests. People here live in peace and harmony and vie with each other in good deeds and charity. Although my humble self is the ruler, I dare not tax the people. All my subjects are free from poverty. There is no begging, robbery, and no punishment. Since ancient times, the ruler and the ruled have been in great harmony and the whole country has been at one with Nature. To tell you the truth, this is a land of utmost happiness.[33]

Confronting social reality, Luo, like Spenser, also tries to establish an orderly Philosophers' Utopia. Even the Country of the Heavenly Paradise surrenders and pays tribute to China, the Celestial Country. Nevertheless, this Country of the Heavenly Paradise expresses Luo's vision of a timeless Golden Age to which a suffering humanity will eventually return. The Buddhist Master Jin Bifeng, the author's ideal hero and human savior, puts the entire country of Safa into such a paradise for five years to let its people escape a three-year disaster.

Jin fails to find the State Seal of China by the end of the voyage. Many Chinese commentators say that this failure suggests the author's pessimism,[34] a response that resembles Western criticism of Spenser's bleak vision at the end of Book VI. I disagree with this viewpoint, for just as Spenser eventually manifests his faith in Nature's victory, Luo demonstrates optimism in his vision of an ideal court with a virtuous, gentle Emperor, who summarizes the seven-year sea voyage as follows:

> During this voyage warriors as well as generals underwent great hard-ships. With the help of the Heavenly Master [the Daoist priest Zhang] and the State Master [Jin Bifeng], our royal virtues spread to the West and won great admiration overseas. However, it was not a good thing to hunt for rare animals and precious stones. Animals like lions and elephants consume food worth ten thousand coins a day, which can well support the life of dozens of people. Therefore, let fierce animals be in zoos and keep them from hurting people and set flying birds and harmless animals free.[35]

Emperor Zhu serves as a symbol of unity in the book, as does Gloriana in Spenser's epic; but unlike Gloriana, who never develops, Emperor Zhu reveals a transformation of character. At the beginning, he cares only for a State Seal carved in precious stone and is bent on overseas expansion. He becomes at the end of the novel a gentle ruler concerned with people's lives and virtuous justice. The transformation of Emperor Zhu suggests, perhaps, the author's belief that an ideal ruler and an ideal court can be found in China rather than abroad.

Symbolic Invention of Female Monstrosity

Both Spenser and Luo employ women as symbolic tools in their common dream of establishing a world utopia by conquering human evils and mastering newfound territories. Indeed, Spenser uses con-flicts between Protestant and Catholic during the Reformation to structure his underlying binary oppositions, but he employs women to represent the concrete objects of the alien. Similarly, Luo uses con-flicts between the Daoists and the Buddhists, but as a superficial an-tithesis. His religious conflicts are reconciled repeatedly, whereas the more deeply rooted, barbarous forces remaining to be conquered are, always, women. Both Spenser and Luo use female sexual power to project their seductive, corrupting lands of Cokaygne, employing female reigns as examples of political anomaly and emasculating monstrosity—the most dangerous obstacle in the path to their Philoso-phers' Utopia.

In constructing the paradisiacal Cokaygne, Spenser either por-trays women as passive sexual objects or as active enchantresses, according to social, cultural, and literary stereotypes. Florimell and her double, False Florimell, are both sexual objects.[36] False Florimell is portrayed as the prize for men in a free-for-all fight, and Spenser's witch constructs this false model of Florimell with negative female qualities, as suggested by snow (false beauty), mercury (inconstancy), and a sprite (wiles). False Florimell's choice of Braggadocchio as her companion reveals women's love of false honor. Florimell, who embodies the associated ideas of woman, beauty, and sex, sparks all men with lewd desire. Even Arthur is momentarily distracted from his quest for Queen Gloriana "in hope to win thereby / Most goodly meede, the fairest Dame aliue."[37] Florimell, therefore must resort to constant flight in protecting her virginity; but she is punished by encountering a more lustful predator each time she rejects a man. Rejection of a man is regarded as a form of female pride, a fault for which Mirabella accepts heavenly punishment. Florimell stops fleeing only when her female pride is taken away by Marinell's first rejection of her love. Florimell's dilemma reflects the conflicting double demands men pose on women—that they both excite sexual desire and possess the grace of virginity or chastity. These double demands are embodied in Florimell's girdle. Signifying the former, the girdle is given to False Florimell when she wins the beauty contest judged by men. As a touchstone of chastity, it enables the Squire of Dames to guffaw at the hidden wantonness and unchastity of the frail sex. Such wantonness and unchastity are heightened in the character Hellenore, who is portrayed as both an enchantress and a sexual object. She seduces Paridell as an enchantress, and Paridell, in the role of a Don Juan, abandons her as one of his many pickup-and-throwaway sexual objects. Hellenore's body and her sexuality also are regarded as Malbecco's private possession.

Florimell, False Florimell, and Hellenore are allegorical women representing basic male perceptions of negative femininity: false beauty, sensual temptation, sexual seduction, fatuous pride, and vanity. Spenser's female portrayals follow a longstanding tradition that begins with Homer. Drawing on such well-established paradigms of negative femininity, he models his other female characters, such as the enchantress Acrasia in the Bower of Bliss, the haughty queen Lucifera in the House of Pride, and Philotime (false honor) in the Cave of Mammon. As sexual objects, women are fantasized as naked dames and mermaids. As a sensual temptress, Damsel Phaedria guides men to Pleasant Island in the Lake of Idleness, thus diverting them from their public concerns. As a sexual enchantress, Acrasia either imposes a death curse on men or turns them into swine.

Spenser also associates women and their sexual power with worldly appetites, the senses, and the flesh of the earth.[38] In a less disguised portrayal, these wanton women are summarized in the image of the Giantess Argante, who was begotten through the incestuous mating of the Titan Typhoeus and his own mother, Earth. Arthur kills Maleger by severing him from his Mother Earth, symbolically purging himself of the flesh of the earth. The Paradise of Cokaygne is the world of flesh. In employing women as the embodiment of flesh, Spenser, consciously or unconsciously, engages men in the war against women and their sexual power, as men struggle to set themselves free from the chains of lust and lewd desire. Proteus originates an evil prophecy for chaste men such as Marinell to avoid women as his nemesis and the mission of Sir Guyon, champion of temperance, is to rid Faeryland of Acrasia and destroy her Bower of Bliss.

Spenser's knights fight with women in the paradise of Cokaygne on private and spiritual levels, while their war against women in the Philosophers' Utopia is fought on a political and social plane. As the image of social evils, woman, combined with Satan, becomes a half-woman and half-dragon monster. The Red Cross Knight's beheading of such a monster, called Error, foretells his eventual defeat of the monstrous Dragon (Queen Mary and Roman Catholicism) and releases Una's parents (humanity) from its scourge.

Spenser stresses the close relationship between man's inner purification and his social quest, as he sees a kinship between woman's sexual power and her political power. The mythological figure combining both is Duessa. A wanton hag in the guise of an innocent damsel, Duessa deceives the Red Cross Knight with her beautiful appearance (the scarlet robe), makes him desert the truth (Una), and guides him to lustful indulgence and the House of Pride. When her sexual enchantment fails in Book I, Duessa reemerges in Book V as the veiled Queen Mary and engages in a political plot to overthrow Queen Mercilla (Elizabeth) and seize her crown. Duessa's double play of sexual and political tactics culminates in the willful rule of Radigund, Queen of the Amazons, in Book V.

Book V is an important turning point in the development of Spenser's utopian impulse. In his earlier books, Spenser examines the correlations between the private virtues of holiness (righteousness), temperance, chastity, and friendship, and their public functions. In Book V, he shifts to society and law. The subject of Book V is justice. Spenser begins the book with his lament over the loss of the Golden Age and attempts to set the chaotic fallen world in order by means of justice. Artegall, a champion of justice, has been trained in his principles by the Goddess Astraea. In earlier adventures, with the help of Talus, the iron man with the flail, Artegall has succeeded in discerning and punishing social injustices, such as treacherous extortion, seditious egalitarianism, property rivalry, and falsehood. Although those successes well illustrate the scope of Spenser's concept of justice, the theoretical argument about justice and injustice is more explicit in the episode of Artegall's plight in the state of the Amazons, which is presented as a fierce war between the sexes.

When Artegall journeys near the realm of the Amazons, he finds a crowd of women preparing to hang a knight. Scorning to fight women, he sends Talus to disperse the Amazons. From Sir Terpin, the knight in distress, Artegall learns that Radigund, Queen of the Amazons, hates all men and knights in particular because Sir Bellodant rejected her love. In her vengeance against men, Radigund becomes a monstrous emasculating agent:

> For all those Knights, the which by force or guile
>   She doth subdue, she fowly doth entreate.
>   First she doth them of warlike armes despoile,
>   And cloth in womens weedes: And then with threat
>   Doth them compell to worke, to earne their meat,
>   To spin, to card, to sew, to wash, to wring;
>   Ne doth she giue them other thing to eat,
>   But bread and water, or like feeble thing,
> Them to disable from reuenge aduenturing.[39]

Horrified at this perversion of the natural and social order, Artegall swears to avenge the injustice and shame inflicted on the knights by Radigund. Artegall defeats Radigund in single combat, but he drops his sword on discovering her beautiful features. Consequently, Radigund captures him and forces him "t'obay that Amazons proud law."[40]

> Amongst them all she placed him most low,
>   And in his hand a distaffe to him gaue,
>   That he thereon should spin both flax and tow;
>   A sordid office for a mind so braue.
> So hard it is to be a womans slaue.[41]

Because Spenser portrays the knight's most horrible fate as working like a woman, evidently he recognizes that women are oppressed and he regards their work as inferior. Yet, Spenser does not have social satire in mind, for he shows no protest against the oppression of women but against their unjust rule that enslaves knights. In Radigund's subjugation and womanization of Artegall, the "faery knight," we can see that Radigund bears all the negative qualities Spenser has been building up through different female monsters. She represents the early Duessa's false appearance, Lucifera's pride and ambition, Acrasia's seduction, and the late Duessa's political usurpation. In addition to all of these, Radigund overtly declares war against all men and subjugates them to the Amazons' law. Furthermore, Radigund resembles the Giant with scales in her demand that Artegall engage in single combat with her and obey the winner's law as a precondition to fight. In positing women's rule as injustice, Spenser denies women's equality with men in politics and opposes government by women.

In the sixteenth century, the reign of Elizabeth I (1558–1603) aroused a great controversy over gynecocracy. Puritan extremists headed by John Knox, with his notorious *The First Blast of the Trumpet Against the Monstrous Regiment of Women*, opposed female government, arguing that "according to the laws of God, of nature, and of nations, women have neither the right nor the ability to rule."[42] Anglicans, headed by John Aylmer, spoke for gynecocracy, maintaining that "women are qualified by nature to govern, and that any woman called by God has the right to do so."[43] To support Queen Elizabeth, the British Parliament proclaimed the legal right of a female ruler, declaring that "the Regal Power of this Realm is in the Queen's Majesty, to be as fully and absolutely as ever it was in any of her most Noble Progenitors, kings of this Realm."[44] Moderate Puritans, headed by John Calvin, insisted on a distinction between the elect woman ruler in particular and the ability of women to govern in general; they denied women the right to rule but made Elizabeth—the woman specially raised by God—an exception. According to James E. Phillips, Spenser's position was "precisely that of the moderate Calvinists."[45] In his poetic rage at the imprisonment of Artegall, a symbol of justice, Spenser quite indignantly articulates a Calvinist position:

> Such is the crueltie of womenkynd,
>> When they haue shaken off the shamefast band,
>> With which wise Nature did them strongly bynd,
>> T'obay the heasts of mans well ruling hand,
>> That then all rule and reason they withstand,
>> To purchase a licentious libertie.
>> But vertuous women wisely vnderstand,
>> That they were borne to base humilitie,
> Vnlesse the heauens them lift to lawfull soueraintie.[46]

This Calvinist position, however, is actually a mask to disguise Spenser's subversion to Elizabeth's reign. If in Book III, he expresses a sincere attitude towards female rule and sexual equality, his later disillusionment with the Elizabethan order causes "a shift in his concept of female sovereignty and the relationship between the sexes,"[47] which is well reflected in Book V.

In using the Amazonian myth of Radigund, Spenser raises three theoretical objections to female rule: (1) the female ruler denatures herself by being "halfe like a man" and men by emasculating them;[48] (2) female rule suggests an inversion of the hierarchical order that is the core of Renaissance justice; and (3) the aim of female rule is to "purchase a licentious libertie."

Chinese traditional hierarchy absolutely denies the validity of female rule and regards the dominance of *yin* over *yang* as the cause of social disorder. In *The Western Ocean*, the domination of *yin* is portrayed by women's participation in men's policy-making and in the system of polygamy. Xie Wenbin, a Chinese man residing in the Country of Luohu, resists Sanbao's expedition on the advice of his wives. Sanbao is surprised: "The husband is the master of the wife. How could a wife teach her husband?"[49] The answer is that the Country of Luohu is accustomed to obey women; all important decisions are made by women, who are believed to be wiser than men. When Sanbao points out that the advice given to Xie is not quite wise, the captive explains that the Country of Luohu encourages its women to engage in adultery with Chinese men. They honor every adulteress by holding banquets in her name and rewarding her with gold. Being born a Chinese man, Xie has attracted many wives and consequently is confused by their contradictory commands. In contrast, the Country of Zufar has many more men than women. Several men share one woman and her number of husbands is indicated by the number of horns shaped on her cloth turban. Some women have three or five and others show a dozen. Obviously due to the predominance of *yang* over *yin*, the Country of Zufar is portrayed as an affluent society, in which people are tall, healthy, and beautiful, and their language is honest and plain; their women do not bother to steal a glance at men. Ironically, this reversal of normal polygamy bears some resemblance to a matrilineal society.[50]

In using *yin* over *yang* to portray the savage western world, *The Western Ocean* is strikingly similar to *The Faerie Queene* in employing women's sexuality to embody temptation, and female rule to suggest political perversion. In the Country of Jinlin Baoxiang, the first western country Sanbao encounters, Sanbao's ships are surprised by seeing numerous flying female heads at midnight. The eyes in those heads have no pupils. These heads swarm in with flames and tumble all over the ships, crying for scraps of food. They belong to a type of woman, known as a Shizhiyu, who can simultaneously fly her head to the south sea, her left hand to the east sea, and her right hand to the west sea, in spite of thunder and hurricanes. The woman warrior Huang Jinding uses them as her last means to stop Sanbao's invasion into her country. This final strategy symbolizes the first sexual temptation of Sanbao's warriors; according to the Judge of Hell, those Shizhiyu are incarnations of lascivious women, who desert their husbands and elope with outsiders for sexual pleasure.

Women's sexuality is more violently portrayed in a metaphor of female rape that is associated with men's death and decay. Sanbao's ships pass a small country called Jilidimen. In this country, men and women both have hair cut short, wear short dresses, and sleep naked at night. When ships pass, it is a common practice for women to board and trade. Nine out of ten travellers raped by those women are bound to die. The first moral victories Sanbao achieves in his expedition are the elimination of all Shizhiyu and the abolition of the libertine sexual customs in the Country of Jilidimen.

Women's political power, like that in *The Faerie Queene*, is exercised through the violence and might of women warriors. In the Country of Jinlin Baoxiang, Sanbao's warriors kill its loyal minister Jiang Laoxing; Jiang Jinding, the daughter of Jiang Laoxing, comes forward to defend her country and avenge the death of her father. At first, Sanbao slights the female warrior: "It's unnecessary to kill a chick with a butcher's knife. Why do we need four good warriors to deal with a woman?"[51] But the fact is that no man can subdue this woman. Jiang Jinding, like Duessa, hides her thirst for blood and honor behind her innocent beauty. Like Radigund, she does not really win through her might but through her tricks. Captured three times, she escapes through the leniency of the Buddhist Master Jin Bifeng. She refuses to surrender even when terribly mutilated by the swords of Sanbao's warriors. Using magic, she escapes again. Her stubborn resistance to Sanbao's expedition is interpreted by the narrator as falsehood: in the guise of defending the country, she vents her private hatred for Sanbao because of her father's death.

In the Country of Zhuawa, the woman warrior Wang Shengu is portrayed as a bandit who captures Yao Haigang and makes him her husband. She then fights Sanbao's warriors on behalf of her country and husband. She, like the Monkey in *The Journey to the West*, can assume seventy-two different shapes. Her magical power, like that of Jiang Jinding, is associated with the five elements of earth. Assisted by Mother Fire, Mother Water, and Mother Mount Li, mother of Pangu who created the world, Wang Shengu cannot be subdued by human or supernatural power; she can only be constrained by the power of Buddhism. Only through a curse recorded by the Buddhist Master Jin Bifeng, is she finally trampled to death under the hooves of hundreds of battling horses. Wang Shengu's Country of Zhuawa is the most savage country conquered on Sanbao's route.

In the Country of Women, women's sexual perversion and violence converge. Scorning the use of a sword against women, Sanbao himself seeks out the queen of the Country of Women and asks for permission to pass through her territory and for a paper of surrender. Sanbao is a eunuch, and subsequently his castration is exposed in the queen's attempted rape;[52] the queen fails to find his "heavenly column [phallus] in the front but a ditch behind."[53] This has symbolic implication. According to Chinese creation mythology, heaven is supported by four heavenly columns. The reign of a dynasty symbolically depends on the heavenly column (capable and loyal ministers). Sanbao's missing phallus compares with China's loss of the heavenly column, suggesting the theme of emasculation by the force of *yin*. To further illustrate Chinese emasculation, Luo portrays Chinese warriors becoming pregnant by standing on the Reflecting Bridge and drinking from the Mother-Child River. To cure their pregnancy, three warriors are sent to fetch water from the Spring of the Holy Mother. The Gold-headed, Silver-headed, and Copper-headed princesses guarding the spring embody material and sexual temptations.[54] The three princesses fight among themselves, out of sexual rivalry, and are eventually slain by the warriors. This fight on an allegorical level parallels the struggle of men against women on the battleground.

The Country of Women resembles Spenser's Amazon state in political structure. It is an all-female realm with the male invaders shut in prison. Women have laws and a court as in any civilized society, with their own ministers, scholars, troops, and military commanders. Wang Lianying, the General Army Commander, captures Tang Zhuangyuan in single combat. Falling in love with her captive, as does Radigund, she attempts to use the price of her entire country and the position of emperor to tempt Tang into marrying her. When Tang rejects her, she shuts him in prison with Sanbao and prepares to execute them both. Tang's rejection becomes a categorical denunciation of women who govern in place of men as usurpers who defy father and sovereignty, and Tang accuses Wang of being more pernicious than the fang of a snake and the sting of a wasp: "the cruelest [thing] is a woman's heart."[55]

An educational myth—of a gentleman who suffers through humility—permeates the structure of Spenser's Book V and Luo's episode of the Country of Women. In each work, a monstrous regiment of women imposes humility on the hero, in a way that defines his character. Louis Montrose points out that what Spenser intends to fashion in *The Faerie Queene* is "not merely a civilized self but a male subject, whose self-defining violence is enacted against an objectified other, who is specifically female."[56] It appears that in their works Spenser and Luo intend to establish not only a Philosophers' Utopia, but a patriarchal one, whose transformation will be achieved through conquering female power. In effect, man's conquest of woman becomes a victory of soul over body, and his conquest of women's rule becomes a purgation of the abnormal or unnatural.

Legitimate or Monstrous: Britomart vs. Hellenore and the Amazon State

The alien forces found during Spenser's and Luo Maodeng's utopian explorations are chiefly composed of female characters with sexual and political powers. In combating these forces, Spenser and Luo create a type of legitimate woman, who turns a war between the sexes into a war among women themselves. This war between legitimate and monstrous women is essentially still a disguised war between men and women, because these particular legitimate women fight on behalf of men. In Spenser's gallery of female portraits, we find not only a troop of wanton maidens and vengeful and rebellious Amazons, as discussed earlier, but also a number of positive female characters. They can be divided into three groups: the innocent beauties; the good queens and goddesses; and the legitimate warriors.

Spenser uses the innocent beauties to represent genderless, abstract ideas. Una represents truth or the one true religion; Medina is "the golden Mean"; and Pastorella incorporates the simple pastoral life. As women, these characters appear passive and conventional. Una, the epitome of a weak, submissive maiden, is easily abandoned by St. George for her alleged wantonness, yet she accepts his male double standards without question. She welcomes him back from his sexual indulgence with Duessa and gives him love and hope. When he fights the dragon, she prays, weeps, and cheers. When betrothed, she stays home as St. George departs to do his six years of service to Fairy Land. Pastorella, like Amoret, is a passive object of abduction. Florimell's active life is very much limited to fleeing from male predators. The textual life of these innocent beauties extends only to the point of their betrothal.

The Calvinist acceptance of the elected woman ruler as an exception to women in general stimulated Spenser to produce a series of good queens. He employs them as icons, however, and presents them as impersonalized objects, as opposed to the plasticity of the innocent beauties. Gloriana, the Fairy Queen, embodies the glory that all knights, and Arthur in particular, seek through their heroic deeds. Queen Mercilla obviously stands for clemency or equity, which Spenser considers a feminine virtue important to his gentle politics. Queens such as Belge, Irena, and Mercilla are portrayed as objects in need of male protection, just like helpless damsels in distress. The good goddesses in *The Faerie Queene*, like its good queens, stand largely for abstraction or divinity. The goddess Astraea, who "symbolizes justice in the Golden Age,"[57] enables Artegall's mission and principle of justice to appear divine. Nature, with her supreme power over all gods and men, is the only goddess who can restore human faith in the ultimate return of the Golden Age. These goddesses, with bad goddesses as their counterparts, have no real gender representativeness.

The Faerie Queene contains three impressive female characters, who burst the skin of their intended allegories: Britomart, Hellenore, and Radigund. Recent Western criticism of *The Faerie Queene* has increasingly emphasized Spenser's protofeminist consciousness.[58] I recognize that in characterizing Britomart Spenser asserts "the natural ability of women to excel in the same fields as men" and their possible sexual equality in matrimony.[59] He projects also his vision of an ideal woman who combines feminine passions with masculine rationality. Nevertheless, I insist that Spenser is unambiguously opposed to gynecocracy. Britomart is Spenser's legitimate woman because she embodies Spenser's notion of chastity and justice and subjugates the Amazons to men's rule. In Book III, he uses Britomart to evoke the allegory of chastity and Hellenore to construct a contrasting allegory of unchastity. In Book V, he lets Britomart act as the dispenser of justice for the imprisoned Artegall and lets Radigund represent injustice. From the perspective of history and women's roles, Britomart appears quite confined by social codes and most subversive to the notion of female rule. Thus, Spenser employs sexual chastity as a metaphor for political virginity to consolidate the order and harmony of society and family. As James W. Broaddus perceives, Britomart's imaginative power, which "gives ethical coloration to those images which have a sexual content," is "controlled by the single image of a virtuous knight, Artegall."[60] Therefore, Britomart's destiny reveals that Spenser essentially celebrates a male-centered and procreative chastity.

In the sixteenth century, female chastity was regarded as a woman's entire value and life: "chastity was the one absolute demand made on virtuous womanhood."[61] Britomart learns the importance of chastity from the examples of Florimell and Amoret. The image of Florimell is that of beauty in a girdle that symbolizes chastity. When she loses her girdle, she is in constant danger of male sexual violation. Amoret, like Florimell, is all femininity, and represents natural love or passion unbridled by rationality. When Britomart puts on a male guise, she assumes the garment of rationality that enables her to overcome sensory illusions and threats produced by "the male imagination" and by "all the instructions of culture."[62]

Spenser uses Palmer (the male) to stand for the voice of reason and treats rationality as characteristic of masculinity. Actually, the notion of chastity itself is a product of patriarchal rationality. Britomart's rationality is, therefore, her rein of power as well as her girdle of self-restraint. The words Britomart sees on the doors in the House of Busirane—"Be bold" and "Be not too bold"—simultaneously encourage and warn women.[63] Rationality gives Britomart the strength to strive ahead, but at the same time binds her to the idea of female chastity—"true feminitee" and "goodly womanhead."[64]

By the end of Book III (in the 1590 version), Britomart watches the hermaphroditic tableau of Amoret and Scudamour,[65] featuring female passion submitting to male rationality. The Hermaphrodite symbolizes "the power of the one parent—Hermes, god of language —over the other—Aphrodite, goddess of love;"[66] the male logos of rationality subdues the female pathos of desire. In sculpting the Hermaphrodite, Spenser captures the moment in which the female enters the male, or rather, the male receives and protects the female: "Lightly he clipt her twixt his armes twaine / And streightly did embrace her body bright,"[67] thus achieving the Renaissance ideal of chastity within marriage.

In advocating chastity within marriage, Spenser opposes the extramarital love and female dominion common in the aristocratic tradition of courtly love.[68] Thus, as far as women's emancipation in sexual love is concerned, Spenser seems rather conservative, as demonstrated by his attitude toward the character of Hellenore, whom Spenser intends to be a bad woman to act as foil to Britomart, champion of chastity. Following Spenser's intention, Eric Sterling denounces Hellenore for lustfulness and rationalizes her imprisonment by saying that "the only manner in which Malbecco may preserve the virtue of the woman he loves is confinement."[69] As did Sterling, most critics simply dispose of Hellenore as a whore or a symbol of unchastity. Yet, Hellenore is the most sympathetic figure in the whole romance; through her we get a glimpse of the cruel social reality regarding women. According to Woodbridge, the connection between women and property was "deeply engrained in Renaissance thought."[70] Malbecco, the one-eyed miser, who is blind to Hellenore's beauty and value, keeps her as a prisoner. His old age, ugliness, and inability to arouse her sexually justify her rejection of this patriarchal tyrant. Hellenore is hardly seduced by Paridell, as "Ne was she ignoraunt of that lewd lore."[71] Her complicity in the seduction, her cruelty towards Malbecco in the fire accident, and her eager elopement with Paridell demonstrate her revengeful "despight" toward her "vnfitly yokt" marriage.[72] From her abuse by her husband to her abandonment by her lover, Hellenore represents a fate of women in patriarchal society. It is no wonder that she is happy with her life as an ordinary working woman in the satyr community; and it is not surprising that she soon forgets both Paridell and Malbecco.

Critics use terms such as "common concubine" as labels for Hellenore, but there is no evidence in the poem that the satyrs have a marriage system. The lines "With them as housewife euer to abide, / To milke their gotes, and make them cheese and bred, / And euery one as commune good her handeled" simply indicate how civilized men interpret a woman's role among the shepherds.[73] Perhaps, Spenser intends Hellenore's work as a degrading punishment for a fallen lady. Yet, he vividly describes Hellenore's joyous life in nature. Satyrs worship the beauty of her sex as they worship the beauty of truth in Una.[74] Hellenore is proud of her "new honour" as their "May-lady"[75] and she receives from each satyr a kiss as a token of affection and love, rather than lust. At the night scene, Malbecco watches Hellenore making love with only one "*Satyre* rough and rude, / Who all the night did minde his ioyous play."[76] This love scene is different from the gang-rape metaphor often used by feminist writers to suggest the abuse of women in civilized society. Hellenore—Hellen-over—turns over a new life when she finally makes her own choice:

> Tho gan he her perswade, to leaue that lewd
>   And loathsome life, of God and man abhord,
>   And home returne, where all should be renewd
>   With perfect peace, and bandes of fresh accord,
>   And she receiu'd againe to bed and bord,
>   As if no trespasse eure had bene donne:
>   But she it all refused at one word,
>   And by no meanes would to his will be wonne,
> But chose emongst the iolly *Satyres* still to wonne.[77]

Hellenore's preference is an action against the mores of civilization: "Monogamy is unnatural for the kind of disposition embodied in Hellenore"; therefore, she "finds her proper place and realizes her ideal of domestic bliss by withdrawing from civilization to the primitive and innocent pastoral world of the satyr community."[78]

Confined by moral codes of Renaissance society, however, Spenser frequently refers to woman's promiscuous nature, and a male double standard permeates *The Faerie Queene.* For instance, the Red Cross Knight becomes enamored of the witch Duessa the moment he deserts Una as a wanton. But, virtually no Renaissance poets or critics hold man accountable for unchastity. Spenser, reflecting the assumptions of his era, sees a serious moral problem in Hellenore. He even "apologizes to women readers for including Hellenore's sexual orgies with Satyres" and claims that "good women should not be offended, since he censures only the bad."[79] Only by reading against Spenser's authorial intention can we perceive a bold feminist vision in Hellenore's final resolution. Traditionally, Helen of Troy is an emblem of doubleness: goddess and scourge.[80] Although most critics see only the image of scourge in Hellenore, from a feminist perspective, we discover a goddess within the downtrodden whore. This goddess brings us a vision of shared sexual life that frequently appears in contemporary feminist utopias.

Britomart and Hellenore obviously belong to different classes. Britomart, the lady of royal lineage, seems to stand "on a footing of perfect equality with men,"[81] as shown in her fight to a draw with Artegall. In fact, Britomart is more restricted by social codes for women than are Hellenore and Radigund. As did upper-class ladies of the sixteenth century, Britomart uses male guise as a means of self-assertion, but she asserts rather than transgresses "the ideals of female chastity, silence, and obedience set forth in Puritan domestic ideology."[82] Spenser's positive use of transvestism in characterizing Britomart is not outside of a pattern found in English Renaissance poetry, where "writers attempt to overcome the threat which the unruly female poses to men: here, the female transvestite uses her unorthodox position to defend women's chastity, promote traditional marriage, and thus furthers the reinforcement of patriarchy."[83]

Justice is a social and political virtue seldom attached to the feminine. Indeed, in Book III, Britomart, in male guise, plays the role of a woman to assert the traditional feminine virtue of chastity; and in Book V, she actually plays "Artegall's male part as Justice."[84] As Judith H. Anderson says, "Justice is the most inclusive and exalted moral virtue in *The Faerie Queene*"; but it "governs relations among men" to maintain hierarchy.[85] Nevertheless, Spenser's concept of justice seems questionable. Except for internal distributive justice, there is hardly any true formal justice in Book V. In the area of international politics, Spenser's notion of justice speaks for the imperialist attempt to establish a worldwide Utopia under the central rule of Britain. In the politics of female rule, his justice articulates the Anglican views against gynecocracy, which regard women's governance as being against Nature and limit women to the domestic realm. At best, a virtuous, capable woman like Britomart can only be a consort to male justice. Radigund embodies injustice because she turns the system upside down. Bieman remarks, "The specific injustice in the Amazonian regime is that of robbing man of dignity and freedom and fitting him into a perverted social order."[86] Although we recognize the necessity of analyzing *The Faerie Queene* according to the criteria of sixteenth-century justice, in appreciating Spenser, we should not stop short of the question: where does justice for women lie in that unjust social hierarchy?

In Radigund's dungeon, where Artegall and his companions suffer as women's wage slaves, we get a glimpse of the working conditions of lower-class women in the sixteenth century. According to Merry E. Wiesner, "Women were independently involved in a huge number of textile-related occupations well into the fifteenth century."[87] In the late sixteenth and early seventeenth centuries, however, the work of a lower-class woman became "increasingly invisible whether she labor[ed] outside the home or within it (as a spinner, for instance), and whether she live[d] in the countryside or, as increasingly occurred in England, in the capital city whose population swelled with peasants uprooted from their farms by the practice of enclosure, [and] her wages tend[ed] to be substantially lower than those of male workers—when she receive[d] them at all, that is."[88] In *The Faerie Queene*, the invisibility of woman's work is accomplished by placing the workers in a dungeon. Although Spenser is probably among the first to portray wage slaves in English literature, he "explicitly equates the female sex and people who work for wages, considering the activity appropriate to both groups unworthy of a 'mind so braue' as that of an aristocratic soldier."[89] Radigund lets Artegall, the minister of patriarchal justice, have a taste of social injustice towards women. Her action of reversal should be interpreted as a justified action rather than as injustice. If Artegall is humanized by his experience in the workhouse, Radigund rather than Britomart is his true "humanizer."[90]

Spenser uses Radigund's transvestism to reflect the power of female cultural misrule in his own society. But it is in this type of transvestism, rather than Britomart's, that we can find "the challenge to the existing socio-sexual hierarchy."[91] The anonymous *Hic Mulier; or the Man-Woman*, published in 1620, actually cites Spenser's description of Radigund's transvestism in Book V.v.25 of *The Faerie Queene* to imply that "man-woman" monsters from all social classes were rampant at the time.[92] Lucas also points out that "men fashion the female transvestite as a mirror image of masculine violence."[93] Spenser's portrayal of Radigund's injustice and violence reflects male jealousy and the fear of female power.[94] Radigund is actually Britomart's double and represents the pride and threat in Britomart—she is, in fact, the Britomart who is "too bold." Radigund's death, with "both head and helmet cleft" by one stroke,[95] resembles Penthesilea's death by a blow to the brain.[96] By killing Radigund, Britomart destroys all her own potential to become a female ruler and reduces herself to a tamed consort:

> And changing all that forme of common weale,
> The liberty of women did repeale,
> Which they had long vsurpt; and them restoring
> To mens subiection, did true Iustice deale.[97]

So, finally, the engulfing Amazon is overcome by the nursing Virgin,[98] as Ruth Kelso observes: "Theory does not divide women into two groups, the rulers and the ruled. . . . Practice did just that, but not theory. Theory said that all women must be ruled."[99] In such a way, the legitimation of Queen Elizabeth as an exception is ultimately subverted. In fact, both literary and pictorial representations of Elizabeth as Amazon were popular during her reign; and "the Amazons were the foremost ancient examples of feminism. The sixteenth- and early seventeenth-century attitude toward them may therefore reveal men's real, secret opinion of the new tendency."[100] The final thrusting of Radigund's Amazons under the yoke of man reveals Spenser's ultimately conservative attitude toward the feminism burgeoning in his age.

In literary works by men, women's rule is nearly always subverted by a woman who represents the male position. Spenser's use of the motif in which female fights female is, perhaps, unintentionally malignant, for three reasons. First, fighting within the female sex exaggerates the stereotype of jealousy in woman's nature. Britomart's first reaction on hearing of Radigund's capture of Artegall is sexual jealousy. When the two women meet like "a Tygre and a Lionesse," they not only fight with "equale greedinesse,"[101] but also hurl "spitefull words" at each other because of one man—Artegall:

> At last proud *Radigund* with fell despight,
>   Hauing by chaunce espide aduantage neare,
>   Let driue at her with all her dreadfull might,
>   And thus vpbrayding said; This token beare
>   Vnto the man, whom thou doest loue so deare;
>   And tell him for his sake thy life thou gauest.
>   Which spitefull words she sore engrieu'd to heare,
>   Thus answer'd; Lewdly thou my loue
>   deprauest,Who shortly must repent that now so
>   vainely brauest.[102]

Radigund's hatred for knights is caused by her unrequited love; out of love's revenge, Britomart's fight with Radigund is, as portrayed, "far bloodier than even Britomart's second battle with Artegall."[103]

> Where being layd, the wrothfull Britonesse
>   Stayd not, till she came to her selfe againe,
>   But in reuenge both of her loues distresse,
>   And her late vile reproch, though vaunted
>   vaine,
>   And also of her wound, which sore did
>   paine,
>   She with one stroke both head and helmet
>   cleft.
> Which dreadfull sight, when all her warlike traine
> There present saw, each one of sence bereft,Fled
>   fast into the towne, and her sole victor
>   left.[104]

Such a portrayal enhances the fallacy that women are naturally crueler to women than to men. Typical of male readers, Hamilton says, "Not even regeneration on the natural level can come of this, woman's violence against woman."[105] Second, by having woman fight woman, Spenser puts male standards into the mouths of women. The surrender of Britomart leads the reader to believe that women are willing to be submissive and subordinate to men, and that they are happy and content with their nonpolitical feminine roles. Thus, Humphrey Tonkin reads Britomart as "a reluctant knight" with a psychological "longing for hearth and home and femininity."[106] Third, Spenser's elevation of Britomart is more subversive to the rule of Queen Elizabeth than to patriarchy. Not only does she hand over her political rights and retreat to her proper role as Penelope, she shall produce a line of British kings who will rule out gynecocracy forever. Here Spenser anticipates the reaction of male successors to Elizabeth's rule: "Partly in reaction against Elizabeth, the Stuarts aggressively promoted the image of the monarch as a father and husband of his country."[107]

As seen at the beginning of Book III, Britomart seems a combination of the queen's two bodies; Gloriana is the body politic, and Belphoebe is the body natural. As a device for textual unity, Gloriana, often mentioned in name, never appears in a physical body. Such a tactful treatment of Gloriana, nevertheless, betrays the British male's desire to make his sovereign queen a trunkless figurehead. Spenser's attitude towards Belphoebe's "rare chastitee" is ambiguous. As "a most vertuous and beautiful lady,"[108] she is essentially a sexual being—"an object of sexual desire," who enables Spenser to bring in the clowns and create laughter at "the doubled erotic and political power of a female."[109] Critics generally recognize Spenser's enlightened attitude toward sexuality within virtuous marriage. The sensual Britomart is, in my view, intentionally subversive to the virgin Belphoebe, whose sexual rigidity is reflected in Spenser's description of her marble legs. As a woman, Queen Elizabeth had to confront patriarchal expectations in her time. "In 1559, a parliamentary delegation urged their new, young, and female sovereign to fulfill her destiny by marrying and bearing an heir."[110] Refusing to enact the female paradigm desired by her male advisers, she proudly created the image reflected by the following words on her tomb: "Here lyes interr'd Elizabeth, / A Virgin pure untill her Death."[111] Comparing history with literature, we can see that the female paradigm desired by the Renaissance male, but rejected by Elizabeth, finds its eternal existence in Britomart.

Natural or Monstrous:
Huang Fengxian vs. the Country of Women and Mrs. Bai

During the Renaissance, British gentlemen argued over the question of gynecocracy. No such controversy can be found in the history of Chinese thought. It is more than clear that women cannot rule because *yin* should never be dominant over *yang*. That a reversal of this order creates social chaos is Luo's imaginative spur. His western world, of *yin* over *yang*, is overwhelmed by female wantonness, female warriors, and female reign. All the powerful goddesses and women warriors are on the side of *yin* because of their female gender, and all the gods from heaven and the male warriors are on the side of *yang*. To turn the tables, Luo makes all goddesses conciliate with men, abandoning their earthly sisters, and sentences all women warriors, except Huang Fengxian, to the executioner's sword under the pretext of chastity and piety.

Huang Fengxian, like Spenser's Britomart, is the legitimate woman warrior created by the author to subvert women's rule. Her major function in the novel is to subdue the Country of Women. Unlike Britomart, whose legitimate power stems from her royal lineage, Huang Fengxian gains her legitimacy in the world of men by openly betraying her all-female society. When Sanbao and his men invade the Country of Women and are captured, Huang Fengxian, like Spenser's Amazon Clarinda, is put in charge of male prisoners. For their inability or refusal to have sexual intercourse with the queen, Sanbao and his followers are put into prison. As Radigund does with Artegall, Wang Lianying, General Commander of the Country of Women, captures Tang, the Chinese Number One Warrior, and falls in love with him. Resembling Britomart's fate as foretold by Merlin, Huang Fengxian has the feeling that she is destined to marry the handsome Tang. She sets Sanbao and Tang free as an exchange for her marriage to Tang. Huang and Wang fight most cruelly, less out of loyalty or justice than sexual jealousy. Huang finally cuts off Wang's head without pity and forces the Country of Women to surrender.

It is not a coincidence that in both *The Faerie Queene* and *The Western Ocean* male warriors are given missions by the court, whereas the woman warrior, whether in a high or a low position, has one destiny: marriage. Radigund is "a projection of Britomart's womanly pride,"[112] and "Britomart's double, split off from her as an allegorical personification of everything in Artegall's beloved which threatens him."[113] Similarly, apart from Wang Lianying, who embodies unbridled love, Luo uses the Red Lotus Princess and Mrs. Bai to suggest Huang's intractable qualities that must be cast off before or after marriage.

When the Queen of the Country of Women agrees to surrender to Sanbao, the Red Lotus Princess refuses to yield to China because of her pride. Every time the Princess is defeated, she tries to report the combat to the queen as a victory so that she will be able to continue to fight Sanbao's warriors. But each time she lies, with a distorted face, she screams, "Spare my life! Please spare my life," as though she were tortured by a blue-faced devil. She is eventually subdued by the Buddhist Master Jin Bifeng. Sanbao stamps his gold seal on her back and expects her to surrender herself to China during the Moon Festival (the following mid-August). Sanbao takes the paper of surrender from the Country of Women and gives its citizens women's hats, gowns, and shoes, thus restoring them to their proper feminine position.

The subduing of the Red Lotus Princess symbolizes the subduing of Huang's maiden pride by Chinese men before she becomes a wife. A further "taming of the shrew" is portrayed in Huang's fight with Mrs. Bai, the wife of Bai Liyan, General Commander of the Country of Yinyan. She can use a nine-blade sword and walk hundreds of miles a day on her three-inch-long lotus feet. She has a long spear, two golden hooks, and a bell that breaks any man or husband's heart when he hears it ringing. The bell is a symbol of her sexual charm, for Mrs. Bai is known as "an unchaste wife." After her husband's death, she offers to command the army and defend the country, but the king suspects her of a woman's trick. Huang Fengxian, who cannot defeat Mrs. Bai by force, collaborates with her husband to destroy her through sexual politics, pretending to welcome Bai as her husband's concubine.

Thus, Mrs. Bai is politically destroyed in front of her own king. After Mrs. Bai is killed by Tang, she asks the Judge of Hell why she was tricked into death since she observed the proper motto: "Husband is the master of the wife and the wife avenges the husband's death."[114] The Judge replies: "Mrs. Bai, in your earlier life you were a long-footed wife. You ran from house to house and visited door to door. You never listened to your mother-in-law. Every time she bid you to do something, you shook your head. Therefore, today you have been tripped over and beheaded."[115] After her pride, unchastity, and shrewishness are purged vicariously through the characters of the Red Lotus Princess and Mrs. Bai, Huang Fengxian, like Britomart, becomes a symbol of prosperity and procreation, bringing a gold child and a silver child across the western ocean to China. When the voyage ends, Huang Fengxian becomes the Second Mistress at court, an honorary position with no political function.

The Western Ocean can be called a free allegorical work, as it uses the entire western world as a metaphor for otherness and contains allegorical figures, such as the Gold-headed, Silver-headed, and Copper-headed princesses; however, it does not have Spenser's sustained allegory, developed from the Western medieval tradition. Thus, Huang Fengxian does not epitomize a moral allegory as does Britomart, and she fails to speak for patriarchy. In turning herself over to China, she obeys the Confucian concept of international justice, but she commits the crimes of disloyalty to her native Country of Women and of unchastity by purchasing marriage with her betrayal. Because of this contradiction, the Judge of Hell, the mouthpiece of Confucianism, recognizes Wang Lianying, slain by Huang, as a filial woman and explains that her death is merely a minor punishment for eating a hen behind the back of her mother-in-law in an earlier life.

Huang Fengxian, who fails to conform to an allegory of traditional chastity, appears as a sixteenth-century feminist figure. Her marriage is based on an equal footing: Huang is *Zhuangyuan* (Number One) in both the liberal arts and martial arts in her country, as is Tang in China. When they come together, they demonstrate a dazzling match in beauty, intellect, and physical might. Huang surpasses Tang in every area. They fight together against the western warriors at the front, and Huang shows her superiority over all male warriors in archery and single combat, as Britomart does in her defeat of all knights except Artegall. Britomart vanishes into femininity after she slays Radigund, whereas Huang embarks on Sanbao's expedition after marriage. She is sent as a scout to enemy countries; and in this role, she resembles Wang Ming, the man with a magic herb that makes him invisible. Once when she returns, her husband Tang asks her about the foreign situation. Huang replies that she must report to General Sanbao first, because though husband and wife have a private bond, the mission is public work; hence, the roles of the wife and the husband are reversed. Huang further turns the Confucian codes for women upside down by teaching Tang the magic arts she knows. She also demonstrates female moral superiority when Tang affirms that spouses part in crisis like birds, but Huang insists that husband and wife, bound by true love, live and die together.

Should such a woman who defies all Confucian codes be put to death? The Judge of Hell, who does not know anything about her behavior in her earlier life, says yes. But Luo's attitude is ambiguous, given his ideological and ethical contradictions. In *The Western Ocean*, Daoism and Buddhism are often in conflict with each other; but both serve Confucianism, as represented by Sanbao. The Confucian ideology that penetrates the whole book checks as well as spurs Luo's moral imagination. Confucian hierarchy attempts to perpetuate the order of Emperor-Minister-Son *(Junjun Chenchen Zizi)*, which does not permit usurpation or transgression. Safeguarding this order is the moral system of Loyalty *(Zhong)*, Piety *(Xiao)*, and Justice or Righteousness *(Yi)*. For women, Confucianism further demands "Three Obediences and Four Virtues" and, above all, Chastity. According to the hierarchical order of Emperor-Minister-Son, Sanbao commands the western countries to obey China as ministers to the emperor, or as sons to the father. Luo's western countries merely assume the names and follow the geographic positions discovered by the historical figure Zheng He in his seven sea expeditions. Their ideology and moral principles are still those of China. Luo, as Ji Mulin says, is "indeed writing fiction," describing less a historical overseas expedition than a spiritual pilgrimage within China itself.

Unfortunately, Confucian morality often thrusts Luo into an insoluble dilemma. According to the concept of Loyalty, the warriors of the western countries should fight to death in defense of their kings. According to the concept of Piety, the sons and daughters of those countries should avenge the deaths of their fathers, but meanwhile, they also break the code of Confucian international Justice that demands a small country's piety and submission to a larger one. Consequently, moral contradictions follow in the wake of Sanbao's expedition. In the Country of Jinyan, the Third Prince fights for the king as a filial son and Ha Lihu fights for the king as a loyal minister. In defeat, they both prefer suicide to surrender. After Sanbao drives them to their deaths, he sets up a tombstone inscribed with a poem to praise them:

> The Prince dared to take orders in a crisis,
> The minister makes great self-sacrifice.
> Nothing is virtuous but loyalty and piety,
> One to the King, the other to the blood kin.[116]

This moral contradiction is particularly evident in Luo's handling of women warriors. Jiang Jinding follows the example of Hua Mulan and fights for her country in place of her father: "The King questions: 'You have a female body, combing your hair in three tassels and wearing blouse and skirt. How can you wield a sword to slaughter men in the battle field?' Jiang Jinding replies: 'Mulan went to the West to fight instead of her father. Wasn't she a female?'[117] Although Jiang embodies the stubborn alien force, Luo can only have her yield in the end, not die by Sanbao's hand. In order to kill Wang Shengu, Luo has to recall an act of impiety in her earlier life: "The Judge of Hell: 'Wang Shengu, you never respected your parents-in-law and obeyed your own parents. You did not do your womanly duty and committed the crime of breaching the Seven Codes for women (Three Obedience and Four Virtues) . . . Today you deserve to die under hooves . . . Send her to the Department of Punishment to suffer through the eighteen hells.' "[118]

Apart from his insistence on piety, Luo's advocacy of female chastity is overtly shown in Sanbao's praise of aspects of that virtue. When Sanbao arrives in the Country of Mayidong, he is quite touched by its custom: when a husband dies, his wife will shave off her hair and refuse to eat for seven days. If she survives the seven-day fast, she will jump into the flames to be cremated alive with the body of her husband. In case she cannot be burnt to death, she will stay a widow and never remarry for the rest of her life.[119] This custom mirrors the Chinese Lienü tradition. Sanbao rewards these chaste women with gifts and sets up a monument adorned with the words, "The Land of Chastity."

Beset by moral contradictions at home and abroad, Luo seems to feel the inadequacy of Confucianism as the Chinese spiritual pillar. His superhero Jin Bifeng saves him from this spiritual crisis by elevating to the status of gods all those who were justly killed according to Confucian international justice but died without guilt according to its moral criteria of Loyalty, Piety, and Chastity. Luo finally purges his utopian impulse by pursuing suzerainty and drives towards Jin Bifeng's Buddhist vision of Great Harmony:

> China has sages and how can
> > Buddhists not exist in the West?!
> The world had been a harmonious unity
> > before wars started.
> Then the Boat of Mercy appears
> > in the vast sea of sufferings,
> Turning all fields and mulberry trees
> > into homes of happiness and peace.[120]

The Western Ocean and *The Faerie Queene*, as Abby Wettan Kleinbaum says of the latter, employ women "as vehicles for male transcendence,"—often done in classical texts—and use the defeat of female reign to "affirm the strength and the ability of [Western] men to conquer and master these newfound worlds."[121] Both works express men's desire to negate female rule and consolidate the primacy of male dominion. In Spenser's and Luo's utopian designs, women are employed as symbols. Spenser and Luo both use female sexuality to construct their lands of unbridled pleasure and depict their female sovereigns as emasculating horrors. The unnatural female, as sex or power, is exiled and punished. The legitimate women who have no territory of their own are a supplement to men and are employed to serve men's noble patriarchy as extensions of men's tongues or arms.

No woman is good for her own sake, because the real value of woman is not in her self but in feminine virtues detached from the female body. Spenser's pastoral utopia in Book VI is headed by a courteous patriarch. In this paternalized Golden Age, Pastorella, as a symbol, merges with the three Heavenly Graces: chastity, innocent courtesy, and harmonious concord. In Spenser's Philosophers' Utopia, Fairy Land, Britomart is incorporated into the ideal patriarchal rule as the embodiment of chastity and equity. Women are not even present in Luo's description of the Country of the Heavenly Paradise, which is ruled by a fatherly king. Huang Fengxian becomes a symbol of prosperity and procreation fit to enter Luo's ideal court—the well-ordered hierarchical rule of a gentle emperor. Feminine virtues, such as mercy, charity, and chastity, are not even gained through the medium of the female, but by the Buddhist Master Ji Bifeng, who holds a proper equilibrium between *yin* and *yang*.

In using women and female reigns as symbolic tools to serve their utopian purpose, *The Faerie Queene* and *The Western Ocean* represent the conflict between textual center and margin in the traditional literary representation of women. Spenser's and Luo's concerns for women, marginal or accidental, are both encouraging yet worthy of despair. The historical rule of Queen Elizabeth, however, gives Gloriana a substance beyond the textual power of *The Faerie Queene*. Lady Florence Dixie will use Gloriana as the name of her utopian protagonist, but reverse Spenser's treatment of female reign in order to imagine a woman prime minister, who leads a new Amazon regiment and rules on behalf of women. Chen Duansheng, encouraged by imaginary characters such as Huang Fengxian, who excel over men in every field, will dare to choose as her destiny in the next life "state rule" as a replacement for marriage—women's eternal and universal destiny. With the appearance of feminist utopias, women and female rule begin to occupy the entire stage of the text and direct authorial intention.

3

As Women's Destiny

The Destiny of the Next life
and *Gloriana; Or, The Revolution of 1900*

C hen Duansheng's *Destiny of the Next Life* (1796) and Lady Florence Dixie's *Gloriana; Or, The Revolution of 1900* (1890) are
consciously feminist Utopias written by women. Although *The Next
Life* is the protesting song of a solitary nightingale in a dark feudal age,
and *Gloriana* is a bugle call for women's rights in an era of social
change, they both offer a daring dream in which a female hero gains
political power through concealing her sexual identity. By means of
utopian fantasies, Chen and Dixie demonstrate women's superior abil-
ities in politics, education, and all other fields in a world dominated by
men. By playing the politics of competing with men, however, Chen
and Dixie both take the path of reform, rather than advocating a
radical overthrow of patriarchal hierarchy.

Feminist Utopia as Women's Destiny

The Next Life, consisting of seventeen books in poetic form, is
Chen Duansheng's lifework, dream, and swan song. She was born in
Hangzhou, Zhejiang Province, in 1751. Her grandfather was a presti-
gious official of his time, and her father had also assumed various posts
in Shandong and Yunnan. Little is known about Chen Duansheng's
own life except through her self-sketches at the beginning of each of
the seventeen books of *The Next Life*. From those autobiographical
fragments, we can gather a portrait of a young lady who occasionally
traveled in the screened cabin of a ship on her father's official inspec-

tion and learned poetic art from her mother. Although the world of reality for her is always a secluded, screened maiden bower, with her own form visible in silhouette by the window, dreaming to the rhythm of the pattering rain, the world of her imagination soars like a kite in spring. Her body is sedentary while her mind travels in the open world, competing with men, outdoing men in battlefields and examinations, and questioning the order of patriarchy.

Traveling seemed to have inspired Chen Duansheng's dream of striding into a masculine world, while the "mad and foolish things" (i.e., poetry) taught by her mother led to her abandoning womanly work.[1] She also admired those women characters in Chinese literary tradition who became warriors and scholars by concealing their female identity. Under these influences, Chen Duansheng began to write her utopian work at the age of eighteen. There seems to have been a spiritual collaboration between mother and daughter, for, according to Chen Duansheng's allusion in Book Seventeen, her "kind mother frequently guided me in my mad dreams."[2] She had finished sixteen books by the age of twenty when her mother died, and grief over the loss of her mother almost ended her literary career.[3] At the age of twenty-three, she married Fan Tan, apparently a man of no great intelligence, who later committed the crime of asking a substitute to take the national examination for him and subsequently was exiled to Yili in Xinjiang. Her husband's failure doubtlessly contributed to her belief that women were not inferior to men and deserved equal opportunities in the world. Though Chen Duansheng left her work unfinished at her death in 1796, her last book, the seventeenth, reveals her irreconciliation with the patriarchal system. As she tells us in her self-sketches, the respectful elders, possibly women, had bidden her to complete the marriage between two of her characters, Huangfu Shaohua and Meng Lijun;[4] but she could not, for a thematic principle in her work lay in Meng Lijun's lifelong resistance to marriage. To avoid this dilemma, she deliberately left her work open-ended.[5]

Chen Duansheng viewed the writing of *The Next Life* as her unique destiny and, perhaps, a disparity between her worlds of reality and imagination compelled her to use writing as a wish-fulfillment. Nevertheless, she had a firm grasp of her artistic objectives, as conveyed by her prefatory sketches: she sought to create a masterpiece in *tanci*,[6] to reverse the utopian dreams of man and woman, and to write for women readers.

The Next Life, written in the form of *tanci,* belongs to the traditional category of telling-singing literature.[7] According to Zheng

Zhenduo and Tan Zhengbi, early Chinese popular literature has two generic forms: the "book for telling" and the "book for singing." In the Yuan and Ming dynasties, the telling book developed into the popular novel, while the singing book was transformed by *taozhen* into *tanci*.[8] The Ming Dynasty produced the longest works of *tanci*, including the trilogy *Anbang Zhi*, *Dingguo Zhi*, and *Fenghuang Shan*, largely historical romances. But in the Qing dynasty, the form turned into fiction and became a genre almost exclusively for women writers.[9] Zheng Zhenduo observes:

> Women loved *tanci* most. . . . By and by they started to write the type of *tanci* they particularly liked. They wove their minds, miseries, and dreams into *tanci*. *Shi* [poetry], *ci* [poetry written to certain tunes with strict tonal patterns and rhyme schemes], and *qu* [a type of verse for singing, which emerged in the Southern Song Dynasty and became popular in the Yuan Dynasty] are men's literary games. Those forms were not suitable for women, and the heavy oppression of tradition made it hard to develop their special talents and express their own ideals. In *tanci*, they found freedom to release their passions and project their dreams.
>
> A part of *tanci*, therefore, became the literature of women, for women, and by women.[10]

Because of its subversion of feudal codes on women, *tanci* was often disparaged by the patriarchal authority; and because of its popularity among women and lowbrow audiences, it was also rejected by mainstream Chinese literature. Chen Duansheng's grandfather Goushan (1702–1772), an eminent scholar of the Qing Dynasty, "strongly despised the genre of *Tanci*," and Chen Duansheng "had to write *The Next Life* secretly during his stay in Hangzhou."[11] Even if others regarded *pingshi* (*tanci* in the south) as "dumb doggerel,"[12] Chen Duansheng intended to produce a masterpiece in this genre. Indeed, she pours all her spirit into her brush and concentrates all her interests in her composition.[13] To her, writing is always composing delicate poetry, like "a fairy weaving with clouds" or "a peacock unfolding its beautiful feathers."[14]

At the beginning of Book One, she states that her title, *The Destiny of the Next Life*, cannot be slighted, for the following reasons:

> Its earlier thread is stitched
> in *The Destiny of the Jade Bracelet*,
> A romance spinning around one head man—Xie Yuhui.

Born in the great Dynasty of Song,
His life glistened in riches of gold.
Behold his portrait:
Still a young man yet in Purple Gown,
With many beautiful wives milling around;
Thrusting his painted halbert,
He scatters all Hoos [invaders] like frightened sheep
      without a shepherd.
Banners of honor flutter afar,
Transmitting his name's magic power.
He gathers honey of fame and position
      happily like a bee;
Daughters like orchids and sons ivory trees
      bow to his knee.
Such fulfills his fate and
      leaves wonderful traces;
After a hundred years of dust,
He returns to the immortal void of grace.[15]

The Destiny of the Jade Bracelet, to which this passage refers, was probably written jointly by a daughter and her mother sometime by the end of the Ming Dynasty.[16] A typical imitation of men's *tanci*, it portrays a masculine utopian dream of having wealth, wives, children, fame and position, and finally immortality.[17] In *The Next Life*, instead of further glorifying Xie Yuhui, Chen Duansheng composes a radical revision in which Zheng Ruzhao, a perfectly virtuous but victimized concubine of Xie Yuhui, turns into Meng Lijun in her next life. Her character becomes an avenging agent who resists a woman's fate of marriage and reaches the position of *Zaixiang* (prime minister). On the other hand, Xie Yuhui becomes Shaohua in his next life, a man tortured endlessly by notions of fidelity and piety, who pins his life and death on a predestined marriage as does a pitiful woman. Through this deliberate revision, Chen Duansheng visualizes an alternative future for woman and consciously subverts the order of patriarchy.

Because of Chen Duansheng's attentiveness to both aesthetic value and feminist ideals, *The Next Life* was already well known throughout Zhejiang Province,[18] before she wrote Book Seventeen. Chen Duansheng's readers then were largely women, for in Book Three, she declares that she would rather keep her manuscripts among women than have them published and judged by vulgar men.[19] This might explain why Chen Duansheng's book did not appear in print until 1821, when Hou Zhi (a woman scholar) adapted and published it under the title of A *Woman Hero.* Her expressed wish may also account for the strange phenomenon that in the past two hundred years A *Women Hero* has been ignored, yet hand-copied manuscripts of *The Next Life* have been always in circulation.[20] Chen Duansheng's dream for her next life is quite representative among the talented women. For instance, Wang Yun of the early eighteenth century complains in one of her poems: "Being buried in the boudoir for dozen years, / a woman can be neither an official nor an immortal. / Every reading roused my admiration for Ban Chao, / Every drinking leads me to the poetry of Li Bai. / In spite of my high aspiration, / I have no luck to be Mulan or Chonggu. / Since I have no share for the Jade Palace and Gold Horses, / I can only pour my fantasies into a dream."[21] Because of its representativeness, Chen Duansheng's book became a seminal text for later women's *tanci.* There have been two declared sequels (*The Re-Creation of the Heaven* and *Flowers from the Brush*) and many other imitations.[22] *The Jade Dresser* by Ying Qing, published in 1924, still echoes Chen Duansheng's fantasy.[23] Jiang Ruizao says of *The Next Life,* "No women of talent and ambition in traditional China had not read it."[24] Xie Bingxin (1900–), a famous woman writer, is known to have read Chen Duansheng's text in her girlhood. *The Next Life* is indeed a dream for women. It is women's love for this dream that keeps it intact and alive from generation to generation.

Gloriana mirrors Lady Florence Dixie's own experience. Unlike Chen Duansheng's life, which was largely immobile and sedentary, Dixie's was full of adventures. She was born in 1855 into the family of the eighth Marquis of Queensberry and was raised the same way as her twin brother, James. All sorts of masculine activities, such as playing ball games, hunting, and racing, "turned her into a Tomboy."[25] From childhood, "She thought of herself as a boy, she spoke of herself as a boy, throughout her life she rode astride her saddle like a man. 'Come kiss your boy,' she instructed her mother in a youthful poem, 'He'll try to be a good chap till he dies'."[26] She married Sir Alexander Beaumont Dixie at twenty, but marriage did not confine her to conventional femininity; she embarked on hunting and travelling again when her baby was only two months old and depicted her exciting life in several travel books. Subsequently, she became "the first of the women war-correspondents" to Africa.[27] As a political activist, she succeeded in her public advocacy for a Zulu king and influenced parliamentary debates about Ireland. Moreover, as a feminist activist, she became one of the vice-presidents of the Women's Franchise League of Great Britain and Ireland during 1890 and 1891, and published many articles on the question of women. "In 1891 she told the Scottish Society of Literature and Art that 'she hoped before she died to stand in parliament,' a prospect that political events had pushed further from her grasp."[28] Dixie died in November 1905, just before the militant suffragettes in the Women's Social Political Union were reorganized. Her enthusiasm for the women's movement, however, had found expression fifteen years earlier in her novel *Gloriana*.[29] Lady Florence, like her protagonist Gloriana, proved by her own life that women are capable of being equal, even superior, in male-dominated fields.

Gloriana represents Dixie's political and social feminist ideas. In 1890, she published "Short Papers on Woman's Position" in *Women's Penny Paper* and "Women's Position" in *The Modern Review*. In these articles, Dixie argues seven major points: (1) rights of women are endorsed by God/Nature and by the law of evolution; (2) "Girls and boys should be *reared together, should go to school together, and to college together;*"[30] (3) English laws made by men represent "cruel inequality and injustice as between the woman and the man;"[31] therefore, women should have legislative power; (4) men's rule results in chaos, war, and abject poverty; therefore, women should have political rights and the right to rule; (5) women must be educated, must organize themselves, must open their minds, and must change their way of thinking by participating in masculine activities; (6) women must improve their physical conditions and change their dress; and (7) women should welcome men of justice as allies in their cause for emancipation. All these points are the fundamental ideas conveyed by the novel *Gloriana*, which Dixie took to be her most important book.[32] In 1890, she sent a copy to the German emperor, with a message asking "What right have men to settle what work women shall or shall not do, without taking the opinions of women on the subject?"[33] In 1893, when a rich gentleman offered Dixie 135,000 pounds to edit a popular woman's daily, she gave him a copy of the novel and wrote him that "the contents would give him an idea of my views and the lines on which I proposed to conduct the paper."[34] She eventually turned down the offer, because the gentleman wanted considerable space devoted to fashion.

Dixie seemed to be fully aware that, in her time, legislative and ruling power were beyond a woman's reach and women in general did not have the privileged social position and education that would enable them to compete with men. Those obstacles for women drove Dixie to contrive *Gloriana* as a personal as well as a collective utopian dream. The portrait on the front page of the first edition, showing her as a handsome boy in a sailor suit, indicates that Dixie puts herself in the role of Maremna, whose dream *Gloriana* portrays. Under Mother's influence and encouragement, Maremna dreams that she is Gloriana, the protagonist who can express her ideas of reform through attaining the position of prime minister. Thus, *Gloriana* represents Dixie's overriding concerns for women and her belief in obtaining social reforms through the organized strength of women.

The names of both authors' protagonists are equally suggestive. *The Next Life* is better known by its protagonist's name *Meng Lijun*. As Chinese writers often play word pronunciation, "Meng Lijun" also means "a fair emperor in the dream." Furthermore, Chen Duansheng names the "male" Meng Lijun "Li Junyu" by cleverly moving her personal name forward to replace her family name and chooses "Mingtang" as "his" style name,[35] which, again, reveals the author's feminist deliberation. Mingtang sparks a historical association with the female emperor Wu Zetian. When Wu was assuming the throne, she pulled down the Qianyuan Dian (The Palace of the Male Emperor) and built Mingtang—a great inauguration hall and a political center where Wu exercised her sovereign power. Sculpted on the roof of the hall was a giant, golden phoenix uplifted by nine dragons. Traditionally, the dragon is a symbol for a male ruler and the phoenix for female sovereignty. In the phoenix's overpowering of the dragons, Wu's intention is obvious.[36] By using Mingtang as Meng Lijun's style name, Chen Duansheng implies that a woman ruler is not subordinate to any male rulers. Similarly, Dixie chooses "Gloriana," the name of Spenser's fairy queen, as the name for her protagonist, but revises the theme of Spenser's *Faerie Queene*. Her Gloriana is no longer a static symbol of honor as is Spenser's, dictating from afar men's heroic pursuits. Her Gloriana is an active hero, the "mighty Champion of Women's Freedom and the Savior of her People."[37] When Gloriana puts on a male guise and names herself "Hector D'Estrange," she becomes the greatest Trojan hero reborn, though her new image will take time for men to recognize. Another significant revision can be seen in Dixie's complete reversal of Spenser's Amazon myth. The "monstrous regiment of women" becomes the women's White Regiment, a revolutionary force that directly threatens the patriarchal state. The novel also highlights the Hall of Liberty and Democracy as a rallying center for women signifying female ruling power, as did the Hall of Mingtang in Wu Zetian's reign.

Dixie, an active feminist, and Chen Duansheng, a victimized wife, each consider creating a utopia of female power as her unique destiny.

With a strong sense of historical mission, Dixie writes the following dedication:

To

All Women

and

Such Honorable, Upright, and Courageous

Men

As, regardless of Custom and Prejudice, Narrow-mindedness and long-established Wrong, will bravely assert and uphold the laws of Justice, of Nature, and of Right; I dedicate the following pages, with the hope that a straightforward inspection of the evils afflicting Society, will lead to their demolition in the only way possible—namely, by giving to Women equal rights with Men. Not till then will Society be purified, wrongdoing punished, or Man start forward along that road which shall lead to Perfection.

Critique of Patriarchy: Parodic Use of Popular Romance

Feminist utopian writers do not hesitate to adopt or remold the most popular literary genres. Chen Duansheng planned to write her utopia in twenty books with four chapters in each—the mode of her time—though she finished only seventeen books. She writes primarily in the seven-syllabic *pingshi* form, with variations of three-three-four syllabic quick lines characteristic of *tanci*, and occasional brief narrations. Although *The Next Life* is intended for reading, it preserves the vividness of telling-singing-performing in the art of *pingtan*. Similarly, Dixie writes *Gloriana* as a standard Victorian "three decker" in one volume and makes use of conventions found in romance and detective stories to serve her feminist purpose, as do many women utopia writers of the twentieth century in employing the form of popular science fiction.

Unquestionably, the conscious borrowing of the most popular literary mode by feminist utopian writers is a political tactic designed to reach the largest readership possible, especially female. *Gloriana* went through four editions in Britain and was reprinted in America in 1892.[38] *The Next Life* has been known popularly in southern China as *Meng Lijun*, and dramatic versions have been frequently staged in the country, even to this day.[39]

The authors of both *The Next Life* and *Gloriana* employ the conventions of romance in their plots, only to twist those conventions ironically to reveal the patriarchal oppression of women, as well as women's rebellion, through acute conflicts arising in the plot development. As there exists no translation of *The Next Life* in any foreign language, I shall provide a plot summary before further discussion.

The story of *The Next Life* is dazzlingly complicated. Set in the Yuan Dynasty, its central conflicts involve three noble families and the imperial family. Meng Lijun is the daughter of the ex-examiner Meng Shiyuan. Her beauty and intelligence have won two suitors: Huangfu Shaohua, the son of the Governor of Yunnan, and the emperor's uncle, Liu Kuibi. In a dilemma over whom to marry, Meng Shiyuan decides that the two suitors should compete with one another in archery. Shaohua wins in shooting and becomes the expectant groom. As a result, Liu Kuibi attempts to burn Shaohua to death in his garden, but Lui's sister Yanyu saves Shaohua's life, making him promise to marry her in the future. His first scheme to rid of himself of his rival having failed, Lui Kuibi asks for the hand of Shaohua's sister, Zhanghua. Again he is refused. Vengefully, he makes use of the power behind his father, Liu Jie, to persecute Shaohua's family, and Shaohua's father, Huangfu Jing, is sent to fight at the frontier. When Huangfu Jing is captured by the Koreans, Liu Jie accuses him of being a traitor, which leads to Emperor Chengzong's order to kill Huangfu's whole family. Shaohua's mother, Yi Liangzheng, in order to preserve the seed of the Huangfu family, helps her son escape when she and her daughter Zhanghua are arrested. As they are being sent to the capital for public execution, the imperial guards are attacked by rebels in the mountains. The chief of the bandits, a woman in male disguise called Wei Yong'e, saves Yi, and her daughter, and accepts Yi as her stepmother.

With the fall of the Huangfu family, Liu Kuibi, through the power of his elder sister, the Empress, makes the emperor issue an order to force Meng Lijun finally to marry him. To escape marriage, Meng disguises herself as a man and escapes with her maid. Before she leaves, she draws a self-portrait with a poem in it expressing her ambition of "exchanging the marital hairpin for an official cap."[40] Fearing imperial punishment, Meng's parents must use Lijun's maiden companion, Su Yingxue, as a substitute. The unfortunate Su Yingxue is secretly in love with Shaohua and hates the scoundrel Liu Kuibi. At the wedding, she attempts to stab Liu. When she fails, she jumps into Kun Ming Lake, but is saved by the examiner, Liang Jian, and his wife, who adopt her as their daughter and change her name to Liang Suhua. Meanwhile Meng Lijun, as a man, has changed her name to

Li Junyu and assumed the style name Mingtang. After great hardships in escaping, she is adopted by the merchant Kang Xinren as his son. As Li Mingtang, Meng wins three first places in national examinations and marries the examiner's adopted daughter, Suhua—her earlier maiden companion; and they live together as husband and wife.

Liu Kuibi, in order to pursue the beautiful Zhanghua, volunteers to wipe out all the mountain rebels and is captured by Chief Wei Yong'e. Just then, the empress dies in childbirth. The emperor's mother is bedridden with grief. Li Mingtang (Meng Lijun in disguise) saves the sick dowager's life, through her knowledge of medicine, and is promoted to the position of defense minister. In order to defeat foreign invaders and allow the Huangfu family to rise again, Li Mingtang advises the emperor to summon brave men of all ranks, including criminals at large, to defend the country. The escaped Shaohua answers the call, after having studied two years of martial arts with Xiong Hao under a hermit called Huang He. Shaohua is appointed by Li Mingtang as General Commander of the Eastern Expedition. Wei Yong'e brings her army of rebels, and Zhanghua organizes an army of women to join the expedition, under the banner of "The Army of Filial Daughters." Overcome primarily by the forces of Wei Yong'e and Zhanghua, the invaders are completely routed. Commander Shaohua is promoted to the position of King of Loyalty and Piety and marries Liu Yanyu to keep his earlier promise. Although he has never seen his promised first wife, Meng Lijun, now believed to have died a female martyr, he resolves not to sleep with Yanyu for three years on the principle of fidelity.

For her merits in promoting the right men to defend the country, Li Mingtang is appointed as a minister of examination, like her father, who is restored to his original post. Although working side by side with her father, Li Mingtang refuses to be recognized as his daughter. At the bedside of her "dying" mother, however, she can no longer hide her feelings and reveals her true identity. When Shaohua hears her secret, he reports it to the emperor, attempting to use imperial power to force Li Mingtang, who is now prime minister and above all men except the emperor, into marriage. However, the emperor has long been stirred by Li Mingtang's beauty and wants her for himself. At this moment there arrive two girls, both using the name of Meng Lijun, who come to marry Shaohua. The emperor orders Shaohua to marry one of them. Judging from Meng Lijun's self-portrait, Shaohua knows they are impostors and falls sick with sorrow. His sister Zhanghua, who has meanwhile become empress, plots hand-in-glove with the emperor's mother to make Li Mingtang drunk so that they can reveal her true sex by taking off her boots and exposing her golden lotus (bound feet).

But, the maid who takes off Li Mingtang's boots and steals the inside lotus shoes is intercepted by the emperor, who forbids her to report the truth to the empress and his mother. The following day, the emperor visits Li Mingtang privately in an attempt to forbid her to reveal her true identity as Meng Lijun, so that he can marry her as his concubine; he gives her three days to choose between death and marriage. Under tyrannical pressures from all directions, she becomes frustrated and despairs that her revealed female self is nothing but a sex object in all men's eyes. She feels her heart burst with anger and bitterness, and the blood spurts from her mouth, spotting her official gown. Here, at this climactic moment, Chen Duansheng puts down her pen forever.

Although *Gloriana* is a much shorter and simpler book, it is no less dramatic and intriguing. It can be seen as the dream of the next life for Maremna, or Dixie herself, who desires to relive her life differently by assuming a male identity. Its plot bears parallels with *The Next Life*: Lord Altai shoots Speranza's lover Harry Kintore and Liu attempts to burn Shaohua to death in the garden; Lord Westray kidnaps Speranza as a sex object and Liu seeks to capture the Beauty Zhanghua; Flora Desmond and her White Regiment attack the prison van to rescue Hector D'Estrange and Wei Yong'e and her gang attack the imperial prison cart to save Zhanghua and her mother; the Duke of Ravensdale's intimate friendship with Gloriana mirrors the emperor's intimate friendship with Meng Lijun; Flora is Gloriana's right arm, as Suhua is Meng Lijun's shield; and Flora and Suhua both fall in love with the man who loves the protagonist, which intensifies the conflict between the comradely love of woman for woman and the sexual love of woman for man and underscores the nobleness of the former (a revision of female jealousy in the traditional romance). The final revelations of sexual identity, trials, and the betrayal of the protagonist by the female in *Gloriana* have their affinities in *The Next Life*. Although professional detectives are too modern for the story of *The Next Life*, there are concerted espionage activities aimed at discovering Meng Lijun's sexual identity. The final shipwreck and the attempted assassination of Gloriana echo the final destructive scene of Meng Lijun's life when the blood spurts from her mouth while she is under patriarchal pressures from all directions—and both sexes.

To some extent, all love romances, classical or modern, are variations of one basic pattern, which universally reflects the relation between sexes in a patriarchal society. In their ironic uses of this pattern, Chen Duansheng's and Dixie's romances, if we may call them romances, offer us not erotic love or passion on the part of their female protagonists, but conflicts, to catch our attention. Most Western utopian writers, including feminist writers of the nineteenth and twentieth centuries, resort to dialogues and verbal wittiness. Romance enables Chen Duansheng and Dixie to ridicule and satirize patriarchy by showing, rather than by arguing. For instance, patriarchal hegemony is well reflected through the male's conventional "carrot and stick" policy towards a woman—offering her a choice of either marriage or death. But Chen Duansheng's and Dixie's female rebels dare to thrust a dagger at the man who sees them as mere sex objects (in *The Next Life*) or to grasp the blade of a man's butchering knife with naked hands (in *Gloriana*). For these writers, every action and development in the foreground becomes a daring thought in the background, which contributes to their utopian intention and adds a brush-stroke to their feminist expression. It is in this sense that Dixie regards *Gloriana* as a romance. She says in her preface to *Gloriana*, "There is no romance worth reading, which has not the solid foundation of truth to support it; there is no excuse for the existence of romance, unless it fixes thought on that truth which underlies it."[41]

Both author's parodic uses of romantic plots to embody feminist ideas is innovative; they do not simply borrow the conventions of the popular literary mode of their time, but experiment with the borrowed mode to generate a new form. In employing the conventions of romance for feminist purposes, *Gloriana* is no longer a romance, but an experimental melodrama that concentrates on plot rather than characters and shapes "a dream world inhabited by dream people."[42] To enhance its political effectiveness, *Gloriana* reduces all its characters to archetypal strip figures of sharp, black-and-white delineation. Lord Westray represents the stubborn and desperate patriarchy, the archenemy of women. Evie represents the "honorable, upright, and courageous men" who are allies of women. The artificial Lady Victoire undoubtedly represents the unawakened "sluggards amongst women,"[43] who are deceived by men and willing to help sabotage the women's movement. Gloriana is portrayed as a legendary figure, or culture hero, and after she disguises herself as a boy called Hector D'Estrange, we hardly see her as a person. She is openly declared by the author to be the "idol" and "Commander-in-chief" of women. She is everywhere and nowhere. She is believed to appear in several places at the same time and is simply beyond the power of the police. In a word, she is none other than the specter of the feminist movement. But unlike most political or religious novels or allegories, *Gloriana* does not smack of dull didacticism but keeps the liveliness of a thrilling romance. It reads very much like a fable.

Rachel Blau DuPlessis observes that the revived apologue in the utopia and Bildungsroman contains "embedded elements from 'assertive discourse'—genres like sermon, manifesto, tract, fable."[44] In *Gloriana*, the authorial voice is declarative and fully articulated, and its assertive discourse carries the power of political agitation. Its long declarations about women's emancipation and rights would appear to be polemics, if they were not required by the protagonist's announced mission and the climate of revolution in the background. Dixie's artistic arrangements have made *Gloriana* a stirring utopia of action without excessively heavy-handed, political intrusions.

It is hard, however, to praise *Gloriana* as a literary masterpiece. For Dixie, the fiction (or the romance) appears only as a garment for her ideas; it did succeed, however, in its political intention and, at the time of its publication, received serious critical attention. One reader wrote to Mrs. Gladstone: "It [*Gloriana*] is not an ordinary novel, but writes of a woman who has wandered over the world and studied women's position and condition through it."[45] Another reader wrote to the editor of the *Women's Penny Paper* that *Gloriana* exposes the things men do not want women to know and "boldly investigates social evils."[46] The *Women's Herald* hailed its publication as Dixie's "advocacy of Women Rights."[47] Although the editor of *The Atheneum* took a snobbish attitude towards the book's writing style, he confessed that "The evident earnestness of the author forbids the reader to regard *Gloriana* as an elaborate joke," adding that the novel earns respect for its author's "warm sympathy for the poor and apparent honest conviction that 'the monstrous regiment of women' is the only cure for social evils."[48]

Like *Gloriana*, *The Next Life* is a rare, experimental flower grown out of an old mode. Classified as telling-singing literature, once considered vulgar, it failed to attract scholarly attention until 1954, when Chen Yinke published his "On *The Destiny of the Next Life*," praising its poetic skills and considering it a match for the beauty of the Greek and Hindu epics: "People of the world are often stunned by the fame of the Greek or Western epics; but they do not know that our country also has this genre."[49] It is, perhaps, injudicious to bring *The Next Life* and Homer together for comparison, as Chen Yinke suggests, since they differ greatly in spirit and social contexts; but in its modern concerns, subtle irony, and satirical tone, *The Next Life* certainly does bring to mind Byron's *Don Juan*.[50]

The Next Life possesses a subtlety in containing no political harangues. Though it never directly challenges the injustices of patriarchy, a spirit of repudiation permeates every page. For instance, when a girl is born, the father despairs; when a boy is born, the same father praises Heaven; in a crisis, women must let men escape; the son, even when he is a criminal, is still the man of the family, whereas the daughter remains insignificant however great the contributions she may make to family and country; and, finally, the discovery of an ambitious woman's female identity amounts to a sentence of death.

Unlike the archetypal strip characters in *Gloriana*, the characters in *The Next Life* are complicated, round, and individualistic. Liu Chongyi comments in the foreword of the book: "In *The Next Life* women always surpass men . . . female images are much more vivid and individualistic than male images. And the author puts forth more creative effort."[51] Male as well as female characters, however, are multifarious beings. Strong feminist figures such as Zhanghua and Su Yingxue are still confined by their feudalistic judgment of virtue and chastity. The emperor does not merely embody imperial power, but often acts as the humane and enlightened ally of women; and as a male, he is also the utmost patriarchal authority. Although Shaohua is Meng Lijun's archenemy in upholding the feudal doctrine of loyalty and chastity, he appears as a most charming prince and pathetic lover. Yet, despite its complex characterization, *Next Life* possesses all the archetypes present in *Gloriana*.

Apart from utilizing the associations and conflicts of these archetypal characters to subvert patriarchy, Chen Duansheng's poetic novel gives great psychological depth to individual characters, particularly to the protagonist. In 1960, the world-renowned poet Guo Moruo (Kuo Mojo), after reading *The Destiny Of the Next Life*, said that he was no less enchanted by this book, as a man of seventy, than he had been by *The Water Margin* and *Dream of the Red Chamber*, as a teenager. He affirmed Chen Duansheng's judgement from a poetic perspective and added:

> As far as vividness, precision and spiral unfolding in narration, characterization, and psychological description . . . are concerned, the skills of Chen Duansheng can be compared to those of the English and French writers of the eighteenth and nineteenth centuries, such

as the British Scott [1771–1832], the French Stendhal [1783–1842] and Balzac [1799–1850]. But these three came up later than Chen Duansheng and all began to write in prose form in their mature years while Chen Duansheng used poetic form and began to write at only eighteen.[52]

Indeed, *The Next Life* should be regarded as a great novel in poetic or epic form. It surpasses the famous novels of the Ming and Qing dynasties in its psychological exploration of character. Moreover, the protagonist's psychological reactions, repression, and argumentative rebellion converge to form and strengthen the overall feminist/utopian theme. Li Qingzhao (Li Ch'ingchao 1081–c. 1141) is recognized as the greatest female poet in Chinese classics, but Chen Duansheng also should be recognized, not only as a great poet/novelist, but as the first conscious feminist utopian writer in Chinese literature.[53] The belated discovery of *The Next Life* by literary critics may be attributed to a traditional silence about popular literature as well as a patriarchal ignorance of women's utopian yearnings.

Both *The Next Life* and *Gloriana* use popular romantic plots largely because these plots are typical products of patriarchal society. When used parodically to propagate feminist ideas, they become most subversive in meaning. In addition, the liveliness, intensity, and suspense of romance set this utopian fiction free from a Western utopian tradition that relies heavily on an *argumental discourse*. The beginning of Maremna's dream in *Gloriana* is beautifully poetic, and its underlying strategy and dramatic intensity appeal to oriental taste. The aesthetic achievement of *The Next Life* shatters the common belief that there exists no truly great literature in utopian writings by women.

The Politics of Concealing Sexual Identity

The most prominent feature shared by these two utopian dreams is their use of sexual disguise. N. P. Ricci says, "In a Foucauldian framework, then, the question of woman comes down to a question of knowledge and power."[54] For a woman to gain knowledge and power in a male-dominated society requires that she have an equal opportunity in education and politics. Naturally a desire to escape the imprisonment of her sexual gender and become equal with men, or even surpass men, has become a woman's dream. Both *The Next Life* and *Gloriana* use concealment of sexual identity to express such a utopian dream, which involves revision of literary traditions, repudiation of patriarchy, and assertion of feminist ideals.

Sexual disguise appears in both Eastern and Western literary traditions. In China, a woman disguised as a man appears in two of the most popular traditional tales: "Liang Shanbo and Zhu Yingtai" and "Hua Mulan."[55] In the former, Zhu Yingtai, disguised as a man, goes to school with Liang Shanbo and later falls in love with him. But, her father forces her to marry another man, who is rich and old. Consequently, she and Liang both die and are transformed into a pair of butterflies. This story, which says nothing about female intellectual ability, is a dream of free love, growing out of either man's or woman's fantasy. In the latter tale, Hua Mulan conceals her female identity and goes off to fight at the frontier, replacing her aged father and demonstrating a female capability for war. As soon as the war is over, Hua Mulan again puts on her female makeup and retires to her boudoir. This tale has been handed down as a story of loyalty and dutifulness from generation to generation. In *The Next Life*, a butterfly dream of love may be seen in the character of Su Yingxue, who is bold enough to thrust a dagger at Liu Kuibi but remains a captive of her dream of love for Shaohua. The shadow of Hua Mulan may also be seen in the character of Zhanghua, who fights as the head of the Army of Filial Daughters. When the war is over, in spite of the fact that she marries the emperor, she gains no political power and becomes a childbearer. It may have seemed to Chen Duansheng that these two types of women had become so accepted by society that there was no need for them to conceal their sexual identity.

More so than even the warrior-wife-slave paragon, the female martyr has stood as the paragon of the Chinese female. A wife committing suicide by dashing her head against the tombstone of her husband could gain a name as a martyr. Su Yingxue, as Meng Lijun's substitute, jumps into a river rather than marry Lui Kuibi, and the imperial court issues an order to erect a monument for the presumably dead Meng Lijun, who had kept her virginity intact for her contracted husband. Chen Duansheng ridicules the "piety" fostering this paragon tradition of the female martyr and warrior. In Luo Maosdeng's *Sanbao's Expedition to the Western Ocean*, Wang Lianying and Mrs. Bai both imitate Hua Mulan in avenging their husbands on horseback; but they are both sentenced to death for their unwomanly or impious behaviors according to the Confucian doctrine of the Three Obediences and Four Virtues.[56] Chen Duansheng is shrewd enough to see the hypocrisy in the woman-warrior model produced by the patriarchal culture. She creates new types of women by using concealment of sexual identity as a political tactic.

Chen Duansheng's tactic of concealing sexual identity enables the new feminist figure of Wei Yong'e to establish a utopia of the margin, in opposition to the imperial court, as men did in *Outlaws of the Marsh*.[57] Wei Yong'e acts as the protector of her sex, capturing and punishing the stubborn patriarchal scoundrel Liu Kuibi, and her rule fulfills the prediction of "a new emperor who practices justice and does not sink into sexual pleasure."[58] For Chen Duansheng, such a new emperor must be a woman, and the character of Wei Yong'e embodies the female desire for an oppositional power.

The radical significance of concealing sexual identity as both a device and a theme is discernible in the development of the protagonist, Meng Lijun, who never succumbs to the conventional woman's fate. She abandons needlework and reads books and poetry. Her talent, superior to her brother's, makes her confident in having a public career. At the beginning of the story, she is treated like a Helen, as a prize for male competition. But, the Emperor's order to force her to marry makes her determined to seek an alternative way of life— "exchanging the marital hairpin for an official cap." How could a woman realize such an unwomanly ambition in the dark age of feudalism, in which women were yoked under the laws of "God, Emperor, Father, and Husband"? The only plausible way would be to steal a fair chance among men by hiding her female identity.

As early as the Five Dynasties (907–960) in the State of Shu, a prefectural governor called Zhou Xiang wanted to marry her daughter to a handsome officer named Huang Chonggu for his superior intelligence and ability. Huang wrote a poem, including the line: "I wish the Heaven could soon turn me into a man," and signed her title as *Jinshi* (a successful candidate in the highest imperial examinations). Her story originates the term *Nü Zhuangyuan* (the female Number One Scholar at the highest imperial examinations).[59] The dramatist Xu Wei (1521–1593), acknowledging women's talent and capturing their fantasy of sexual equality, wrote a play called *Nü Zhuangyuan*, in which the female protagonist, by concealing her sexual identity, passes all levels of examination and achieves the title of Zhuangyuan. Nevertheless, Xu Wei's *Nü Zhuangyuan* is essentially a quest for ideal marriage—the female Zhuangyuan of letters matches the male Zhuangyuan of martial arts. Xue Wei's play seems to have stimulated female characterization in popular literature henceforth.[60]

That a woman becomes Zhuangyuan by means of concealing her

sexual identity was already conventionalized in *tanci* during Chen Duansheng's time. Before Meng Lijun escapes in a male guise, she takes Xie Xiang'e and Liu Qingyun as her role models. Xie Xiang'e, sister of Xie Yuhui in *The Destiny of the Bracelet*, achieves the title of Zhuangyuan through male impersonation, but winds up her fate as the wife of a prince. Liu Qingyun,[61] a character in *Small Gold Coins*, also becomes Zhuangyuan under a male guise, but must kneel at court with a sword on her back to beg imperial pardon for the crime of concealing her true sex. She is ultimately reduced to a wife and a governess for the imperial concubines. Comparing Xie Xiang'e and Liu Qingyun with Meng Lijun, it is clear that though Chen Duansheng attributes the origin of her imaginative sexual concealment to earlier *tanci* works, she rejects them by political revolt—resisting marriage, negating her sexual concealment as a crime, and refusing to give up the political position she has achieved by being equal with men. Unlike Xu Wei's female Zhuangyuan, or Xie Xiang'e and Liu Qingyun, who are destined to marriage, Meng Lijun appears as a new type of woman who desires political power. By borrowing a man's guise, she demonstrates not only her intellectual superiority but, especially, her capability for governing. The moment she discards her traditional feminine self to a portrait, she chooses running state affairs as her career. She becomes prime minister at the age of eighteen and proves herself to be the most efficient, upright of ministers—"the heaven-column" of the state. In her absence, the court is paralyzed; documents pile up and disorder reigns.

In the West, as early as in the classical Greek age, Aristophanes had used the device of concealing sexual identity in his comedy *Ecclesiazusae*, in which a group of women disguised as men seize power by vote. They eventually abuse power, as men do, and demonstrate little political ability. Aristophanes's concealing of sexual identity is used to provide a political alternative without a feminist intention. Spenser's employment of concealing sexual identity, or transvestism, in *The Faerie Queene*, typically represents two classical intentions: to defend patriarchal chastity, as Britomart does; and to embody a denatured savage force, as with the land of Amazons headed by Radigund. Dixie is aware that concealing sexual identity by itself is not necessarily feminist. In her novels, a woman concealing her sexual identity may be a traitor—an instrument of man—or a feminist hero. Both images appear in *Gloriana*. Little Leonie appears to be a detective boy. She is cut off from the female tradition represented by mothers and sisters and brought up completely by men. Thus, she is unable to think, mechanically completes her "duty" given by Mr. Trackem—the running dog of patriarchy, and betrays Gloriana. On self-awakening, however, she sacrifices herself to save Gloriana's life. The concealment of her sexual identity in the character of Leonie implies no feminist necessity. Instead it resembles Virginia Woolf's device of crossing sex in *Orlando*. When dressed as a man, Orlando behaves like a perfectly patriarchal male who hurls "at the faithless woman all the insults that have ever been the lot of her sex;"[62] when a change in herself dictates "her choice of a woman's dress and of a woman's sex,"[63] she grows into a new woman. In this case, "clothes are but a symbol of something hid deep beneath."[64]

Dixie uses concealment of sexual identity as a conscious thematic device for feminist assertion in her character Gloriana. Like Meng Lijun, Gloriana demonstrates female intellectual superiority in surpassing all male students in Eton and Oxford. But when Meng is in a man's guise, she is forced to behave like one and to govern the country within the existing structure. Although she reaches the highest position possible, she is unable to make any new laws concerning women, as does the female Emperor Wu Zetian in *The Flowers in the Mirror*. We must consider, however, that the protagonist is confined by her male disguise, as the author herself is restricted by the conditions of her age. Dixie's Gloriana is different, for she is consciously brought up to assume her historical mission, as is Galahad, the illegitimate son of Lancelot, in Arthurian literature. As a champion of the women's movement, she avenges her mother and fights for the emancipation of all women. Both Meng Lijun (at the age of eighteen) and Gloriana (at the age of twenty-eight) reach the position of prime minister. Meng Lijun is promoted by the emperor, while Gloriana enters Parliament by the votes of women. In Parliament, Gloriana "presents a complex bill with four clauses, each calculated to redress an aspect of women's dispossession: equal education with men, free entry to the professions, the right to stand for Parliament, and inheritance by primogeniture. The last two clauses form a radical assault on masculine politicians; the right to stand for Parliament introducing women into the House of Commons, and primogeniture introducing them into the House of Lords."[65]

Gloriana's male guise never serves as an obstacle to her actions or speeches on behalf of women. In characterizing Gloriana, Dixie employs the device of concealing sexual identity to propagate her politics of competing with men. Dixie finds inspiration for this in political reality rather than in any previous literary tradition. In her treatise "Woman's Position," she openly encourages women to conceal their sexual identity in order to find their place in society:

Look at Woman in the political world. . . . She is a pariah, outside the pale of human rights. She may not even vote for the male who is to represent her, unless she does so by stealth and fraud; for it will surprise some people to know that there are not a few voters in the United Kingdom who are women in men's clothes, who have been forced to adopt that attire in order to obtain work, and who, posing as men, exercise those rights which are denied to them as women. I myself know several of these people, and am willing to confess that I have advised them and helped them to play their role. It is man's shame that woman should be driven to such a subterfuge to obtain liberty, protection, employment, and the commonest of human rights, the vote. I, for one, shall always advise women to act thus when it is convenient to themselves to do so, and where their position makes it necessary. At this moment I know a woman who is captain of a ship, her sex being unknown to her employers.[66]

Aside from its political function and thematic importance, the device of concealing sexual identity has a crucial technical necessity. It enables Chen Duansheng to produce a feminist discourse by inventing a rebellious private voice and an open voice of supremacy and it helps Dixie to put feminist discourse in a masculine voice. Both authors are sensitive to relationship of voice and gender in a patriarchal society. When a woman adopts a man's name and disguises her body as a man, her voice takes on the masculine gender to the audience. In *The Next Life*, the suspicion of Li Mingtang's sexual identity leads to two trials of gender. At both trials, Li Mingtang defeats her prosecutors with a man's voice, full of audacity. The imperial court finds her guiltless on the ground that she does not show "any feminine traits" or womanliness in her emotion and voice.

When Li Mingtang is disguised as a man and promoted to the highest of position, she can no longer use her own voice and, ironically, defends patriarchal ideas. She often has to wave the flags of loyalty and piety. She advises Shaohua to take concubines and denies the possibility of women getting to any official position. It is easy for the reader to perceive that she deliberately says such things only to hide her sexual identity. Since the protagonist cannot express her feminist ideas in her public voice, the author resorts to her private voice. When she is alone, she often protests, "Why should I give up my golden marten fur and jade belt [which signify a man's high position]? Why should I change them back to a green hairpin or a red skirt?"[67] In the final chapter, when her sexual identity is being exposed, she uses her private voice to denounce Shaohua as "the stinking Confucian disciple" and protests,

> I am not hidden in the deep chamber of a lady.
> We frequently meet in court and chat in private.
> The beauty of me you have often seen.
> Why should you insist on marrying me
> If it is not because you cannot bear being
> My subordinate and me being your master?[68]

Rebellious as this private voice can be, it is still a muted or repressed one. To overcome its deficiency in defending the author's utopian vision, Chen Duansheng invents an open voice of supremacy and boldly puts it into the mouths of the emperor and of his mother, whose voice has an even higher authority.[69] Both the emperor and his mother have double faces: the Emperor is the impartial judge as well as the selfish male, while the Emperor's mother is the powerful feminist as well as the conservative mother who plots to discover Meng Lijun's lotus feet. When the emperor and his mother stand for the highest authority of justice, they serve as the author's mouthpiece. For instance, when Meng's beauty first arouses the suspicion of her shrewd eye, the emperor's mother remarks: "If the minister is really a female, it is lawful for the state to be governed by the Mother."[70] When he is apprised of Meng's crime in concealing her sex, the emperor's immediate reaction is:

> What a wonder!
> If the Prime Minister is Meng Lijun
> What crime has she committed?!
> I cannot punish but reward her.
> Since the creation of the world
>   there is no such a woman like her.
> She won three first places in examinations
> and rose to the position of Prime Minister.
> She has managed the state affairs of *yin* and *yang* wisely
>   and brought the country to order!
> She is, indeed, a genius in statecraft.
> Who has ever seen such a woman in history?
> Only a muddle-headed emperor would take her as guilty.[71]

The private, protesting voice and the open voice of supremacy, which protects and justifies the former, combine to forge a powerful feminist prophecy in a dark age of feudalism.

Meng Lijun cannot speak for women while in man's guise, therefore, Chen Duansheng invents a voice for her of supremacy more powerful than that of any man who could speak for women. Dixie also exposes prejudice against the female voice in a male-dominated society and invents a powerful masculine voice speaking from the throat of a feminist. In nineteenth-century England, women were the silenced sex. As Dixie says, "the mouth of Eve was closed. Her voice is still hushed."[72] When the women's movement enabled the feminist vanguards to speak, the sound of their voices was often ridiculed as "shrieking"—so jarring on men's ears that it was likely to rouse more resentment than sympathy. In the second trial scene of *The Next Life*, Meng's mother is brought to court. She insists on recognizing her genuine daughter, while her daughter in the disguise of man refuses to be recognized. Because Li Mingtang has the advantage of the male voice, her mother's truth is silenced. Meng's father is laughed at and fined by the court one-half year's salary for revealing the fact that he obeys his wife at home—being a hen-pecked husband. Similarly, in the trial scene in *Gloriana*, when D'Estrange's mother is brought to court, she tells the truth "in a firm clear voice, without hesitation or faltering."[73] Yet, because of the female gender of her voice, her words are treated by the judge as a hallucination—"Is it possible that such horrors reflect the truth?"[74] She is "cross-examined"; but, when the Duke of Ravensdale "corroborates the statements made by Hector D'Estrange," his voice is listened to "with marked attention," and he is not cross-examined.[75] In representing different treatments of a man's voice and a woman's voice in court, Chen Duansheng and Dixie directly challenge men's legislative power. Chinese law and the English law each tells "its own tale of cruel inequality and injustice as between the woman and the man."[76] Man's legal power, as in Lovelace's imagined rape trial in Richardson's *Clarissa*, is "dependent upon his ability to silence women in court."[77]

In an age of prejudice against the female voice, the device of concealing her female sex provides Gloriana the advantage of propagating feminist ideas through a voice of the male gender, so that her words can carry more weight and make it easier for men, or even some women, to accept her and become her allies. When Mr. Trevor reads the Eton boy D'Estrange's "Essay on Woman's Position," he says "it's deuced clever and original," and he is moved by the essay. He feels guilty for his past attitudes towards women and begins to change his attitude towards his wife.[78] If the essay were written in an undisguised female voice, we might rightly wonder whether he would have bothered to read it or think twice about it at all.

Dixie is aware of the necessity not only of disguising oneself as a man to do what a woman, as a woman, could never achieve, but also of masculinizing the female's voice and discourse. The discourse Chen Duansheng invents is "the language of the night," which tries to let "the truth against the world" sink through by private mutterings and a nightingale's warblings.[79] The discourse Dixie tries to forge is the language of the day, "the language of the torrent's roar:"[80]

> And hark! a voice with accents clear
> Is raised, which all are forced to hear.
> 'Tis woman's voice, for ages hushed,
> Pleading the cause of woman crushed.[81]

Chen Duansheng's feminist discourse negates received feudalist ideas about women by means of irony, while Dixie's masculinized feminist discourse eradicates notions of women's spiritual and physical slavery, producing words of daring action on behalf of women.

In creating a new discourse, Chen Duansheng and Dixie are both concerned with the effect and authority of voice on the audience. By exposing prejudices against the female voice, these authors urge their readers to reconsider bias produced by conventional images associated with the female sex and to listen to the voice of truth—the new female discourse is not, after all, "hallucination."

Revelation of sexual disguise generally leads to the climax of a novel. In feminist utopias, it intensifies the conflicts between the different sexes as well as within the same sex, thus giving the utopia a closer contact with reality. In a patriarchal world, female sex is treated as a birthmark of inferiority and as a crime, if one tries to conceal it. When D'Estrange reveals her identity as the female Gloriana, men's shouts of "Guilty!" "Condemned to death!" "Hector D'Estrange a Woman!" pass "through the court, along the corridors, and out into the street beyond."[82] For centuries, a woman's sex revealed in court would convict her or even inflict on her the death penalty. Gloriana's self-revelation of her sexual identity, however, signifies a great feminist victory. She is able to declare her female identity both at court and before the whole country: "Hector D'Estrange, whose advancement has been rapid and unparalleled almost in the annals of statesmanship [a Member of Parliament for seven years and the current Prime Minister], must be no longer known to you under that name. The time has come when I must confess myself. Before you, you see one of the despised and feeble sex, the unfitted to rule, the inferior of men. I am a woman!"[83] This feminist victory drives Lord Westray and his follower

Mr. Trackem into their last-ditch struggle. Lord Westray, who first treats Gloriana as a love rival and then as an archenemy—a substitute for the mother, employs the naive woman Little Leonie in his plot for Gloriana's death.

The protagonist's sexual revelation also inevitably intensifies the struggle between women liberated and women still subscribing to the conventional style of love and marriage. The unawakened sluggard Victorie, under Mr. Trackem's deception of love, attempts to assassinate Gloriana. Similarly, Meng Lijun is betrayed by women. The Emperor's mother and Empress Zhanghua, who are feminists in many ways but also stubborn upholders of feudal marriage and virtues, plot to reveal Li's sexual identity by using a poisonlike wine to make her unconscious. Zhanghua also plans to give the discovered Meng Lijun —proven a superior prime minister—to a man (Shaohua) as a reward.

Gloriana reveals her sexual identity when she and her feminist army and allies have grown powerful enough. Her revelation cannot harm her anymore and enhances the courage of women during the intensified conflicts between the sexes. Conversely, the revelation of Meng Lijun's sexual identity highlights a double mutilation—physical and political. The political mutilation of a Chinese woman is embodied in the binding mutilation of her feet, normally to three inches. Because of Meng Lijun's unwomanly ambition, a more severe political mutilation is signified by her extraordinary footbinding to 2.7 inches. Simone de Beauvoir points out that a woman "is called 'the sex,' by which is meant that she appears essentially to the male as a sexual being. For him she is sex—absolute sex, no less."[84] When her feet are discovered, Meng Lijun is not only mutilated in action and speech, but reduced to a mere sexual object in all males' eyes. On discovering Li Mingtang's true sex, the Emperor, as the patriarchal tyrant, privately visits her and threatens to kill her whole family to force her to marry him. Shaohua's family also experiences antagonism from the Emperor because of Shaohua's competing for Meng Lijun. But, Meng Lijun defies all their male chauvinism, and as a result of indignation over her womanly fate, blood bursts from her mouth and dyes her official gown.[85]

As we know, The Next Life was left unfinished at this climactic moment, and writers who have offered various endings have failed to understand Chen Duansheng's true feminist intention. The writer Liang Desheng attempts to marry Meng Lijun off in her added ending;[86] and Guo Moruo, the famous Chinese critic and poet, believes that Liang distorted Chen Duansheng's authorial intention and insists that Meng Lijun must die to complete her ambition to "change the marital hairpin for an official cap" and "return to the void without touching the pollution of dust."[87] But, critics Zhao Jingshen and Liu Chongyi point out that a happy ending is the fashion of Chen Duansheng's age and thus within her authorial intention. Actually, two possible happy endings are implied in the book: one is that Meng Lijun will marry Shaohua but remain Prime Minister; the other is that Meng Lijun will marry the Emperor and continue to work at court. Both, however, would be impractical in Chen Duansheng's feudal society and, more importantly, would fail to realize Chen Duansheng's feminist ideal. Of course, Meng Lijun could die, but if she does, her death will be the death of Chen Duansheng's utopia; and if Meng Lijun marries, her marriage will have violated her wish to "exchange the marital hairpin for an official cap." According to feudal codes of loyalty and piety, Meng Lijun commits the crime of disloyalty by hiding her true identity from the emperor and the crime of impiety by denying her own parents; but Chen Duansheng presents Meng Lijun as the most loyal minister in defending the country and running state affairs, and a most humane character in caring for Shaohua, Suhua, and her own mother. When Meng Lijun hears that her mother is dangerously ill, she goes to see her at all costs, only to find out that the illness is a trick to test her sexual identity. As stated in the first chapter of the first book, Meng Lijun is predestined to be Shaohua's first wife. Yet by the end of the book, it is not hard to see that Shaohua—King of Loyalty and Piety—is Meng's most dangerous enemy, an obstacle to women's emancipation, and that Meng has used her whole life to struggle against the predestined fate for women.

The Next Life is Chen Duansheng's lifelong work. Comparing the first book of *The Next Life* with its seventeenth book, we can see a sudden deepening in Chen Duansheng's observation of reality. That she did not finish the epic may have been because she was stopped short by insoluble conflicts between her dream for the "next life" and the reality of a patriarchal society some three thousand years old. She, instead of her utopian hero, died in order to protest the fate of women. A similar conflict between a woman's suppressed masculine ambition and her inescapable feminine fate is portrayed in Dixie's last novel *Izra, or, A Child of Solitude* (1905). Its female protagonist, with all her feminist ideas, has to stay "a proper Victorian wife and mother at home, but lives a secret life dressed as a male, with all the freedom that this allows."[88] Like Chen Duansheng's *The Next Life*, *Ezra*, a long romance of seven hundred pages, was left unfinished with its author's death; the conflict throws the author and her protagonist both into the abyss of solitude. But *Gloriana*, Dixie's earlier book, is a much more heartening feminist utopia; in 1900, Gloriana becomes the legal prime minister; after her, Flora governs for twenty years; by 1999, many of Gloriana's reform plans have been carried out.

Utopian Visions for Women

One of the values of utopian literature lies in its projecting of new directions and alternatives. *The Next Life* and *Gloriana* provide similar visions. They both insist that gender difference is a cultural product and that when women are free from prejudices against them, enjoying the same opportunities in education, politics, and all other aspects of life, they shall be capable of being equal to men and will become proven beings "who can reason, and who can study humanity in its various phases, and act on her own responsibility."[89]

Both works imply that a female, rather than male, government is more efficient in bringing order and prosperity to the country, because women, coming out of the ranks of the oppressed, are more eager for reform. In *Gloriana*, Duke Ravensdale relinquishes his position of prime minister to Gloriana, for "she alone has the right to carry those great reforms. The person who conceived them alone has that right."[90] *The Next Life* shows not only that it is natural for women to govern but that the country becomes paralyzed without women's participation. Women are "the Column of the Heaven," and the deeds of Meng Lijun and Wei Yong'e are reminiscent of those of the mythological goddess Nüwa, who supports and mends the falling sky.

Both *The Next Life* and *Gloriana* provide women careers within the academy and in open society as alternatives to the traditional secluded and man-centered life. In breaking away from the bondage of family, marriage, and traditional feminine traits, Meng Lijun is even more radical than Gloriana. In *Gloriana*, with the influence of revolution, the number of marriages is diminished, and increasingly more females are set free from their "unnatural and one-sided position in society" and take women's causes as their career.[91] Yet, Gloriana still "blushes" and "her last vision of the life which she is quitting, is the face of Evie Ravensdale,"[92] and we are told of her marriage in the epilogue. Meng Lijun raises the question of why a woman must marry at all. She enjoys working with the emperor and Shaohua as colleagues but treats them mercilessly as opponents when they see her as merely a sexual object. She challenges, "Why can't I, Meng Lijun, remain an official all my life? . . . Being married to a man is not that important; I'd rather leave my name in history as a good minister."[93] Marriage seems to be a curse to Meng Lijun. But in an imagined egalitarian context, marriage is cherished by Dixie. Although the character of Evie in *Gloriana* is underdeveloped, Dixie's representation of him as an ideal, equal partner is quite clear. In her added ending, Liang Desheng, attempting to follow Chen Duansheng's train of thought, depicts an ideal marriage in which woman and man are like mandarin ducks in bed (a Chinese traditional image of ideal love for couples); the woman not only helps at home but participates in public affairs; and both enjoy composing poetry in their leisure time—behaving like best of friends.[94] Yet, this dream of ideal marriage is still phallocentric. When Liang was adding the three books to *The Next Life*, she was already nearly sixty. She confessed that she was too old and sick to care for fame and honor; so she "fuzzed up the story" and made Meng Lijun and Shaohua marry each other.[95] Again, Chen Duansheng's intention is violated by such additions, for she seems quite firm in her conviction that women should have the freedom of remaining single and being independent.

Both *The Next Life* and *Gloriana* create a vision of female comradeship. In *Gloriana*, the mother serves as the backbone for the new woman (Gloriana), who is the protector and educator of the younger woman (Leonie). Among members of the same generation, Flora Desmond is Gloriana's right arm. They both fall in love with the Duke of Ravensdale, but there is no jealousy between them. They hold sisterhood higher than love between sexes. In *The Next Life*, Su Yingxue is deeply in love with Shaohua, the man Meng Lijun is predestined to marry. Yet, to help Meng Lijun in her disguise, she sacrifices her own desire and marries Meng Lijun. The marriage of the two women foretells the ideal lesbian relationship. They are confidantes and treat each other like blood sisters. The love between them surpasses that of a real husband and wife. Meng Lijun even says openly, "It is possible for a woman to marry a woman; but it will be a wonder if two males can ever live in cooperation!"[96] Her view anticipates Gilman's in *Herland*.[97]

The device of sex-role reversal implies that one rules over the other. Nan Albinski remarks: "Dixie engages in a symbolic role-reversal, for while her Gloriana is called Hector, the Duke is usually referred to as 'Evie'."[98] But, sex-role reversal runs counter to Dixie's egalitarian vision of the sexes in all aspects of life. In *Gloriana*, the gender reversal of their names signifies the transcendence of "sexual identity, into a new landscape where men can be women and women

men."[99] As early as 1890, the editor of *The Woman's Herald* regarded Gloriana as "typical of the coming woman: the woman who manages to combine . . . all those qualities which men have hitherto believed to be incompatible."[100] As far as I know, *Gloriana* is the only utopia written by a woman who openly declares her book written with "no antagonism to man" and welcomes righteous men as allies to the women's cause.[101]

Gloriana, unlike feminist utopias that insist on women governing alone, upholds an egalitarian principle between man and woman. The central question for Dixie is not whether a man or a woman should govern, but how one governs. Although Dixie affirms the right of women's rule and suggests that women should take the lead in governing because they, as society's victims are more capable of reforming, she does not exclude the right of men's rule. If Gloriana had not survived, Evie, not Flora, would have been the prime minister. Using the voice of the people, Dixie writes: "I don't see what it matters whether Mr. D'Estrange is a man or a woman, sir. He's the people's friend, sir; he wants to help us poor folk."[102]

Amazonian images appear in both utopias. Zhanghua and Wei Yong'e represent two oriental types of Amazons. The ideal feminist Meng Lijun rejects the lifestyles of Zhanghua, for its required "dutifulness" and total annihilation of woman herself, and Wei Yong'e, for its undisciplined wildness. Meng Lijun herself governs through discipline and knowledge. She is a kind of new feminist Amazon, who "does not mime the male principle but denies it in order to unite the two fundamental forms of life in paradisiacal harmony which had been divided by the Great Mother."[103]

The Western Amazon tradition does not involve filial duty to the father, as does that of the woman warrior in China. In *Gloriana*, the White Regiment of the Women's Volunteer Companies surpasses the Army of Filial Daughters, headed by Zhanghua, and the utopia of marshes, commanded by Wei Yong'e, in the conscious aim of battling for women, particularly in their discipline. Through the mouthpiece Hector D'Estrange, Dixie says: "One of our most heart-stirring writers —I allude to Whyte-Melville—has left it declared in his writings, 'that if a legion of Amazons could be rendered amenable to discipline they would conquer the world.' "[104] By "discipline," Dixie means organization. The strengths of strong women in *The Next Life* work in isolation from one another. In *Gloriana*, the women have all been united to become a powerful social force in revolution. Meng Lijun, confined by her male disguise, could only be a strong political figure, but Gloriana is able to establish a new type of woman in power, who battles for all women and for the rest of humanity.

Both Chen Duansheng and Dixie play the role of the invisible, rational thinker in their utopias. Both writers refuse any patriarchal notion of a female nature, or essence. They rationalize woman's participation in governing a masculine world by invoking women's innate rights and repudiate men's laws intended for women's degradation as "false to nature."[105] In over three thousand years of civilization, the female's subordination to the male has been regarded as a natural law. Subversion of this so-called natural law is central to *The Next Life* and accomplished through the literary device of a woman disguised as a man. Meng Lijun's greatest crime in concealing her female identity lies in her breaching the law of *yin* and *yang*. The narrator repeatedly accuses Meng Lijun of turning this law upside down, but the complaint becomes ironical when we realize that the Chinese also call state affairs, or official matters of right and wrong, affairs of *yin* and *yang*. Meng Lijun, by her excellent administration of "things of *yin* and *yang*," fully proves woman's natural, political, and governing rights and smashes the tradition that keeps woman under man. In *The Next Life*, the country is saved by women and governed in an orderly way. It is apparent that when the country is in the hands of men, things get out of hand. *Gloriana* offers a more straightforward argument in renouncing the law of male over female as one of "the artificial laws" concocted by men. Dixie's novel regards "the cause of woman" as "the cause of Nature," which is "unconquerable."[106]

In the area of feminist utopian criticism, one often finds discussions of patterns of feminist utopias in ideas or technique. *Gloriana*, which has not been reprinted since 1892, seldom appears in contemporary utopian criticism. There are two possible reasons: *Gloriana* is treated as a popular romance more than a significant utopia; and it does not fit into feminist utopian patterns prevalent in the West. Carol S. Pearson, in her examination of feminist utopias by women in the nineteenth and twentieth centuries, finds in them an anarchic pattern in politics: "The feminist Utopian ideal is a decentralized, cooperative anarchy in which everyone has power over his or her own life. There are no laws and no taboos, except for cultural consensus against interference in another's life. The basic unit of social organization resembles an extended family, but without biological basis. People do not live together because they are related, but because they choose to be together."[107]

Such political anarchy is missing in *Gloriana*. Moreover, it is interesting how anarchic perceptions of feminist utopianism echo Daoist utopianism. This may explain why ideal orientalism is often given a female gender by Western feminist critics. This political model of ideal anarchy also shows what is commonly perceived to be feminist moral superiority: on one hand, a disapproval of competition, fame, discipline, pragmatic political power, and written knowledge—all essential elements of patriarchal civilization; on the other, a preference for nature, peace, and an elemental human relationship. This tendency has been carried even further since the 1970s, so that utopia now depicts an "inner vision" or "a state of mind."[108] In the 1920s, Lu Xun wrote two short plays, "Passing the Pass" and "The Rising Dead." His first play satirizes the politically impractical Zhuang Zi as a hypocritical sage, and his second ridicules Lao Zi as a useless escapist. If Lu Xun were still alive today, he would view female moral superiority in a marginal utopia settled only by women as an unconscious form of escapism from the real political world.

Similarly, Pfaelzer observes that Gilman's Herland still reflects "nineteenth-century patterns of belief that justified the economic and political inferiority of women while at the same time preserving an image of their moral superiority."[109] Pfaelzer's critical observation may even apply to some feminist utopias of today. But, Dixie represents late Victorian women, who "were far more interested in asserting their right to be co-inheritors of the power structures of current male-dominated culture than in claiming versions of a domestic-based, devalued, restrictive moral guardianship as their own visionary ideal."[110] As does Dixie, Chen Duansheng deliberately ignores the issue of female moral superiority. She openly advocates competition with men for position and honor in the outside world. Instead of establishing a utopia of the margin, she tries to seize half of the political and cultural arena from men. The protagonists of both The Next Life and Gloriana maneuver in the field of knowledge and in political cities. They emphasize discipline and rational thinking, rather than any ideal form of anarchy. Through their protagonists, both authors demonstrate the strength of a politics of competition.

Though women striding into the masculine world may affect gender-power relations, a politics of competition is fatally flawed. In their anxiety to enter, rather than challenge, the existing political structure, Chen Duansheng and Dixie are both trapped by an intrinsic conservativeness. Meng Lijun, though climbing to the position of Zaixiang, is entangled in a structure that never allows her to justify herself. Guo Moruo observes that the weapon Chen Duansheng uses to fight against feudalism is still feudalist: "She uses feudal ethics to deny feudal order, fame and position to oppose woman's inferiority to man, the Emperor's power to deny parents, the doctrine of master to deny the husband, and codes of female virtue and martyr to challenge the imperial court."[111]

Influenced by socialism, Dixie suggests that the "greatest evils we have to face are the social ones" and emphasizes that Gloriana "has the mass of the working classes of the country on her side—certainly nearly every woman amongst them."[112] But, being herself from an aristocratic family, she never touches upon the British crown or the royal family in her writing. Her Gloriana, following the parliamentary system, fails to eliminate the gap between rich and poor. In 1999, her utopia still maintains a federal imperial system. As part of her strategy to play a "fair game," Dixie insists that "both on the throne and in peerages, and in succession to estates, it should be the first born, not the eldest son, who succeeds."[113] As early as 1890, a reader had challenged Dixie on this by asking, why does she "disfigure her charter of women's emancipation by retaining and extending to both sexes such a relic of barbarism as the right of primogeniture?"[114]

Although *The Next Life* and *Gloriana* share striking similarities, there is an essential difference. *Gloriana* carries the force of the nineteenth-century's women's movement, whereas *The Next Life* remains very much an individual's dream, which cannot help showing its isolation. *The Next Life* lacks a collective consciousness—the nucleus of the modern feminist utopia. Although many strong female characters are to be found in *The Next Life*, they are not united. They are more like the multiple portraits of the author's possible self in her next life; though, in choosing Meng Lijun as her ideal model, Chen Duansheng does revise the feudal codes of the female paragon tradition. In an age of European revolution and women's movements, *Gloriana* carries the full swing of its age. Its banner is the cause of all women; however, Gloriana still appears to be an individual superhero to her sisters, and the women's organization still differs from female collective rule. Yet, in spite of their limitations, Chen Duansheng's and Dixie's works succeed in their feminist intentions. *The Next Life* is a daring dream in a dark age, while the immediacy of *Gloriana*, placed in historical conditions at the turn of twentieth century, makes Dixie's utopia a dream of action—a fulfilling dream. Both dreams express "stern reality, / Mingled with visions of a future day."[115]

—ಬಿ—

Both Chen Duansheng and Dixie are pioneers in experimenting with popular literary forms to write feminist utopias. What makes their novels most exciting is their feminist vision. By concealing their female identity, the heroes in both novels assert female intellectual superiority, political astuteness, and "masculine" ability in running all affairs. The concealment of sexual identity, functioning as a neutral device, enables both *Gloriana* and *The Next Life* to avoid the disadvantages of a sex-role reversal that creates further antagonism between sexes by maintaining the domination of one over the other.

Both novels repudiate patriarchal ethics, draw feminist strength from a rebellious female tradition represented by mothers, and create a plausible utopia for women. Although Dixie's advocacy of the women's cause is more powerful, Chen Duansheng's bold divorce from the traditional conceptions of family, marriage, and love through imagination is no less radical. They both challenge the so-called natural law of the female's subordination to the male and visualize an egalitarian relationship between the sexes. Although their politics of competition with men in the masculine world show a historical practicality, the inherent problems they fail to address as feminist works, such as political conservativeness and a lack of female collective rule, point to the necessity of a complete separation from the patriarchal superstructure and a strategy of setting up female autonomous worlds. Those qualities are the hallmark of *Herland*-type utopias and the ultimate utopian vision Li Ruzhen offers to women in his *Destiny of the Flowers in the Mirror*, which we shall explore in the next chapter.

4

Separation from the Patriarchal World

The Destiny of the Flowers in the Mirror and *Herland*

A t first glance it seems rather risky to compare Li Ruzhen's *Destiny of the Flowers in the Mirror*[1] with Charlotte Perkins Gilman's *Herland*. The former was first published in 1828 by a male scholar, who wrote in an oriental, feudal environment; the latter was first published in 1915 by a female, who was an activist in the women's movement and under Western capitalism. However, as Steven Goldberg observes, patriarchy is universal—"be the society feudal, capitalist, or socialist, autocratic, communist, or democratic . . . it makes no sense to explain patriarchy in feudal societies in terms of feudalism, in capitalist societies in terms of capitalism, and the like."[2] Although feminism crosses social divisions to encompass all women in one oppressed class united against patriarchy, writers who fight for the cause of women are by no means restricted to the female sex. Despite their temporal and contextual differences, *The Flowers* and *Herland* are strikingly similar in their powerful attacks against patriarchy, their visions for women, and particularly their treatment of women as the source of a potential collective power that demands separation from a world dominated by male values.

Background and Critical Reception

Li Ruzhen was born in Hebei Province near Beijing, in 1763, and died about 1830. Because he disliked the Qing examination system based on the "eight-legged essay," he never received any degree higher than that of Xiucai.[3] Still, he became a famous scholar, completing three works during his lifetime: *The System of Phonetics* (6 vols. 1805); *Handbook of Chess* (1817); and *The Destiny of the Flowers in the Mirror* (1828). Although Li Ruzhen's professional life was largely devoted to philology and phonetics, he is now remembered primarily as a novelist because of the influence exerted by his last work.[4]

Why did Li Ruzhen choose to write about women's problems? Were there influential women in his life? Li's biography reveals little information about his private life and none about his association with women. We know only that he married the elder sister of Xu Guilin and Xu Qiaolin, who were both well-known phoneticians. In answering the question, then, we might look at the conditions for women during his time. The Qing Dynasty was the darkest period in Chinese women's history. The severe persecution of Chinese scholars by the Manchus made Li Ruzhen deeply sympathetic to women, who resided at the lowest levels of society. In attacking patriarchy, Li found the most effective metaphor for attacking the "entire social code and cosmology" of his era.[5]

Despite a general snobbery towards vernacular fiction in the Qing Dynasty, Li Ruzhen not only dared to write fiction, but took "ten-odd years of labor" to complete *The Flowers* (1810–1820), a novel centered on women.[6] The title of the novel suggests several closely associated and significant meanings that apply to women and art separately. "Flowers" refers to women; the "mirror," to life, which, according to the Daoist concept, is an illusion; and "the destiny," to a divine mission designated for an individual or a group of people. Tang Ao's destiny is to rescue twelve flowers (women), who have been cast abroad, and bring them back to China to attend the imperial examinations. The destiny of the incarnated flower, Tang Xiaoshan, and her ninety-nine sisters is to complete their earthly mission of demonstrating sisterhood and female superiority. Before she falls to the earth, the Flower Fairy, who is later reborn as Tang Xiaoshan, is already aware of this destiny: "I wonder whether this Jade Monument has something to do with my destiny. Although we are immortals, we remain, after all, female bodies. In the future, scholars who flourish and win fame will be recorded on this monument. If all names inscribed on it are Confucian disciples without a single woman, isn't it a shame on us?"[7] Tang Ao's destiny is obviously auxiliary to Tang Xiaoshan's. The book, therefore, is devoted to the destiny of women on earth.

The image of the flowers in the mirror traditionally refers to poetry.[8] Li Ruzhen believes that the aesthetic value of fiction is like that of poetry, but that its method is more straightforward in revealing truth. He believes that writing a fictional history of women is his destiny, as unprecedented as the hundred women's destiny of winning honor at the imperial examinations. At the very end of the novel, Li Ruzhen makes up a mythical tale to explain how the Flower Fairy commanded her White Ape to find someone to record the glorious history of these women heroes. In the tale, three hundred years later, the White Ape found the historian Liu, who had written *The History of Late Tang*, but Liu refused to compile a history of these inferior women. During the Song Dynasty, the White Ape asked the historian Ouyang, author of *The New Book of Tang*, to write their tale, but Ouyang had no time for women's history, a history of marginality or wilderness. It was not until the Qing Dynasty that the White Ape found the author, who was a Daoist descendent, and simply threw to him the records of the history of the hundred flowers. Li Ruzhen thus found his destiny to write this book. He boasts that he spent thirty years composing this "flower in the mirror" and believes that the power of truth lies within his novel: "The mirror reflects the truly talented scholar; the patterns of the flowers entirely renew the unofficial records of those obscure women."[9] He also reveals to the reader that his novel captures only a fragment of women's history. If one wants a view of the entire picture, one has to wait for its sequel. In fact, Li never intended to write a sequel himself, but left this call for more books about women.

The Flowers contains a hundred chapters, as is the fashion of vernacular novels. The story is set in the reign of Wu Zetian, the only woman emperor in Chinese history, who ruled from 684 to 705 under a dynasty of her own called the Zhou. The novel can be divided into two parts, fifty chapters each. The first part begins with the drunken Emperor Wu ordering all of the flowers on earth to bloom in the winter. The hundred flower spirits in heaven are intimidated into obeying her. But they are banished to earth as one hundred mortal women to "suffer through the bitter sea of transmigration."[10] The Fairy, who is in charge of the other ninety-nine flowers is born into Tang Xiaoshan, Tang Ao's daughter. Twelve flower spirits are cast to lands beyond China. As dictated by Providence, Tang Ao, a talented scholar deposed by Wu Zetian, journeys into many outlandish countries with Merchant Lin to rescue those twelve girls (flower spirits incarnate).[11] After completing his destiny, Tang Ao becomes a Daoist immortal, and concludes his journey at the fairy mountain of Little Penglai. His daughter, the Flower Fairy, continues her quest for the father. At Little Penglai, a woodcutter delivers to her a letter from

Tang Ao, which dictates that the daughter change her name into Tang Guichen and win a title at imperial examinations before he receives her. At Little Penglai, the daughter also reads about the predicted success of one hundred women (flower spirits) at the imperial examination on a tablet placed inside the Pavilion of Weeping Ladies. She copies the inscription on the tablet and returns to China.

The second part of the novel describes how Tang Guichen and other women, including the twelve girls rescued by Tang Ao, participate in all levels of examinations for women held according to Wu Zetian's decree and in subsequent banquets for celebrating women scholars. At those banquets, women play various games and discuss mathematics, medicine, philology, and other academic subjects. After the banquets, four talented women leave to govern the Country of Women; Tang Guichen resumes her quest for her father and becomes an immortal at Little Penglai; other talented women either get married or return to their parents with honor. In an earlier part of the novel, rebels against Wu Zetian act as a force against the Providential will; yet in a later development, they become a force that tries to purge the corruption of Wu's court. Many talented women fight against Wu's court along with the loyalists. Finally, with Tang Guichen's magic help, they break the Four Gates of Wine, Wrath, Sex, and Wealth deployed by Wu's army and restore the court to Wu Zetian's son, Tang Zhongzong. The story ends as Wu Zetian, dethroned but still in power, continues to hold imperial examinations for women.

The Flowers is a well-designed feminist work depicting women as the sole participants in all the major actions and using the concerns and activities of a band of superior women as "the single most important unifying element in its plot."[12] The narrative, however, is fragmentary, digressive, and centrifugal. Critics such as Lu Xun and Liu Dajie put *The Flowers* in the category of "novels of the scholars" of the Qing dynasty. Lu Xun thinks Li's intellectual breadth handicapped his fiction writing, while Yu Wang-leun insists that the novel's importance lies in its scientific innovations. In the introduction to the English version of *The Flowers in the Mirror*, Lin Tai-yi comments on its originality, "It is one of the most original works in Chinese literature, and there is nothing like it in Western literature either, unless we think of a work which has the combined nature of *Grimm's Fairy Tales*, *Gulliver's Travels*, *Aesop's Fables* and the *Odyssey*, with *Alice in Wonderland* thrown in for good measure."[13] The encyclopedic digression of the novel creates a rare complexity, which has led to widely differing interpretations by scholars.[14]

As a feminist utopian novel, however, it has received the most critical attention. In 1923, Hu Shi, in his Introduction to *The Flowers*, pointed out that it discusses the question of women, a question that had been ignored during more than two thousand years of Chinese history, and affirms that Li was the first to advocate that "men and women should receive equal treatment, equal education, and equal opportunities for selection."[15] In addition to this introduction, Hu Shi published successive articles in the same vein, such as "A Chinese Declaration of the Rights of Women" or "A Chinese Gulliver on Women's Rights." After Hu Shi, most critics, including Lu Xun, Lin Yutang, Lin Taiyi, and Li Changzhi, have accepted *The Flowers* as a novel concerned with women's problems and Li Ruzhen as an early "champion of equal rights for women."[16] Writing in 1977, Nancy J. Evans accepts Hu Shi's feminist interpretation but concludes that Li, suffering from the "effect of conditioning," fails to "revolutionize all his ideas about women."[17] F. P. Brandauer's "Women in the Ching-hua yuan" (1977) starts with describing *The Flowers* as a conscious feminist work in its narrative unity and structural design, then confines Li's ideas about women to Ban Zhao's Confucian ideal, and ends by blaming Hu Shi and his followers confusing "the Confucian ideal toward which this moves with the fairly recent idea of sexual equality."[18] In the same year, C. T. Hsia completely rejects any feminist interpretation, pointing out that Li did not contradict the Confucian assumptions of male privilege and dominance over women.[19] You Xinxiong believes that the feminist interpretation is caused by a superficial reading, which neglects Li's thematic message of nationalism.[20] Whether exhausted or discarded, interest in *The Flowers* as a feminist utopia almost disappeared by the 1980s.

The stagnation of feminist readings of *The Flowers* may have resulted from confining Li's feminist ideas to Confucian ideals. It is true that Li Ruzhen wrote under the influence of two indigenous intellectual movements: the School of Han Learning and the School of Mind.[21] The former is a revival of Classical Confucianism, while the latter emphasizes the spiritual search for one's own humanity. *The Flowers* shows an effort to reconcile and unite the two cultural experiences in the search for a future for women and for spiritual salvation for all of humanity. But my analysis will show that the danger of treating *The Flowers* as a feminist novel lies not in associating Li's feminist ideas with modern notions of sexual equality, but in neglecting Li's subversion of the very Confucian ideals held by Ban Zhao, and in underestimating its significance in straddling the nineteenth and the twentieth centuries, or the traditional and the modern China.

According to You Xinxiong, C. T. Hsia, and F. B. Brandauer, feminist interpretations of Hu Shi and his followers stem from misreading; yet, if any misreading is involved, it is a dynamic misreading. Such misreadings have caused *The Flowers* to shed a strong influence on the early Chinese women's movements and to occupy "a glorious place in the history of women's rights in China," as Hu Shi predicted.[22] Li's criticism of foot-binding and favoring of sexual equality have been recorded in nearly all books concerned with the history of feminist thought and women's movements in China, including Chen Dongyuan's *History of Chinese Women's Life*; Li Youning and Zhang Yufa's *Documents on the Feminist Movement in Modern China, 1842–1911*; Esther Yao's *Chinese Women: Past and Present*, Ono Kazuko's *Chinese Women in a Century of Revolution, 1850–1950*; and Gao Dalun and Fan Yong's *History of Chinese Feminists: 1851–1958*.

Like *The Flowers*, Charlotte Perkins Gilman's *Herland* reflects the feminist ideas found in the nineteenth and the twentieth centuries in the West. But unlike Li Ruzhen, Gilman drew on her personal experience, the traditions of her family, and her participation in the women's movement to create her feminist utopia.

Charlotte Gilman was born in 1860, into a New England family, and was surrounded by the feminist influence of her great aunts and great uncles. Among them, Henry Ward Beecher was "a president of the American Woman Suffrage Association;"[23] Isabella Beecher Hooker advocated women's right to vote and a matriarchal government; Harriet Beecher Stowe wrote *Uncle Tom's Cabin*; and Catherine Beecher wrote books on "domestic femininity." According to Mary A. Hill, "the work of Catherine Beecher and Harriet Beecher Stowe represented an early and preparatory stage of the nineteenth-century women's movement."[24]

Charlotte's father was a man who loved personal independence. To disentangle himself from family responsibilities, when Charlotte was only two years old, he separated from his wife and left her to suffer alone through the adversity of raising children and endless domestic drudgery. An early abhorrence for the traditional role of wife and mother, and the conflict between a woman's desire for intellectual pursuit and bondage to mothering, brought on Charlotte's depression and a nervous breakdown following the birth of her daughter Katharine in 1885. This painful experience was captured in her famous story *The Yellow Wall Paper*. As in the case of Anna O,[25] feminist activities became Charlotte's only cure. After a divorce, she engaged herself in writing and lecturing on the subject of socialist feminism. She attended the Women's Suffrage Convention in Washington and International Women's Congresses in London, Berlin, and Budapest. Correa Moylan Walsh, the author of *Feminism* (1917), calls Gilman "the foremost American female feminist"of her age.[26]

Unlike Li Ruzhen, who groped in a dark age devoid of modern thoughts and feminist theories, Gilman was influenced by the feminist arguments of Mary Wollstonecraft and John Stuart Mill, Lester Ward's social Darwinism, and Edward Bellamy's socialist utopianism. She herself was recognized as "a major theorist and popularizer for the women's movement in turn-of-the-century America."[27] The integration of feminism with socialism is her special contribution to American feminist theory. At her death in 1935, the novelist Zona Gale rightly praised her as "one of the great women of the two centuries."[28]

Throughout her prolific career, Gilman wrote a number of articles, and treatises, as well as poetry and fiction. During her lifetime, her best-known work was *Women and Economics* (1898), which was not only "the first real, substantial contribution made by a woman to the science of economics,"[29] but a monumental exposé of sex-based inequalities and a revelation of the sources of female strength.

Gilman wrote three utopian novels: *Moving the Mountain* (1911), *Herland* (1915), and its dystopian sequel, *With Her in Ourland* (1916). *Moving the Mountain* is the visualization of a transformed, future America. Its protagonist, John Roberson, falls over a precipice in Tibet in 1910 and loses consciousness; he wakes up thirty years later to witness a change in peoples' beliefs and attitudes toward women. Gilman calls *Moving the Mountain* "a short-distance Utopia, a baby Utopia" which envisions women's participation in a socialized economy and their freedom from domestic drudgery.[30] *Herland* is a mildly humorous story of three young American men—Terry, Jeff, and Van—who discover a country of women that has been virtually hidden from human sight. The three men reside in Herland both as the women's prisoners and as sexual invaders. The ideological conflicts and the communication, as well as miscommunication, between men from the outlying patriarchal world and women in a world entirely settled and ruled by women, highlight the satirical edge of this feminist utopia. It ends with the banishment of Terry, a stubborn, patriarchally oriented man who attempts to rape his wife, and with the woman Ellador's mission, entrusted to her by her country, to investigate the outer two-sexed world for possible communication between the worlds in the future. *Herland* represents Gilman's radical feminist position, which demands an eradication of the entire patriarchal civilization. In her sequel, *With Her in Ourland*, Gilman reverses the viewpoint and looks at our world through the eyes of Ellador. Disgusted by our social evils, both Ellador and her husband, Van, return to Herland, which represents a hope for their newly born son. *With Her in Ourland* reinforces Gilman's indictment against all the social evils produced by patriarchy and further illuminates the values of Herland, a civilization built upon a female tradition more than two thousand years old. The contrast between Herland and Ourland raises the essential question in Gilman's mind: What would human civilization be like if the world had been in women's hands?

Although Gilman today is recognized as "the best-known feminist utopist of the early twentieth century, largely because of the strength of *Herland*,"[31] *Herland* was little known in Gilman's time. It was first serialized in *The Forerunner*, a monthly journal published and written solely by Gilman, which had a very small circulation. It began to receive modern critical attention in 1977, but was not published in book form until 1979.[32]

Since its rediscovery, *Herland* has been recognized as a classic text for its type of ideal world, which includes all-female utopias and occasionally two-sexed egalitarian utopias.[33] Carol Pearson may have been the first critic to note "the surprisingly numerous areas of consensus" in contemporary feminist utopias and *Herland*—the absence of men, de-urbanized and decentralized anarchy, a nurturing ethic, relationships based on the love between mother and daughter, worship of a "mother goddess," and mothering as a social function.[34] Many female critics and a few male critics, such as Peter Fitting, have produced insightful analyses in a positive light.[35] In 1981, in her "Recent Feminist Utopias," Joanna Russ insisted on separating recent feminist utopias from *Herland* on the grounds that *Herland* and *Mizora* were "responding to the women's movement of their time," while recent feminist utopias are "not only contemporaneous with the modern feminist movement but made possible by it."[36] Except for sexual permissiveness, however, Russ did not really demonstrate any difference in principle between *Herland* and its modern cousins.[37] In 1990, Libby Falk Jones declared, "Sixty years later [from 1915], the thesis of Herland is still current."[38]

While *The Flowers* takes the form of a pseudo-historical fiction, *Herland* adopts the genre of science fiction. If *The Flowers* is handicapped by Li Ruzhen's erudition, *Herland* is marred by Gilman's didacticism: "Gilman gave little attention to her writing as literature, and neither did the reader, I'm afraid. She wrote quickly, carelessly to make a point."[39] But, we should keep in mind, as far as narrative structure is concerned, there is always a question of indeterminacy. For instance, Bartkowski observes that Gilman's use of a man as the reader's guide and narrator in *Herland* disguises "some of the ideological trappings of early twentieth century feminism;"[40] while Christopher P. Wilson treats Gilman as a "self-conscious literary craftsperson" and argues for her intentional subversion of narrative conventions in order to forge a feminist and socialist idiom.[41] *Herland* differs greatly from feminist utopias such as *The Female Man* in aesthetic form. As Hoda M. Zaki points out, however, utopian scholars cannot assume that "the process of imagining the form of utopia is a liberating act."[42] Feminist utopian study is essentially a political and ideological one.

The Flowers and *Herland* are both pioneering works. *The Flowers*, written in 1828, had an influence on the Chinese women's movement during the early 1920s, while *Herland*, written in 1915, helped foster the writing of feminist utopias in America during the 1970s. I hope a comparison of these two works, as examples of the third stage in feminist utopias, will demonstrate that, as effective, satirical weapons against patriarchy, they play an important role in the development of feminist thinking. Both Li and Gilman move away from isolated dreams of individual women in envisioning a collective power shared by women who reform and radically change man-made religions and political institutions to establish new relationships among women. Li visualizes two types of separation from our world: sex-role reversal, as in the Country of Women; and spiritual transcendence, as represented by Little Penglai—a Daoist Utopia. Although Gilman's vision of Herland contains sex-role reversal and shares similarities with Daoist utopianism in philosophy, it sows the seeds for modern and more radical feminism by insisting on a separatism, not only from our world but from the male sex.

Critique of Patriarchy: Seriocomic Satire

Feminist utopias differ from other critical utopias by concentrating their criticism on patriarchal superstructures and day-to-day practice. Using dramatic satire as his weapon, Li Ruzhen launches an all-out war against China's three thousand-year-old patriarchal order, with its cosmic philosophy of *yin* and *yang*, polygamy, foot-binding, and the imposition of Four Virtues on women.

Like the feminist utopist Chen Duansheng, Li Ruzhen believes that women must overthrow the deep-rooted patriarchal hierarchy to free themselves from men's perpetual oppression. As has been mentioned, the Chinese traditionally believe that human society corresponds to the cosmic order of *yang* over *yin*. If *yin* prevails over *yang*, the country will be thrown into great chaos. But such is not the case with either the Daoist paradise in heaven or Wu Zetian's reign on earth, as portrayed in *The Flowers*. Li Ruzhen's mythological paradise is occupied by a community of women. Although it still retains a hierarchical order with a token male supreme ruler, the Jade Emperor, he neither appears in person nor exerts any power. The Flower Fairy is punished by the Western Queen Mother for her refusal to let all of the flowers bloom without the order of the Jade Emperor on the Queen Mother's birthday. Her punishment is designed in such a peculiar way that all her ninety-nine flowers are forced to bloom by the mandate of the woman ruler Wu Zetian, and their banishment from heaven permits them to carry out their destiny of winning honor and fame at the imperial court. The Flower Fairy's banishment is hardly a punishment, because she has expressed her desire to have women's names appear in a Jade Monument. Female power dares to defy the law of the four seasons, not to mention the man-established order of *yin* and *yang*. In order to give women full autonomous power, Li Ruzhen even lets the Star of Literature appear in female body. Thus, the destiny of the hundred flowers is entirely controlled by goddesses rather than by any god.

Because the well-ordered Daoist paradise is ruled by the female, the mandated world ruled by Wu Zetian is peaceful and prosperous rather than chaotic. On her seventieth birthday, the Female Emperor issues twelve decrees for women's welfare and orders all talented girls to take the imperial examinations.[43] Women are excited by their good luck, unheard of in the last thousand years, and men praise Wu's good government. The merchant Lin's sick wife, benefiting from the Twelve Decrees, receives timely treatment from the best doctor in town. Tang Ao's brother remarks: "It is rare that an empress becomes the sovereign. In the dozen years since she came to the throne, we have had good annual harvests and the whole country has been in peace and harmony."[44]

According to Li Ruzhen's new cosmic law, heaven does not respond to *yin* or *yang*, but judges in terms of good or corrupt government. The loyalists of the Tang are repeatedly defeated by Wu Zetian because they ignore the omen of heaven:

[When the surprised loyalists were watching the star of Wu Zetian—
The Star of the Heart-Moon-Fox (Antares)—emitting a wondrous
light,] Xu Chengzhi asked: "What kind of good government can so
move Heaven and Earth?" . . . Wen Song said: "On her Seventieth
birthday, Wu issued a decree to reduce taxes and criminal punishment. And she also issued twelve decrees specially for women, such
as to praise good relations between daughters and daughters-in-law,
hold public funerals for the female who died homeless, set free court
ladies for their marriage, take care of widows, set up medical centers
for women, build temples for chaste women, and organize Old
Women's Homes and Girls' Homes. All these are unprecedented
events. As soon as the decrees were issued, the officials implemented
them at once, thus rescuing numerous lives and saving many more
from poverty. The living are grateful and the dead are moved. The
wailing and lamenting has suddenly turned into an atmosphere of
peaceful joy. Such deeds must have touched Heaven."[45]

Wu Zetian is eventually dethroned at the age of eighty-two. Although her dethronement is necessitated by the facts of history, Li
Ruzhen transforms her downfall into a symbolic war that purges the
loyalist rebels of their sins through the Four Gates of Wine, Wrath,
Lust, and Wealth, as well as rids Wu's court of its eunuchs and corrupted officials. During the loyalist war against Wu's court, she herself
is bedridden with an illness. When the war is over, Wu symbolically
recovers through purgation. Although Wu Zetian's son assumes the
throne, Li Ruzhen refuses to deprive Wu Zetian of her political power.
He writes, "The following day, the Dowager came to power and was
honored as "Zetian the Holy Emperor."[46] Li's fictional history of
women thus ends with the success of Wu Zetian's feminist politics:
"Soon after the Dowager recovered, she issued a decree to the whole
country: The imperial examinations for women shall be held again
next year and all the chosen talented women shall reunite at the Banquet of Red Literature for special honors. At once the decree excited
countless talented girls."[47]

If Wu Zetian's government is subversive to the patriarchal order
of *yang* over *yin*, Li Ruzhen further justifies a reversal of this order
in the Country of Women, where the roles of women and men are
entirely reversed. Women and men have not only exchanged their
gender-related names, but have traded their identities, functions, and
activities. Women govern and work in the outside world while powdered, rouged, and delicate men stay at home with housework and
babies.

Like Gilman's *Herland*, the Country of Women assumes a long tradition of female rule. Except for the treatment of men as the second sex, the country is well-governed. "From the King down to her subjects all lead an industrious and thrifty life."[48] Furthermore, "this country is extremely harmonious with her neighbors,"[49] and is open to new technology. Later the female king borrows Flying Machines from a foreign country to get his prince (her princess) back from China. Just as a world dominated by men could be considered the world of men, this two-sexed country is rightly called the Country of Women. Here, the cosmic order has always been *yin* over *yang*.

The paradise in heaven, the Country of Women abroad, and Wu Zetian's reign in China, one mirroring the other, all confound the man-made Natural Law that perpetuates women's subordination to men. While justifying a woman's right to be an equal human being with a man, Li Ruzhen satirizes the Chinese customs of polygamy, female martyrdom, and foot-binding.

The Chinese tradition of polygamy was deep-rooted. In the Daoist myth recorded by Luo Maodeng in his *Sanbao's Expedition to the Western Ocean*, Lao Zi lived to be 996 years old, had 136 wives, and fathered 361 sons. No novelists prior to Li Ruzhen openly challenged polygamy as fiercely as he did. Novels of the Talent Scholars and Beautiful Ladies,[50] though challenging feudal marriage in favor of freedom in love, generally end happily with a polygamous marriage. The plot of the Ming novel, *The Golden Lotus*, is structured solely around the plot of Ximen and his many wives. The Qing novel, *The Dream of the Red Chamber*, does not really oppose polygamy, though Wang Xifeng, one of its major female characters, rivals her husband in a double sexual game. The protagonist of *The Destiny of the Next Life* challenges polygamy by her refusal to marry, but its author is unable to denounce the system openly.

Li Ruzhen criticizes polygamy and the harem tradition through the perspectives of both men and women. In *The Flowers*, the person who embodies the harem tradition is not a male, but the female emperor Wu Zetian, for the notorious Wu keeps a large harem of men to satisfy her desires. Consequently, her country is ruined by corruption and by her gigolos' secret usurpation of state power. This description obviously revises the accounts of a fallen emperor, whose fall is attributed to the maintenance of a harem of concubines and whose loss of throne is due to his indulgence of women and the secret power struggles among their favorite concubines' relatives. Men are so accustomed to the traditions of polygamy and the harem that they never notice the irrationality of these traditions until they see women using men as sexual objects or as entertainment.

Taking the women's perspective, Li Ruzhen names a country in which the husband desires a sexual double standard, "the Country of the Double-faced," to reveal the hypocritical nature of man's practice of polygamy. In that country, the Pirate Chief kidnaps four girls and wants to keep them as his concubines. His wife first seeks suicide, as an ordinary woman would be inclined to do under the circumstances, but then has him beaten almost to death. Her berating words vent the ferocity of all women who have been victimized by sexual inequality:

> Suppose I take a few male concubines and gradually leave you in the cold, would you like it? You men are all like that. When poor, you remain good husbands and have some respect for your wives, but once you are high up and rich and powerful, then off you go like a different person. You begin to think a lot of yourselves and look down upon your friends and relatives and even begin to forget about your wife. As you are, you are all thieves and scoundrels and if I have your body slashed into ten thousand bits, you certainly deserve it! *What do you know about the doctrine of "reciprocity"? I'll have you flogged for thinking only of yourself and not of others, and I am going to flog this idea of "reciprocity" into your head before I quit* . . . [my emphasis]. You either take or don't take concubines; but if you do, you must first get some male concubines for me before I'll give my consent.[51]

C. T. Hsia believes that Li Ruzhen accepts the Confucian male domination over women, and Brandauer blames Hu Shi for his farfetched reading of Li's position on sexual equality. But the italicized lines above show that Li Ruzhen does anticipate our modern idea of sexual equality.

Nevertheless, *The Flowers* is restricted by puritanical moralities. The Tang Dynasty was the most sexually relaxed period in Chinese history. Wu Zetian was against judging either men or women by their sexual behaviors. At court as well as in society, women had freedom to choose their own husbands and lovers, and to divorce or remarry. Wu even helped court ladies find lovers. When Wu was criticized by Minister Zhu Jingze for keeping gigolos, she, instead of getting annoyed, gave him a hundred yards of silk as reward.[52] Li Ruzhen obviously associates sexual behavior with political corruption. He insists on both man's and woman's chastity, and his attitude towards feudal marriage is ambivalent. Love, passion, and freedom of marriage are completely absent from *The Flowers*. Li seems to accept the social reality of his time, including the concepts that all women find their homes through marriage and all marriage should be arranged by their parents or guardians. Nevertheless, he believes marriage also dooms women, not only turning them into commodities, but also demanding their total sacrifice for men. Li Ruzhen has Merchant Lin experience the fate of being bought and sold: "Jewelry and silver and gold" are spread before Lin's eyes when he is chosen to be "the Imperial Consort," and Tang Ao has to buy Lin back with silver when he is found to be useless as a sexual object. Once married, women completely lose their identity, and the worth of their lives is centered either on husband or son: "Those who had sons did not lose courage altogether, and those who were pregnant had some hope, but those who had no offspring wanted only to follow their husbands to the grave."[53] Li satirically removes most of the incarnated flower spirits by letting them either hang themselves to preserve their chastity or run swords through their necks to follow their dead husbands, a gesture reminiscent of widow-martyrs praised throughout Chinese history. This custom leads to Li Ruzhen's belief that life in this world for women is tantamount to being banished to the bitter sea. Only five girls escape the doom of marriage: Three go outside China to govern the Country of Women and two enter the utopia of Little Penglai.

Li's most influential feminist idea is the condemnation of foot-binding, which has been discussed by numerous critics, beginning with Hu Shi. The Country of Gentlemen is generally considered by critics to be a Confucian Utopia. Comparing Confucius's vision of Datong with Li's Country of Gentlemen demonstrates Li Ruzhen's special concern for women. With regard to the evils of foot-binding, Wu Zhihe, Minister of the Country of Gentlemen, compares foot-binding to a regular form of torture for criminals and to amputation, like "slicing a part of a high forehead off," which would entail all kinds of bodily and psychological sickness.[54] In chapters 32–38, Li simply allows men to suffer vicariously for women in the Country of Women. In this farcical episode, Merchant Lin, who is chosen to be the female emperor's concubine, is diminished from an independent man to a helpless willow sprig as his feet shrink to a "dainty size" under beating and torture.[55] He can no longer eat but only nibble; he can no longer walk without being supported. Lin's foot-binding is a perfect symbol of the dependency, helplessness, and submissiveness of females under male subjugation.

It is a grave mistake to confine Li Ruzhen's feminist thought to Ban Zhao's feminine ideal, as Brandauer does. In fact, Li's main effort in *The Flowers* is to subvert and revise the Four Virtues designated by Ban Zhao as the core of that ideal.[56] Ban Zhao (?–116), a famous female Confucian scholar of the Han dynasty, embraced the convention that "*yin* and *yang* were different in nature, so man and woman naturally have different characteristics . . . a man's honor relies on his toughness, a woman's beauty relies on her weakness."[57] Although she wrote *Commandments for Women* intending to help women survive within the patriarchal Confucian system, her Commandments or Four Virtues acted ironically to fetter Chinese women for some two thousand years.

Ban Zhao elaborated the Four Virtues originating from the Confucian text, *The Book of Rites*, as follows:

> A woman must be modest in behavior during her leisure time, must protect her virtue, must control herself to maintain a sense of shame; must follow certain ways in action and at rest. This is called *woman's moral virtue*. A woman must choose what words to say and not use coarse language; to think first, then to speak and not tire others. This is called *woman's speech*. A woman must clean the house, wash away the filth, and keep her clothes and ornaments fresh and clean. She must bathe herself regularly in order not to be shamed by a disgraceful appearance. This is called *woman's appearance*. A woman must concentrate on sewing and weaving and should not joke around; she should neatly prepare the wine and food for guests. This is called *woman's work*.[58]

Obviously, Li Ruzhen's hundred female heroes have nothing to do with these Four Virtues. In Li's notion of morality, loyalty and piety are most important. Yet Tang Xiaoshan's loyalty to her father, who is no longer a patriarchal figure but a medium for passing divine messages, is dictated by her divine mission. Her name later is changed to Tang Guichen, which literally means Tang the Maiden Minister or the Minister of the Tang Maidens,[59] as she is the Flower Fairy in charge of the other ninety-nine flowers (the women scholars of the Tang dynasty). Just as the historical Wu Zetian did in her time, Li changes the customary object of piety from father to mother. Luo Hongju hunts tigers to avenge her mother's death; a girl of the Country of Gentlemen dives into the sea to get sea cucumbers for her sick mother; and Tingting takes care of her aged mother under all circumstances. Li's talented women not only group together and joke around, but speak coarsely, using "fart" and "shit" freely at the banquets. Li

satirizes Ban Zhao's admonition that "women should not watch outside by the door" by allowing them to mingle with men throughout
the novel. When the three male visitors come to the Country of
Women, they are laughed at by "male women": "The beard on your
face proves you are women. Why are you wearing men's clothes and
pretending to be men? I know you dress like this because you want to
mingle with the men, you cheap hussies!"[60] Li even ridicules Ban
Zhao's fastidious demand for the cleanliness of the female body. In
the Country of Women, two strong male ladies-in-waiting wash the
would-be concubine Lin's private parts after each urination. The traditional feminine appearance as portrayed in literature is mercilessly
ridiculed through the reversed role of Merchant Lin: "his eyebrows
were plucked to resemble a new moon," his face was "like a peach
blossom," his eyes "like autumn lakes," and his figure "like a willow
sprig swaying in the wind."[61] The talented women in the novel do not
use ornaments and often appear dressed like either a hunter or a
fisherwoman, like Luo Hongju and Yan Zixiao.[62] Li particularly values
knowledge in plain and ugly women. By convention, Honghong and
Tingting are ugly for their black teeth; their brilliant intellect makes
Tang Ao claim that they are more beautiful than any ornamented
ladies. Li's female characters all abandon their needlework and engage
in non-feminine pursuits: learning, debating, fighting, travelling, and
governing.

At the opening of the first chapter, Li says:

> In former times, Dame Cao [Ban Zhao], in her *Commandments for
> Women*, said "Women should have four qualities: (1) feminine virtue;
> (2) feminine speech; (3) feminine appearance; and (4) feminine
> work." These four are the principal goals for women and are indis-
> pensable. Now in the beginning of this work, why do I take Ban
> Zhao's *Commandments for Women* as an introduction? It is because
> the contents of the book, though but trivial matters of the women's
> quarters and casual affections between men and women, certainly
> resemble what Dame Cao called the "Four Virtues."[63]

One must wonder why Li Ruzhen mentions Ban Zhao's *Commandments for Women* at all. He does so in order to borrow Ban Zhao's
original good intentions regarding women while at the same time revis-
ing the entire contents of the Four Virtues to serve his own purpose.
Moreover, he uses the text to communicate a deliberate irony. Of
course, Li Ruzhen does not really believe that his novel is about the

"trivial matters" of insignificant women, nor does he write of the "casual affections between men and women," like those in Cao Xueqin's *Dream of the Red Chamber*. Li's satire becomes most obvious toward the end of the novel, when the talented girls playfully interpret the "Feminine Virtue" regarding husband and wife in Ban Zhao's *Commandants for Women* as "*Fufo*" (Negating Husband).[64]

Like *The Flowers*, *Herland* challenges patriarchy as unnatural, ridicules traditional marriage, and refutes the prejudices against women located in men's consciousness and subconsciousness, through verbal wittiness, satirical humor, and dramatic conflicts. Combined with the force of *With Her in Ourland*, Gilman here extends her critique of patriarchy worldwide and manifests women's large-minded concern for humanity.

Gilman demonstrates the unnaturalness of patriarchy by creating a vision of a superior female civilization that reflects innate female characteristics. Instead of arguing directly for women's natural right to rule, as Li Ruzhen does, Gilman uses her utopian world to open a new horizon for men. Herland is peaceful and nonviolent. When Terry fires his revolver, five middle-aged Herlanders seize the three male intruders and bring them before "a majestic gray-haired woman" judge. The three captives are given anesthesia and looked after like "yearling babies."[65] Terry calls those women who detain them "the Colonels" simply because he does not recognize female authority as "maternal and benevolent," as opposed to male authority which is "military and despotic."[66] In Herland, female power is exercised as a form of "disciplinary restraint," whereas in the contemporary world male power is exercised through violence.[67]

Terry assumes that men are the sole builders of human civilization. But Gilman shows that Herland, a country without men, has a superior civilization with a higher degree of technology and better utilization of natural resources. Herland has eliminated divisions between countryside and city, and blue- and white-collar work. Ecologically minded Herlanders are engaged in horticulture and cultivation. Their civilization is free of war, poverty, disease, pollution, and overpopulation.

In a tit-for-tat attack on men's biases about innate female nature as "jealous" and "incapable of organizing," Gilman uses biological determinism to prove that men are by nature belligerent and competitive, whereas women are "natural cooperators."[68] In *With Her in Ourland*, Ellador says to Van: "We had such advantages, you see. Being women, we had all the constructive and organizing tendencies of motherhood to urge us on and, having no men, we missed all that greediness and quarrelling your history is so sadly full of."[69] Gilman has obviously paved the way for the contemporary feminist indictment of "men or male institutions as a major cause of present social ills."[70] By demonstrating the superiority of female rule, female civilization, and women's innate nature, Gilman in fact liquidates the existential right of patriarchy.

Gilman never convincingly explains how these three male invaders manage to persuade three Herlanders to marry them on the grounds that a two-sexed society is superior. Their marriages, nevertheless, provide a vantage point from which Gilman criticizes inequality in monogamy. Gilman mercilessly satirizes the Western monogamous system under which a wife "belongs to a man" and becomes man's possession by giving up her maiden name and, thereby, her identity. Gilman's criticism of conventional marriage is not satisfied by satirizing marriage as "a lottery,"[71] but goes further by digging out its root in the idea of "mastering woman." Terry believes that he "has the right" to rape Alima after marrying her.[72] But Alima, no Desdemona like "a mouse" to be smothered by her Othello,[73] refuses to be tamed by man. Instead, she kicks her man, who signifies to the Herlanders "only male—the sex,"[74] and demands his death if he refuses to be tamed by Herland.

To illustrate the patriarchal ideology that permeates man's conscious and subconscious mind, Gilman uses two archetypal characters: Jeff, a courteous knight who is inclined to idolize and protect women; and Terry, rich and powerful, but a most stubborn male chauvinist and playboy. Because of Jeff's poetic idolization of women, Celis has to postpone their love until Jeff learns that Herlanders need no woman-worshipper or protector: "Stalwart virgins had no men to fear and therefore no need of protection."[75] Through Terry, Gilman deals with men's treatment of women as sexual objects. Terry assumes that because women represent sex and game to men, their appearance, dress, and behavior should be geared for sexual seduction. Hearing that Herland has no men, Terry first expects to find "a national harem," then finds the inhabitants woefully inadequate as women. The young Herlanders are both masculine and feminine: "short hair, hatless, loose, and shining; a suit of some light firm stuff, the closest of tunics and kneebreeches, met by trim gaiters."[76] The middle-aged Herlanders are completely devoid of femininity: "They have no modesty . . . no patience, no submissiveness, none of that natural yielding which is a woman's greatest charm."[77] Terry excludes old women from the category of women because of their age and ugliness. To their great frustration, the three men find that as a result of two thousand years without male contact, Herlanders possess neither a sexual psychology nor a sex drive.

Like Li Ruzhen's hundred talented women, Gilman's Herlanders are desexed, showing no love or passion in any traditional romantic sense. Gilman places prudish sexual values—permitting sex only for procreation—against the sexually intensified Western culture and society. Opposed to men's neglect of children for personal pleasure, Herlanders transfer their love and enthusiasm to mothering and communal good. Just as Li Ruzhen's women discard the Four Virtues, Herlanders are also defeminized. Gilman shows that desirable masculine traits are actually general human traits, whereas "feminine charms" are artificial and "merely reflected masculinity—developed to please" men.[78] Gilman thus creates Herlanders as masculinized New Women who have the strength of fishwives and market women, the intelligence of college professors, and the calmness of cows. Gilman also repudiates the convention of treating the female in a delimited way as the "sex" and the male more comprehensively as mankind or "the world."[79] Through a rhetorical reversal, she lets Herlanders represent humanity and men the mere "sex." Somel assures Van that she likes him best because he is "more like us—more like people. We feel at ease with you."[80] Perhaps, the main purpose of her sequel, *With Her in Our World*, is to break this narrowness of *Herland*, to push her critique of patriarchy into the world, and to embrace a broader humanity.

Herland ends with a feminist triumph in the expulsion of Terry, the incorrigible patriarchal tyrant, though on a self-defeating note by treating men as the sex. Ellador follows Van to the outer world in order to expand her horizon: to learn and to criticize. As the three visitors to Herland are Americans, Gilman's criticism necessarily focuses on the Western patriarchal tradition. When Ellador enters our world,[81] she witnesses war and ruin in each region she visits. She discovers that the older the man-dominated civilization is, the crueler is their treatment of women. In chapters 3 and 4, Gilman specifically mentions Ellador's "heartache over the Japanese women, whose dual duty of childbearing and men-service dominated all their lives" and her horror at the Chinese foot-binding practice.[82]

What ideas differentiate Gilman from Li Ruzhen are Gilman's class consciousness and her concern for children. After noting in *Herland* that two-thirds of American women must labor for a minimum wage while raising a maximum number of children, Gilman describes, in *With Her in Ourland*, how Ellador, in a Chinese village, "saw the crippled women; not merely those serenely installed in rich gardens and lovely rooms, with big-footed slaves to do their bidding; or borne in swaying litters by strong coolies; but poor women, working women, toiling in the field, carrying their little mats to kneel on while they worked, because their feet were helpless aching pegs."[83] Ellador also heard "the agony of the bound feet of a child." Van explained that "It is the women, their own mothers, who bind the feet of the little ones. They are afraid to have them grow up 'big-footed women.' "[84] Here, Gilman reveals that patriarchy has polluted women's minds. In fact, the good-hearted mother fears that her big-footed daughter will not have the female charm needed to attract a husband.

Attributing our exaggerated sex-gender psychology to men's need for pleasure and dominance, Gilman is convinced that once the social conditions that have truncated women's natures and ambitions disappear, as in Herland, women will become complete human beings. After staying in Herland for some time, Van comes to understand that women in Herland, like men in Ourland, call up a two-thousand-year-old-civilization, one in which he becomes used to "seeing women not as females but as people; people of all sorts, doing every kind of work."[85]

As Herland is largely intended for the education of men, Ourland instructs Herlanders. After inspecting our world, Ellador learns that "men are people, too, just as much as women are."[86] She and Van bring "a new sense of responsibility, a larger duty" to Herland. The vision of Herlanders expands to encompass all of humanity at last. Care for our world gives Herland "not only love, but the great new spread of life—of work to do for all humanity."[87]

Collective Female Strength

Unlike Chen Duansheng's *The Destiny of the Next Life*, which portrays a single woman striking into the masculine world in male guise, *The Flowers* emphasizes a broad feminist representativeness—sisterhood, collective political rights, and group action. Li Ruzhen uses the spirits of a hundred flowers to represent women of different classes, ages, and occupations. Among these hundred female candidates for the imperial examination, thirty-three belong to aristocratic families. They are excluded from the examination by their fathers, who are supervising the examination, and fear being accused of favoritism until Wu Zetian gives these women special permission. Most of the talented girls, like Tang Xiaoshan, come from middle-class intellectual families. The twelve candidates brought back from abroad by Tang Ao represent several kinds of women in exile: the persecuted, Lo Hongju and Yin Ruohua; the sick, Lanyin; the alienated, Yao Zhixin; and those with neglected talents, Honghong and Tingting.[88] Although Wu Zetian excludes old and poor women from participating in imperial examinations, Li Ruzhen deliberately includes an old woman and a servant girl among the candidates. Tingting's mother, a widow of about sixty, takes the county and provincial levels of the examinations under a false name and wins first place at the latter, gaining the title of the Virtuous Lady of Literature. A maid named Cui Xiaoying also follows her lady to take the ministerial examination at court.

The representative scope of the one hundred female candidates is extremely significant. As Hu Shi points out, in "A Chinese 'Gulliver' on Women's Rights," Li Ruzhen "advocates that the examination system should be extended to women. In making Empress Wu institute a new system of examinations open to women, he was in fact advocating something which was no less radical than granting the vote to women, for in China the state examinations meant proper channels of civic advancement and political participation."[89] Li Ruzhen is particularly sensitive to the relationship between political motivation and education. Once women are granted the right to take the imperial examinations, the entire nation, rich and poor, begins to educate girls in the same way as boys, no longer limiting them to weaving and sewing. The right to take the examination also frees women from their secluded gardens and deep maiden bowers. During the long examination period, girls from all over the country are travelling and staying in hotels. In the capital, Emperor Wu prepares special quarters for groups of women. Consequently, women have the opportunity to live, eat, and study together. For the first time in Chinese history, women strive for the same goal and share the same fears and joys.

All of this mobility and sociability promotes women's sisterhood, so that the candidates address each other as sisters—drinking, laughing and debating on the same footing. Li Ruzhen stresses that "such a sisterly gathering of a hundred women has never been recorded in official or unofficial history or in legends or popular tales."[90] Women not only organize themselves in a manner similar to men's societies of sworn brothers, but demonstrate their sisterly nobleness. Just before the ministerial examination, Tang Guichen hears one of her "sisters" weeping. Tang immediately shows concern for the girl's health and financial situation. But to her surprise, she finds out that the girl has forgotten to bring her registration paper for the examination, and although Xiuying has offered hers, the girl refuses to accept it for fear of depriving Xiuying of her own examination rights. Among the female candidates, there is sincere concern for honor and mutual assistance rather than competition, which is common among male candidates.

From chapters 70 to 95, Li Ruzhen seems to have been carried away by a display of his erudite knowledge of philosophy, flowers and birds, calligraphy, painting, lyre playing, chess, medicine, astrology, phonology, and mathematics. But because the setting is the Banquet of Red Literature, in which the female scholars are the sole participants, Li's often-criticized digression becomes a part of the thematic design. Not only does it open the door to various arts and sciences for women, but it also suggests that the very content of education and examination should be changed in the direction of modern science and useful knowledge. There is also a strong possibility that Li intends to make these areas better known to women by including them in this form of literature. In the Han dynasty, Ban Zhao made "a remarkable plea for equal education of boys and girls from ages eight to fifteen; however, the purpose of educating girls was not to develop the girls themselves but to help them better perform their household duties."[91] In *The Dream of the Red Chamber*, although idle ladies often meet to enjoy writing poems and playing games, they show little interest in politics and none in science or mathematics. On the other hand, Li Ruzhen's female scholars conduct themselves like male scholars, if not in a more enlightened way.

In addition to asserting themselves politically by taking the imperial examinations, talented women take group action to change the male-oriented religion and to combat human corruption. During a visit to a monastery with four other talented women, Tang Guichen discovers that the statue of the Star of Literature is male and asks Weikong to have a female statue placed in the shrine of the Star of Literature. By the end of the novel, thirty-five newly married talented ladies, together with their husbands, go to war against the corrupted Wu Zetian's court. They live collectively in the Barracks of Women Warriors. Without the women's courage and strength, and particularly the spiritual assistance from Tang Guichen, who has already returned to Little Penglai, the loyalist army could not hope to win the battles fought at the Gates of Wine, Wrath, Lust, and Wealth.

Li Ruzhen's treatment of Wu Zetian is complex. Although he often denounces her as a figure of tyranny and corruption, he also lets her sovereignty embody female power, suggestive of collective rule. Wu Zetian, the star Antares, descends to earth with her unique destiny to "reverse the order of *yang* over *yin*,"[92] unlike Meng Lijun, *Zaixiang* of Chen Duansheng's utopian dream, who desires to win personal honor and serve the country like a man. After dethroning her son, Wu first demonstrates her power by daring to "Let a hundred flowers bloom and the four seasons appear at the same time." Wu takes this simultaneous blooming of flowers from the four seasons as a divine sign that talented women will appear to "help her manage state affairs."[93] She even bestows official titles and honors upon the flowers: Flower Luoru is given the title of "Woman Minister of Cultural Campaign" and Flower Qingnang "Woman Minister of Culture."[94]

Emperor Wu does not wish to have a body of talented women to help her rule the country only. At court, she places Shangguan Wan'er above all men. Restricted by history to the facts that all her ministers have to be men and that Shangguan Wan'er can only occupy the position of *Zhaoyi* (the highest office a women can hold), Li Ruzhen has the fictional Wu Zetian treats Shangguan like a *Zaixiang*. She gives Shangguan the opportunity to beat all eleven ministers in composing poems and often issues decrees on her advice. The close relationship between Wu Zetian and Shangguan reveals the political strength of female collaboration.

Wu Zetian is the only ruler who makes substantive efforts to given women legal protection. Although the historical Wu Zetian did make twelve suggestions before she came to the throne, the twelve decrees in *The Flowers* are composed by Li Ruzhen. Of the suggestions, the ninth demands that the father observe three years' funeral rites for the mother if he survives her.[95] Critics have correctly noticed that Wu's intention is to elevate women's social position and prepare for her crowning.[96] Li Ruzhen's fictional twelve decrees are entirely designed to express his ideas for improving women's social conditions.

Although writers from Lu Xun to Brandauer have criticized Li Ruzhen for advocating piety, chastity and feudal marriage, we cannot hope to judge Li Ruzhen fairly by using today's social and ideological environments. A careful examination of the twelve decrees reveals that Li's feminist thinking is governed by two purposes: to elevate women's sociopolitical status and to protect women through socialized institutions supported by the government. In Decrees 1, 3, and 4, the praise for female piety, chastity, and longevity is actually not as important as raising their social status and political influence through public honors and titles and the setting up of memorials for great women. For the same purpose, Decree 2 shifts the concept of respect for elder brothers to respect for women and to mutual respect among women themselves. With the other decrees, Li Ruzhen boldly proposes that the government give economic protection to old, poor, sick, and homeless women. The decrees demand that Old Women's Homes be established for women over forty at both county and prefecture levels to relieve them from poverty, infirmity, and loneliness (Decree 6); that Girls' Homes be opened for poor and disabled female children from birth to age ten; and that Women's Health Centers be staffed with the best gynecologists. In addition, the state will give monthly allowances to widows and dowries to those who otherwise cannot afford marriage. Li Ruzhen obviously also considers marriage an important means to protect women; therefore, Decrees 5 and 9 insist that court maids be set free after five years' service and that the female servants of rich families be properly married off at the age of twenty.

These twelve decrees show Li's concerns as a social reformer, while the Special Decree that establishes a women's imperial examination system expresses his more radical feminist thinking. Li's insistence on giving women the rights of examination is based on the fact that countless talented women, like Su Hui who creates a fascinating palindrome, are buried in history because men are interested only in the feminine charms of seductive women like Zhao Yangtai.[97] Through the symbolic names of Shi Youtan and Ai Qunfang, the two women who win the first and the second places in the state examination, Li Ruzhen claims that "by a thorough examination of women's history I acquire the truth and by lamenting the nameless talented females throughout history, I inscribe this monument."[98] Through Wu Zetian's Special Decree, Li Ruzhen proclaims:

> I believe that the essence of Heaven and Earth is never endowed exclusively in any one sex in particular, and that advisors and counsellors to the throne may very well be sought in exceptional channels. . . . Now the State examinations have long been open to men, while women are still barred from participating in them. This speaks ill of the electoral system, and is not conducive to the encouragement of talents . . . .Moreover, it is evident today that the fine gifts of nature are no longer endowed in the male sex, and that virtue and goodness have long become the attributes of womankind. . . . I have therefore consulted many a sagacious mind and decided to institute a new system of examinations for the women of the Empire.[99]

Li Ruzhen's proclamation indeed carries the spirit of Lady Florence Dixie's feminist declaration.

While the twelve decrees emphasize socioeconomic protection for women, the Special Decree enables a new generation of women to gain political power and economic independence. The hundred talented women achieve not only official titles, such as Women of Letters, Women Doctors, and Women Scholars, but also annual salaries; even their parents and future husbands benefit from their honor and wealth. In Li Ruzhen's pragmatic thinking, women are recognized and protected through the force of the law; in his utopian design, a generation of New Women begins to assert its power as a collective entity.

Like *The Flowers, Herland* moves toward the realization of female collective power, but in an essentially different manner. *The Flowers,* resembling *Gloriana,* belongs to the stage of women's awakening to their ability to exert an organized strength against patriarchy within the existing system. This stage belongs to Herland's past history, when, we are told, its women rose as an oppressed class to put an end to men, along with their polygamy and harems. Where Li stops is the point of departure for Gilman, who imagines what women would have done if they had had the entire world in their hands for the past two thousand years.

Being an all-female world, Herland itself embodies women's autonomous power. To show how radically it differs from the power structure of patriarchy, Gilman places it in a political vacuum, where the patriarchal system and its ideological influence have ceased to exist with the disappearance of men and of older women who remember men. In two thousand years' time, her new race of parthenogenetic women establish a female civilization with a complete system of religion, social order, productivity, social activity, and education shaped by the model of mother/nature.

Herland's religion is Maternal Pantheism. Herlanders worship their great Mother Spirit, who "was to them what their own motherhood was—only magnified beyond human limits. That meant they felt beneath and behind them an upholding, unfailing serviceable love— perhaps it was really the accumulated mother-love of the race they felt —but it was a Power."[100] Their Mother Goddess, though associated with the woman who bore the first five parthenogenic girls and lived in the Temple of Maaia, does not assume the image of "a Big Woman somewhere," but embodies a diffuse, competent love, "a Pervading Power . . . an Indwelling Spirit."[101] Its function is not to dope a person's mind as opium does, but to expand her vision and mind in her momentary confusion or spiritual "hours of darkness."[102]

In its social order, Herland is basically egalitarian in spite of its natural hierarchy, seen as follows:

Great Over Mother of the Land (Queen-Priestess-Mother)
Over Mothers
Mothers
Young Girls
Children

This chart shows that hierarchy is based largely on age differences: the older one becomes, the more service or wisdom one offers; but, in reverse order, children get the most social attention. This natural hierarchy is essentially not oppressive, because it lacks an economic base, and the content of female power is designated by selfless maternal service to children. Apart from the age distinction, all Herlanders are of a new race descending from one mother. Each is considered a full human being; even children are treated respectfully as "people." This natural hierarchy is, in Riane Eisler's words, an "actualization hierarchy" as opposed to a "domination hierarchy."

The idea of nurturing controls Herland's productivity and social activities. Herlanders are largely food producers. To keep their bodies healthy and athletic, they do not eat animal meat and subsist on a diet of fruit. Consequently, the majority are foresters like Elladjor. Their social activities focus on the arts of childbearing and mothering. Children do not belong to their blood mothers and are considered social products to be reared in open social and cultural environments by co-mothers, the selected artists in mothering.

Herlanders have no concept of formal education; for them learning naturally occurs during growth. They "seek to nourish, to stimulate, to exercise the mind of the child."[103] The content of their education involves "a good deal of knowledge of anatomy, physiology, nutrition—all that pertains to a full and beautiful personal life," along with rudimentary botany and chemistry.[104] They have no schooling in our sense; nurse/teachers guide children through designed games, and children learn through their inventive play. The aim of education is to help children gain two powers, "a clear, far-reaching judgement, and a strong well-used will," as required for Herland's citizenship.[105]

Herland, with a family structure centered on women, is characterized by its sisterly based solidarity and uniformity. Gilman pictures the whole nation functioning as one organic body. If one woman is in danger, as in the case of Alima, the whole nation rises up in action. Gilman demands uniformity not only in collective action but also in the individual's consciousness. With the disappearance of private possessions and sexual life, personal pleasure is transferred to mothering or service in the communal good. Consequently, personal psychology, as imagined by Gilman, is replaced by a historical sense that reflects the psychological change of "the succeeding and improving generations" of Herlanders.[106]

Gilman's seeming suppression of individual rights in order to realize a common ideal has led some critics to rank Herland with imaginary societies such as Swift's Houhynhnms in *Gulliver's Travels*, Zamyatin's *We*, and Orwell's *Nineteen Eighty-four*, though Swift, Zamyatin, and Orwell's utopias or dystopias are essentially patriarchal. Gilman keeps her utopia from becoming a totalitarian nightmare by two means. First, she eliminates the division between the public world and the domestic world. With men's disappearance, the so-called masculine world, characterized by competition, greed, and war, ceases to exist; what we normally limit to the domestic realm, such as childbearing and mothering, "is idealized and serves as a building and guiding principle."[107] Hence, Herlanders have no concept of private home or domesticity but only of responsibility and service for the whole race. Second, Gilman eliminates the conflict between the personal and the collective by reversing their serving purposes. Herland's political establishments, such as religion and education, are aimed at helping the individual develop a full personal life, while each Herlander is only capable of thinking only in terms of "we."[108] Anticipating criticism of her utopia as static and limited, Gilman particularly emphasizes the cultivation of Herlanders' individual wills and inquisitive minds, and their readiness to communicate with the rest of humanity represented by men.

Although Li Ruzhen's *Flowers* contains germinal ideas pertaining to women's collective rule and state welfare for women, *Herland* surpasses Li's feminist imagination. In *The Flowers*, Wu Zetian's organized social institutions, such as homes for old women and female orphans and women's health centers, merely supplement the existing system, and the hundred flowers' assertion of sisterhood and political strength at the imperial examinations only prove women capable of being a counterpart to men within the old political structure. Gilman's utopian *Herland* has reversed the value system—women are "the world" and maternal activities become social norms.

Each utopian vision has its own beauty, however. As "conscious Makers of People,"[109] the Herlanders' sole reason for living is to improve the human race. Therefore, the quality of their children becomes their utmost national concern. By advocating the human imitation of Nature's merciless law of mutation, Gilman deprives the physically, mentally, and morally weak women of motherhood, in hopes of breeding out human spiritual vices and physical weakness. She also exhibits racism by populating her utopia exclusively with women of one "pure stalk."[110] Unlike Gilman, Li Ruzhen welcomes ethnic and cultural diversity. He includes two black girls from the Country of the Black-Toothed into the circle of the talented women and creates a female character who can speak thirty-six foreign languages. He also stresses legal protection for the aged, the poor, the sick, and disabled women, including prostitutes, and gives them equal rights of marriage.

Three Types of Separation

Aside from focusing their attention on women's collective strength, Li Ruzhen and Gilman both express the desire to separate from the known patriarchal world. *The Flowers* projects two separations: a country ruled by women outside the sphere of Confucianism; and Little Penglai, a paradise of spiritual perfection. Gilman's separation in *Herland* represents female autonomy.

In light of Chinese utopian traditions, *The Flowers* can be seen as a utopia based on two Daoist myths: that of Peach Blossom Spring (Little Penglai), a secluded, pastoral, peaceful land isolated from our world; and that of Messianism, a political means to rid the degenerate world of its evils. What separates Li's utopia from previous Chinese utopian discourse is his preoccupation with the rights of women.

Li attempts to find a future for Chinese women by going in different directions. First, he explores the Confucian utopia Datong in the Country of Gentlemen. This Country of Gentlemen appears to be an all-male world. Although its gentle Minister Wu denounces the cruel treatment of women in China, he ends his denunciation with a patronizing gesture: "Only by all the gentlemen of this world agreeing to stamp out this custom [foot-binding] can an end be put to it."[111] The Country of the Black-Toothed seems to open a feminist vista; women are engaged in serious Confucian learning and have an opportunity to take the imperial examinations every ten years. Court corruption, however, bars talented girls like Honghong and Tingting from social promotion. Both, as victims of the system, find their opportunities in China during Wu Zetian's reign.

Referring to Chinese history, Li Ruzhen borrows the sovereign power of the only Chinese female emperor to give women access to public honor and official positions and to institute organizations for women's welfare. Although advocating reforms beneficial to women, Li Ruzhen is not very optimistic about women's participation in state affairs in China. When Tingting, an ambitious talented girl from the Country of the Black-Toothed, hears that she is going to the Country of Women, she can hardly hide her excitement. She tells the other girls:

> The ambition of your humble sister is not confined [to Shaobao, a title given by Emperor Wu]; I am happy only because I have my own reason: These three [talented girls] and I, whether staying in the Celestial Country or returning to my home country, can only waste our lives and accomplish nothing. . . . When Sister Ruohua becomes the king, we will combine our strength to manifest our loyalty—in setting up rituals, in amplifying the merits of the court to banish its defects, in purging tyranny to pacify the people, in recommending the truly talented to replace the incompetent, in enhancing people's respect for the law and carefully investigating law cases. We'll help her become a virtuous king. We ourselves will gain the title of "Famous Women Ministers" and enter the records of history. . . . Even if we hundred sisters assemble here annually another dozen times, there won't be any essential change.[112]

Through Tingting, Li Ruzhen suggests that even examination rights are only of ornamental significance under the Chinese patriarchal system. Both the historical and fictional Wu Zetian depended on a body of male ministers to govern. Even if the fictional Wu Zetian expresses her desire to have women ministers to assist her in state affairs, she can only give these hundred flowers intellectual titles and post them in the inner palace, rather than in open court.

The moderate feminist utopian possibilities offered by the Country of Gentlemen, the Country of the Black Toothed, and the Celestial Country during Wu Zetian's reign are fused within the sphere of Confucianism. Through the character of Duo Jiugong, Li Ruzhen traces the root of Chinese patriarchal ideology to Confucianism: "The other day when we were in the Country of Gentlemen, the Wu brothers told us that their customs and culture are shaped by Confucian teachings of the Celestial Country. Now we see that the Country of the Black-Toothed is influenced by the teachings of the Country of Gentlemen. As far as their origins are concerned, our Celestial Country is the fountainhead of all."[113] Tang Ao and Duo Jiugong not only find that their girls have been taught by an old Confucian gentleman, but they also discover that Ban Zhao's *Commandments for Women*, inscribed on one side of the fan that Duo Jiugong took away by mistake, were copied by Honghong at the command of the Confucian Master of Ink Stream.[114]

Although Li Ruzhen is known as a Confucian scholar, he opposes indoctrinated Confucian ethics and particularly its oppression of women. As observed by Liu Zaifu and Lin Gang, "The quintessence of Confucian Culture rests on the deification and ethicization of the power structure of the Chinese patriarchal clan system."[115] But in *The Flowers, Wulun* (the Five Principles of Confucian Ethics), which perpetuate this power structure by regulating the hierarchal relationships between emperor and minister, between father and son, between brothers, between husband and wife, and between friends, are challenged by an old woman called Wang Lao: "If a person born in the world lives happily following his/her own inclinations, why should s/he care about the Five Principles or the Four Principles? Even if you lack a couple of principles [of those ethics], you are still a human being. Aren't you still a human being in others' eyes?"[116] Li Ruzhen seems to be convinced that women's emancipation is possible only outside the Confucian influence. The Country of Women represents one example of this belief. Without the bondage of Confucian ideology and the Four Virtues, women become masters of the country. The picture of sex-role reversal in the Country of Women is marred, however, by its female king's sexual indulgence and by the oppression of men. To ameliorate this picture, Li Ruzhen arranges for four talented women to rule in the Country of Women: Yin Ruohua, the hidden female prince of the Country of Women, who has achieved a balance between masculinity and femininity by coming to China and having no disposition to sexual indulgence or tyranny; Honghong and Tingting, both from the Country of the Black Toothed, who surpass Tang Ao and Duo Jiugong in knowledge but are deprived of the opportunity to rise in their own country; and Lanyin, a girl from the Country of the Fork-tongued, who can speak thirty-six foreign languages and is cured of her physical disease by Tang Ao. These four girls all win the first-ranked academic title, "Women of Letters." With Yin Ruohua as king and the other three as her guardian ministers, Li Ruzhen leaves the reader to imagine the utopian future of the Country of Women under a sisterly based collective female rule.

Reform under a female sovereign such as Wu Zetian, and autonomous female rule in a place outside Confucianism, are viable political solutions in *The Flower*; yet, Li Ruzhen still insists on ultimate separation from the earthly world in having his protagonist Tang Guichen complete her destiny at Little Penglai. There appear to be three reasons for this. First, Li Ruzhen associates power with corruption. Though emphasizing the importance of female sovereignty to the achieving of women's equal rights with men, he is aware that women can abuse power, too. Li Ruzhen reveals his abhorrence of female tyranny in his negative portrayal of Wu Zetian as a female monster obsessed with power and sex, faults that lead eventually to her dethronement. Second, Li agrees with Xun Zi that human nature is inherently evil.[117] One of the satirical fables in the novel has the character Chang Hong caught in a hole of a giant coin. Through the hole, he watches millions of people—intellectuals, peasants, laborers, and merchants, the Three Religions, and the Nine Classes—all struggling for the coin.[118] In the allegorical war, both Tang loyalists and Wu's court are subject to corruption. Third, although Li is a Confucian scholar, the philosophical and religious underpinning of the novel is Daoism, which renounces this worldly life as an illusion or dream. As the creator of the Pavilion of Weeping Ladies, Li Ruzhen sees the life endured by women in this world; they are bound to wifehood and motherhood as a banishment to the sea of bitterness. As the self-alleged "descendant of Lao Zi," he strongly suggests that women participate in Daoist purification to reach their ultimate utopia, Little Penglai.

By separating from Confucianism and the earthly world, Li Ruzhen provides women with a political utopian vision and a spiritual utopian vision. The critic Hsin-sheng C. Kao suggests that Li Ruzhen uses the Daoist concept of spiritual salvation to oppose women's political involvement;[119] but, I believe, Li Ruzhen's two utopian visions for women complete rather than contradict each other. In fact, Li's picture of Little Penglai has greatly changed from the traditional one. Not only does Little Penglai have a community of women, but Tang Guichen, after becoming an immortal, is still involved in this-worldly politics. Without her help, the loyalists would not have been able to win the war against the corrupted court of Wu Zetian.

Gilman also insists on separation from patriarchy and from this world; but her separation is far more radical than Li's in the direction of feminism. Her separation demands the elimination of men, as we know them, along with their patriarchal superstructure and ideology. Li Ruzhen supports the politics of "separate but equal," while Gilman affirms the politics of "separate and superior." Within the existing political structure, Li attempts to set up an independent political area for women by creating a separate but parallel examination system for them. Restricted by historical conditions, he is unable to imagine a different value system. His vision extends no further than allowing women to imitate men in education and politics, to become sworn sisters like sworn brothers, and to gain Daoist transcendence. Unlike Li Ruzhen, Gilman dares to use the symbolic elimination of men to establish a new world of women in accordance with female values. Her daring dream is, perhaps, the result of four special conditions: (1) Being a woman, she most appreciates maternal values, women's desire to have their domestic work recognized as a contribution by society, and their dream of separating personal motherhood from mothering; (2) Lester Ward's Gynocentric Theory, which regards the female as the original "race-type," while the male is only the "sex-type," [120] provides a theoretical basis for Gilman's conviction of women's social, spiritual, and biological primacy; (3) Gilman is influenced by the early nineteenth-century women's zeal for the "Cult of True Womanhood" and womb-worship; and (4) Gilman believes in the philosophy of natural life. Female values are closely related to nature and life, while male values are the props of what she sees as our superfluous civilization. Above all, Gilman's bold imagination shows the new feminist awareness that "the subordination of women could only end when women led the struggle for their own autonomy and equality, thereby freeing men as well as themselves from the distortions that come with dominance." [121]

Although motherhood, mothering, and domesticity are completely absent from *The Flowers*, the Daoist utopian impulse found throughout the novel happens to share most of the values held by Western feminists. Nearly all critics have noticed the influence of Bellamy's socialism on Gilman's utopian vision, but nobody has mentioned the affinities between Gilman's utopian thinking and Daoist utopianism. Gilman's utopian vision resembles Li Ruzhen's Daoist vision in the following five ways.

About the social structure of Herland, Jennings, the sociologist and narrator in the novel, observes that the Herlanders had "no exact analogue for our word home, any more than they had for our Roman-based family." [122] The Roman family, a "house community" that includes several generations, is patriarchal. [123] Gilman's concept of the extended family is modelled after the matrilineal community. Being idyllic and peaceful as well as temporally static and geographically isolated, this ideal utopian social unit particularly echoes Lao Zi's *Dao De Jing*, which says,

In a small country with few people
. . . .
Let the people value their lives and yet not move far away
Even if there is armor and weapons, none will display them
Let the people again knot the cords and use them (instead of
     writing).
Let them relish their food, appreciate their fine clothing,
find comfort in their homes.[124]

Herland's worship of the "Over Mother" of the land resembles Li Ruzhen's Daoist worship of "Queen Mother of the West." Both are symbols of sacred female power. The worship of a goddess as the maker of man can be traced back to Chinese creation mythology.

Herland's primitive communism mirrors the Daoist ideal society "to be found in pre-civilization."[125] Little Penglai is pastoral, with its settlers serving in the roles of fishermen, woodcutters, or herb-gatherers. Similarly, Herland is a "little paradise" hidden in primitive jungles, and the Herlanders are food-gatherers. Although Gilman's vision looks forward, rather than backward like *The Flowers*, which is set in a chosen historical past, *Herland* is unavoidably atavistic in its return to nature from the strayed civilization. It is in this sense that Gilman's ideal and Li Ruzhen's vision join in the ultimate Daoist utopian vision of "the restoration of the Golden Age, a restoration in which past and future are merged."[126]

Gilman's conception of time, her philosophy of "growth" in process, and her claimed nondifferentiation between good and evil echo the Daoist way of nature. The Herlanders' abhorrence of violence and war and their love for harmony and peace resemble Daoist social concerns. Also, the Daoist utopian messianism in the Tang Dynasty "actually inspired revolutionary movements aiming at seeking social betterment."[127] This ideal is reflected in *Herland*.

Both *Herland* and *The Flowers* create a vision of an androgynous being, echoing the Daoist harmonious balance of *yin* and *yang*. E. H. Baruch, in her "Introduction to Visions of Utopia" in *Women in Search of Utopia*, discusses the "psychosocial androgyny" and "biological androgyny" in *Herland*. Gilman's biological androgyny is used only symbolically. In fact, as revealed by *Herland* and its sequel, *With Her in Ourland*, Gilman's ultimate purpose is to create a political androgyny. The same purpose is reflected in Li Ruzhen's vision of the Country of Sexless People in *The Flowers*. All of the people are androgynous —"neither men nor women." But Li's attitude towards their androg-

yny is ambivalent. He disapproves of biological androgyny by portraying them as sterile—they "do not give birth to children." Their
biological infertility makes them "an earthy lot" who "don't like the
fruit which grows on trees, but prefer to eat the soil."[128] Their androgyny, however, is the only way to achieve Li Ruzhen's ultimate political
utopianism. These people do not crave fame, power, or personal gain,
for they understand the essence of Daoism—"death as sleep and life as
a dream"—and see through the dubious value of "wealth and fame."
Existence to them, as to the Herlanders, is a natural process of cyclical
growth. Li Ruzhen and Gilman sculpt the ideal human being—a female man or a male woman, the egalitarian union of woman and man
—in this vision of political androgyny.

Because Gilman and Li Ruzhen have elemental affinities in their
utopian thinking, they both see the absurdity of contemporary civilization. Li Ruzhen advocates equal opportunity for women in traditional
education only to redress social injustice against women. In fact, he
insists on purging all the "worthless knowledge" that burdens mankind. Gilman radically discards all written texts and laws in Herland;
however, she is not a Daoist escapist as is Tang Ao. Gilman is concerned with improving human existence, with high ideals of "Beauty,
Health, Strength, Intellect, Goodness."[129] Her combining of feminism
with socialism, as well as her "consciousness about the human responsibility in the overall ecology,"[130] draws a demarcation between the
modern Herland and the classical Little Penglai.

—⟨ᴍ⟩—

By criticizing patriarchy and elevating female collective power,
both *The Flowers* and *Herland* create practical feminist visions within
ultimate visions of the implausible. Li Ruzhen's idea of sexual equality
has been largely realized in modern China, while his Daoist vision,
though having spiritual significance, will remain a utopian ideal forever. In a similar way, Gilman's practical vision of females as independent working women, who pool their intelligence, skills, and energy in
education, production, the improvement of human surroundings, and
the creation of a better human world, has proved its strength in the
past sixty years, while her fantastic vision of an all-female world peopled through parthenogenesis has triggered a discourse of "feminist
fabulation."[131] After all, even fictional dreams contain embryos of the
"ideal of desirable quality."[132]

Gilman's description of Herland as an ordered, peaceful world
settled purely by women, and her celebration of natural female superi-

ority seem to have evoked the idea of "lesbian separatism" in *Herland*; this interpretation goes against its author's original intention,[133] perhaps because of the limitations and potential separatism in radical feminism—"Gilman insisted she was not a feminist" but a humanist.[134] Gilman's unique female consciousness, however, accounts in large measure for her novel's attraction to later lesbian utopian writers.[135] With the appearance of feminist utopias, such as Russ's *Female Man*, Gearhart's *Wanderground*, Charnas's *Motherlines*, and Sheldon's [Tiptree's] novella "Houston, Houston, Do You Read?" in the 1970s, lesbian separatism became an academic and political arena comprised solely of women. Their politics, falling between Li Ruzhen's "separate but equal" strategy and Gilman's "separate and superior" tactic, have demonstrated their strength in shaping "a female culture sharing center stage with a male world."[136]

In the next chapter, I choose to leap over this group of contemporary all-female feminist utopias to concentrate on the fourth phase of my thematic study. Apart from a shift from motherhood to sisterhood and an acceptance of sexual freedom, the all-female feminist utopias develop in the same direction of collectivism and symbolic separatism as does *Herland*. Their most significant achievement centers on their aesthetic form.

In Spenser and Luo Maodeng's utopian schemes, women are merely accidental or marginal authorial concerns. Although Dixie and Gilman attempt to reach humanity through women, as do Chen Duansheng and Li Ruzhen, their sole or dominant concern is with women's questions. In the fourth thematic phase of female power, women again become the authors' marginal concern, as in Bai Hua's *Remote Country of Women*. Women, as shown in Le Guin's *Dispossessed*, do not even have to occupy textual centrality, but their power and value system continue to dominate the authors' utopian imagination as they explore a better future for modern or postmodern society.

5

From Matrilineality to Anarchism
The Remote Country of Women and *The Dispossessed*

Written on opposite sides of the world, Bai Hua's *Remote Country of Women* (1988) and Ursula K. Le Guin's *Dispossessed* (1974) strike us with their similarities. Both Bai Hua and Le Guin proceed on a utopian impulse with the consciousness of a realist. By alternating between utopia and dystopia, each author stages dramatic contrasts between those two worlds, provoking fundamental questions about contemporary social systems. In view of each author's conscious critique of patriarchy and dream of a world governed by the female principle, or Dao—the Way of Nature, *The Remote Country of Women* and *The Dispossessed*, even if not concerned primarily with the question of women, emerge as powerful, feminist utopian narratives. These novels, seen as feminist utopias of our fourth phase, transfer female power from the realm of women to the larger world of humanity and propose a feminist philosophy within a world view that deals with the possibilities and problems of humankind rather than of women only.

Background and Authorial Intention

Bai Hua, a pseudonym for Chen Youhua, has been recognized as a major contemporary Chinese writer. Born in Xinyang, a small city in the Henan Province, in 1930, he became fatherless at the age of nine, when his father was buried alive by Japanese invaders for his refusal to collaborate. Bai Hua's poetic sensitivity and love of literature

117

were first shaped by his mother's folk songs and her poor, illiterate friends' devotional Buddhist songs. Of his mother, he says that "[she] came from a poor family and had married Father only to bear him sons, for his first wife had died leaving only two daughters."[1] He joined the People's Liberation Army (PLA) in 1947 and four years later began to write poems, short stories, and screenplays. Labeled a "Bourgeois Rightist" in 1957, he was expelled from the army and the party the following year. In 1961, he became an editor and screenplay writer for the Shanghai Petrel Film Company and three years later began his career as a free-lance writer. Since 1985, he has been residing in Shanghai.

A prolific writer, Bai Hua became the target of political movements against bourgeois liberalism in the early 1980s, after his screenplay *Unrequited Love* (1979) was made into the film *The Sun and Man* (1980), which was criticized and banned by the Communist Party. The *The Remote Country of Women*, his first long novel, was published in 1988 by the journal *Literature of the Inland and Overseas* (February), the Renmin Wenxue (May), and Taiwan's San Min (July).[2] As a result of political problems and language barriers, *Country of Women* has received little critical attention either at home or abroad. Consequently, it has not been examined as a feminist utopian novel.

Bai Hua sets his story in two worlds: the utopian world of the Mosuo people, located at the very border of southwestern China, and the dystopian world of China itself during the ten-year Cultural Revolution. The story has two protagonists: Sunamei, a naive, female observer from the matrilineal paradise of Mosuo, who defies all the codes of modern civilization; and Liang Rui, a rebellious seer of chaotic China, yet a man with a patriarchal ego. The story shuttles back and forth from eutopia to dystopia, presenting Sunamei's and Liang Rui's changing mentalities through conflicts experienced in both worlds. Sunamei's happy growth and innocent questioning permit Bai Hua to demonstrate an organic social system embodied in matrilineality; through Liang Rui's imprisonment and ironic perspective, the author exposes the absurdity and horror that reside beneath socialist China's revolutionary slogans.

The plot of the story runs on two tracks. When Sunamei is nearly thirteen years old, PLA soldiers and cadres, sent by the Central Party Committee under the control of the Gang of Four,[3] attempt to force the Mosuonians to accept monogamous marriage, but fail completely. Sunamei, undergoing the rituals of "Changing into Skirt," and worshipping the Goddess Ganmu, grows into an independent woman and enters into sexual relationships with two men, Longbu and Yingzhi, before leaving to join a Dancing and Singing Troupe in the civilized world. On the other track, a young student of fine arts, Liang Rui, the main narrator of the novel, recounts his acts of vandalism in 1966 as the head of a group of Red Guards. Later, he becomes a cowherd on a farm to receive reeducation like other graduates and intellectuals. He happens to know a girl called Yunqian and escapes to her place under medical pretexts. In his attempt to help a returned intellectual, Gui Renzhong, break through "the prison in his mind," Liang Rui, ironically, is betrayed by the honest Gui Renzhong and jailed until the end of the Cultural Revolution. After leaving prison, he discovers that his girlfriend has abandoned him. In utter disillusionment, he volunteers to go to the most remote and primitive area of China to shun the evils of civilized society. Eventually, he is posted as a jack-of-all-trades at a cinema in a county adjoining the Mosuo Community, where Sunamei has become the horror of the town because of the Mosuo women's notoriety for promiscuity; but Liang Rui boldly marries her despite her reputation. From this point on, Liang Rui, formerly the heroic crusader against social evils, dwindles to an ordinary, patriarchal man, seeking to possess and master his wife by bonding her with their marriage certificate. While visiting the Mosuo Community, Liang Rui becomes violent upon catching Sunamei with her earlier lover Yingzhi, and as a result, he is abandoned by Sunamei as well as by the entire Mosuo Community, which embodies Nature. Symbolically, we witness modern man expelled from utopia for his patriarchal ego—the desire to possess.

Four elements in Bai Hua's biography appear to shape the feminist dimensions of *Country of Women*. First, a rebellious spirit inherited from his father, and further inflamed by repeated setbacks in his political life, finds expression in a rebellious feminism, subversive to oppressive authority. Second, the suffering experienced by his widowed mother and her poor women friends has led Bai Hua to often associate his own suffering with the suffering of women. It is not surprising that in *Unrequited Love*, he follows the patriotic model of the poet Qu Yuan (c. 340–278 B.C.) and analogizes the pathos of Chinese intellectuals to a woman's unrequited love for the patriarchal Communist Party embodied by the sun. Third, disillusioned by the Chinese social system and modern civilization, which act very much as a corollary for over three thousand years of patriarchy, Bai Hua turns to matrilineality for moral strength as well as for a vision of the future—matrilineality being considered by him the original model of human society. Lastly,

Bai Hua finds a concrete model for his feminism in the contemporary Mosuo Community, which has preserved its prehistoric matrilineality to this day.

The Mosuo Tribal Communities have long been a subject of interest in China. Located along the Jinsha River and around the Lugu Lake in the provinces of Sichuan and Yunnan, "the Mosuonians still maintain a prehistorical family structure and marital form. They regard the female as the root and trunk and the male as the branches and leaves. The social scientists call them 'matrilineal.' "[4] Accounts of this curious country of women were recorded as early as the Jin Dynasty in *Huayang Guo Zhi: Shu Zhi*, by Chang Qu. The Mosuonians are also known as the Naxi by nationality. In 1981, Zhan Chengxun and three other anthropologists published the results of their investigations on the Mosuo Community in a book titled *Yongning Naxi Nationality's Azhu Marriage and Matrilineal Family*. In 1983, Yan Yuxian and Song Zhaolin published similar findings, but with more theoretical analysis, called *Yongning Naxi Nationality's Matrilineality*. Reminiscent of Frederick Engels's analysis of Lewis H. Morgan's investigation of North American Indian gentes, these two books, both read by Bai Hua,[5] demonstrate how sexual-gender equality and public ownership are possible under a matrilineal system and how the sexual and class oppression and private ownership arise when men come to power.

The Mosuo Community investigations, however, fail to acknowledge futuristic values in this model of matrilineal society. The 1981 study regards the community as primitive and backward. The development of monogamy and the acquisition of modern civilization to secure a better future are among the investigators' predictions. The 1983 study recognizes the vitality of the matrilineal system and respects the rights of a minority people to choose their own system, but still believes that the replacement of matrilineality by patriarchy is inevitable and progressive. Bai Hua has completely reversed these conclusions. The authorial intention of *Country of Women*, as stated in the introduction to the Taiwan edition, is to "use the past as a mirror to see the present," to use the values of his matrilineal model to challenge our conventional evaluations of the primitive versus the modern, the barbarous versus the civilized, and the monogamous versus the promiscuous.

Although Bai Hua is not particularly concerned with women's issues in contemporary China, his novel is undeniably feminist; he sees the future of humanity in the model of matrilineality and raises such questions as, "What are the criteria for human progress? How much have we sacrificed for our material civilization? Why has humankind lost peace after entering the stage of patriarchy?"⁶

Unlike Bai Hua, Ursula K. Le Guin insists on a postmodern gylanic model rather than a primitive matrilineal model for humanity. Her personal experience may in part account for this. Le Guin, generally recognized as a feminist utopian writer of science fiction, was born in Berkeley, California, on October 21, 1929. Raised in a liberal intellectual background, she suffered "no adolescent hangups" or marital problems caused by gender issues,⁷ as were often experienced by women writers of the nineteenth century. Her father, the noted anthropologist Alfred Kroeber, kindled her early interest in cultural anthropology and Daoist philosophy. Her mother, who had a graduate degree in psychology and a well-known book entitled *Ishi in Two Worlds*, greatly affected her daughter's interest in Jungian psychology and her constant fictional theme of cultural contrast. Ursula's marriage to Charles Le Guin ended her doctoral study in 1953, but provided her with a true idea of "partnership."⁸ Her husband, who has encouraged Le Guin in her writing, often reads the first drafts of her works and has shared mothering with her. Her dedication of *The Dispossessed* to "the partner" is a tribute to their friendship, which extends beyond the limits of marriage. It is no surprise, therefore, that among her numerous creative works, *The Left Hand of Darkness* and *The Dispossessed*, winners of Hugo and Nebula awards and her best-known feminist utopias, are both gender-free utopias. The former is "a feminist thought-experiment whereby Gethenians as androgynes become heuristic for determining essential humanity without lifelong cultural conditioning of gender roles;"⁹ the latter is a feminist thought-experiment based on contemporary world politics.

Although both Dixie's reformist utopia and Gilman's all-female utopia focus their arguments on women's problems and issues, they generally reveal a lack of interest in today's world politics. On the other hand, Le Guin, like Bai Hua, deals with national or world problems in which women are only a part of her concern. *The Dispossessed* is a product of global power politics and of revolutionary movements in the late 1960s and early 1970s. As Tom Moylan perceives, Anarres mirrors the isolated People's Republic of China from 1948 to the Nixon initiative, while on A-Io's rivalry with Thu, on Urras, embodies the United States' rivalry with the Soviet Union. The activists on Urras "reflect the various movements of the late 1960s—Anti-war activists, ecologists, school reformers, anarchists, socialists, working-class and poor, Third World revolutionaries."¹⁰ But instead of following "the classical utopian aspirations of Western philosophy: reconciliation in the potential harmony for all," as Moylan and Fekete believe,[11] we find that Le Guin draws strength from the oriental Daoist philosophy that prefigures natural anarchism.

In *The Dispossessed*, Le Guin aims to create a utopian model of a higher form of anarchism, as well as to criticize propertarianism, authoritarianism, and power concentration. Le Guin, like Bai Hua, also uses a double-track narrative; however, *The Dispossessed* has only one protagonist, an intellectual rebel and keen observer named Shevek. The narrative concerning Anarres begins with Shevek as a two-year-old child learning to share, who, since childhood, has often felt alienated from others because of his "disruptive" genius. Encouraged by two women teachers—Mitis and Gvarab, he becomes a physicist and discovers the "Principle of Simultaneity," which he hopes to develop into a device, the "ansible," that will allow instantaneous communication between all parts of space. His idea is exploited by Sabul, who is an anti-Odonian Anarresti in his egoist pursuit of power and fame. Because of the importance of the ansible to the future of the League of All Worlds, Shevek is invited to Urras. The other track begins with Shevek's departure for Urras with a single purpose: to "unbuild walls" in human communication. On Urras, he gradually discovers that his host nation A-Io is attempting to use his theory to advance its national power. Shevek decides to broadcast his theory publicly so that all humanity can share the benefits of interstellar communication. With the aid of the Terran Embassy and the Hainish, Shevek returns to Anarres with his faith in Anarresti anarchism reinforced. He finally breaks down the wall between utopia and our world by bringing a man from Urras to Anarres.

Le Guin's authorial intentions and this plot outline show us little particularly feminist. In fact, Le Guin has been criticized for marginalizing women by using a male protagonist. Critics, such as Moylan, even accuse Le Guin of being antifeminist. "The text [of *The Dispossessed*] reveals a message of male, individual, intellectual, elitist leadership rather than one of collective resistance and common victory. In particular, the power of the women's movement of the late 1960s and early 1970s is silenced in favor of the limits of mainstream male discourse."[12] My reexamination of *The Dispossessed* is a defense of Le Guin.[13] Without the feminist movement of the late 1960s and early 1970s, *The Dispossessed* would not have existed. Furthermore, some feminist writers, including Gilman, refuse to be called "feminist," because they assume that feminism is too limiting. Daphne Patai, in

"Beyond Defensiveness: Feminist Research Strategies," raises the question of how best to overcome women's marginalization of themselves by "simply considering women typical human beings and not arguing about it," writing "as if women, rather than men, were the model for the human norm," and assuming that "the subject is of general human interest and that women constitute the human norm."[14] Le Guin apparently agrees with Patai's broadening of feminism. She actually says that "I didn't see how you could be a thinking woman and not be a feminist."[15] *The Dispossessed* is one of her conscious efforts against what she calls the "baboon patriarchy" found in American science fiction:

> This tendency has been remarkably strong in American SF. The only social change presented by most SF has been toward authoritarianism, the domination of ignorant masses by a powerful elite—sometimes presented as a warning, but often quite complacently. Socialism is never considered as an alternative, and democracy is quite forgotten. Military virtues are taken as ethical ones. Wealth is assumed to be a righteous goal and a personal virtue. Competitive free-enterprise capitalism is the economic destiny of the entire Galaxy. In general, American SF has assumed a permanent hierarchy of superiors and inferiors, with rich, ambitious, aggressive males at the top, then a great gap, and then at the bottom the poor, the uneducated, the faceless masses, and all the women. The whole picture is, if I may say so, curiously, "un-American." It is a perfect baboon patriarchy, with the Alpha Male on top, being respectfully groomed, from time to time, by his inferiors.[16]

It is not surprising that many women readers find Le Guin's *Dispossessed* an exciting feminist utopia.[17] In fact, it is not the textual centrality, or marginality, or even authorial intention that makes a work feminist; it is the author's fundamental feminist consciousness. So, although *Country of Women* and *The Dispossessed* do not concentrate on women's questions, these novels are feminist texts, because they radically challenge patriarchal power structure by replacing the male principle with the female principle.

Critique of Patriarchy: "Sex" and "Property" as Central Metaphors

Feminist utopias are critical utopias in the sense that the utopian past and future are both gauges for criticizing the present, with social conditions created by a patriarchal system, which cause the oppression of women. Their forms of criticism, however, differ. Chen Duansheng uses subtle irony, while Dixie uses open declaration. Li Ruzhen employs satire in a dramatic form, while Gilman satirizes through verbal wit. Bai Hua and Le Guin each choose a central metaphor with which to criticize patriarchy: sex and property, respectively.

"Sex" functions in *Country of Women* as its controlling metaphor to expose the ramifications of patriarchal evils: sexual repression, sexual starvation, rape, prostitution, monogamy, adultery, jealousy, and murder. Mosuonian sexual freedom is viewed as an emancipatory force. In *Country of Women*, sexual repression becomes a disguised form of political invasion. In chapter 1, the Chinese Central Party Committee, headed by the Gang of Four, sends a Work Team accompanied by a troop of the PLA soldiers with guns and bayonets to the Mosuonian region. This invasion comprises a picture of fascist colonization. The invaders seize as criminals all Mosuonian men and women who have been sleeping together without marriage certificates and punish them by "reducing their food ration . . . sending them to jail or reformatory."[18] During the reign of white terror, Mosuonian men and women stop seeing each other rather than yield to legalized monogamy, being confused by this Chinese suppression of their life style: "Why should the leaders of the Central Party Committee give a damn about what's inside a man's pants or under a woman's skirt?"[19] The underlying message is that Chinese authorities regard such primitive freedom as a threat to a civilization based on centralization of power.

Bai Hua also links sexual repression with political automation. Gu Shuxian, the Work Team Leader, rises to power not only by repressing her own sexual instinct but by persecuting other men and women on the grounds of their sexual behavior. She gains her position as Political Commissar in the early revolutionary period and consolidates through her ability to detect and expose adulteries, flirtations, or any kind of sexual ambiguity. She wins praise from all male commanders for torturing their "unchaste" wives. In so doing, Gu Shuxian completely abandons her humanism and becomes "a part in a gigantic political machine. She must turn, move forward and backward with the body of the machine and make the same noise to keep her in unison with other parts of the machine."[20]

Bai Hua believes that sexual suppression is a function of political inequality, enabling those in power to indulge in lust and requiring those without power to suffer sexual starvation. When Mosuo men are not permitted to visit their women at night, the male members of the

Work Team take advantage of these Mosuo women, who have no concept of sin associated with sex. On the other hand, at a political gathering, sexually starved females jump onto the table on which Gui Renzhong is standing to pull his hair and pinch his flesh; one spinster even pulled his "organ which no other but his mother and wife could touch."[21] Bai Hua uses this absurd incident to suggest that not only the female but the male body may become a private possession in puritanical China.

Sexual starvation reaches its climax in prison. Three female prisoners between the ages of twenty and forty "gang-rape" a male prisoner sent to fix their window; but this female gang-rape involves the collaboration of the male prisoner, who is equally starved for sex. Men's rape of women in the novel is always linked with political abuse. With the help of his wife, a senile army commander rapes Jane in broad daylight, while Jane begs him to allow her husband Gui Renzhong to return home from the prison farm. A young man who has risen to power in the Cultural Revolution rapes a woman doctor with the help of anesthesia because she refused his love during their schooldays; and he rapes his former classmate in front of his teacher, because he believes the teacher to be politically dead and thus no longer a human being. In these two examples, Bai Hua uses "rape" to show the utmost absurdity of patriarchal power, which relies on willful corruption and conquest of the rebellious other.

Perhaps because women in China have now largely achieved economic independence, Bai Hua locates the business of prostitution in India, where a woman may still openly sell her body for money. Inside China, Bai Hua uses the case of Liu Tiemei to expose the evil consequences of monogamy. Liu Tiemei, a woman doctor, becomes politically neurotic as a result of bearing three children to a husband who never loves her. She persecutes all the women around, fearing that they are sexually attractive to her husband, and threatens to accuse her husband of being a counterrevolutionary if he dares to associate with another woman. Eventually, Liu breaks through her own sexual repression and commits adultery with a fellow doctor, Yu Shouchen. The result of the breakthrough, however, is her murder of Yu's wife, who accused her of being a whore and stealing her husband.

Taken together, these dramatic tragedies of sexual repression and monogamy comprise Bai Hua's indictment of patriarchy as a cause of all social evils. To Bai Hua, sex is a natural part of human life, but men create laws and entire ideologies that make sex a matter of politics and property. To stress this point, Bai Hua recreates the Mosuo myth of the goddess Ganmu. Being sexually generous, Ganmu takes many gods as her *Axiao* (sleeping friends), but the god Warupula wants to possess her and cuts off the god Zhezhi's penis out of jealousy. In his modern version of the myth, Bai Hua lets any Mosuonian outshine his protagonist Liang Rui. Though a hero struggling against mechanized modern society, Liang Rui fails to overcome man's chauvinist ego. When he discovers his wife receiving her former lover Yingzhi:

> I rushed over and slapped her face fiercely. . . . Yingzhi protected her with his body and began to reproach me. I could not understand his words. . . . What right have you! You dirty dog! To steal into *My* room, get into *My* bed, seduce *My* wife. I will punish him! I picked up a large piece of firewood. The next moment I was striking at Yingzhi. Sunamei screamed like a wild beast. She grasped Yingzhi and dashed out. . . . The kindled wood flew to the roof, the whole building was swallowed by tongues of flame (original emphasis).[22]

In spite of his grandiose "My," Liang Rui becomes completely invisible to the silent, peaceful Mosuo village, symbolically abandoned by Nature.

Bai Hua uses the private ownership of sex as a key metaphor for exposing the evils of the patriarchal system, while Le Guin uses "property" as her central metaphor for refuting patriarchal evils stemming from property ownership: possessors, profiteers, and body profiteers.

Although critics seldom treat Le Guin as a Marxist, her ideas seem to have been very much influenced by Karl Marx's views on the relations between property, profit, and state capitalism.[23] She regards possession as the root of all social evils. In *The Dispossessed*, Le Guin attributes the social problems on A-Io to three types of possession: property possession, knowledge possession, and power possession. Because of the private ownership of property, A-Io has a class hierarchy that polarizes men into two groups: the propertarians or profiteers, and the poor who live in slums. In this hierarchy, women, whether rich or poor, stay at the bottom because, as Shevek observes, women "in the eyes of men are a thing, a thing owned, bought, sold."[24] Through the division of "social status," men exclude women from jobs, such as "running a space freighter" to avoid "the loss of—of everything feminine—of delicacy—and the loss of masculine self-respect."[25] This male "self-respect" requires men to consider half the human race as inferior, whereas women are left with no respect but self-deception. A rich but pitiful woman such as Vea can only play a psychological game by deceiving herself that women "run the men" while men run the world.[26]

Le Guin uses the possession of knowledge to criticize the intellectual hierarchy. In A-Io, titles such as Doctor are foreign to Shevek, who has never heard them on Anarres. In this intellectual hierarchy, women do not seem to occupy any place. Meeting only male physicists, mathematicians, astronomers, logicians, and biologists at the University of A-Io, Shevek asks, "Where are women?" He is told that a woman's place among intellectuals is at the entertaining party as a certain professor's wife. Le Guin also exposes men's prejudices against women using their intellect: Women are incapable of "abstract thought" and "original intellectual work;" they can only be girls' school teachers; the few exceptional "brainy women" not only suffer "vaginal atrophy" but are suitable only to be "technicians" who can "take a good deal of the load off the men in any laboratory situation."[27] Le Guin ridicules the so-called intellectual plight of women in which even the shyest man can gain courage "from his dismissal of the woman from the realms of higher thought."[28]

According to Le Guin's portrayal, the possession of power on A-Io represents an abomination on four counts. First, power is exercised to serve the interests of the propertied class. Second, the power structure excludes all women as one class of inferior beings. Shevek says to Vea: "It seems that everything your society does is done by men. The industry, arts, management, government, decisions. And all your life you bear the father's name and the husband's name. The men go to school and you don't go to school; they are all the teachers, and judges, and police, and government, aren't they? Why do you let them control everything? Why don't you do what you like?"[29] Third, power reaches its highest form of concentration at the stage of state capitalism, which engineers global wars and owns everything: even an idea, a scientific theory, is "a property of the state."[30] Fourth, power, with its army and police forces, bloodily suppresses the working class and all revolutionary activists. As does Herbert Marcuse, Le Guin believes that existing state power is the greatest obstacle to the realization of utopia.[31] Odo is jailed eight times for speaking her Odonianism. Shevek witnesses a peaceful antiwar demonstration, organized by post-Odonians, being suppressed by machine guns and helicopters.

In sum, the possession of property, knowledge, and power produces moral corruption. Therefore, human relationships on Urras are centered around money or profit—one person the profiteer of another. A woman who uses "her sexuality as a weapon in a power struggle with men" becomes a body profiteer.[32] Le Guin portrays Vea as a model of a body profiteer:

> Vea was the body profiteer to end them all. Shoes, clothes, cosmetics, jewels, gestures, everything about her asserted provocation. She was so elaborately and ostentatiously a female body that she seemed scarcely to be a human being. She incarnated all the sexuality the Ioti repressed into their dreams, their novels and poetry, their endless paintings of female nudes, their music, their architecture with its curves and domes, their candles, their baths, their mattresses.[33]

In particular, Le Guin exposes the bourgeois hypocrisy of sexually intensified Western society. On the one hand, women are diminished into sexual dolls, with "baby talk" and a jewel in the naked belly; on the other hand, women have to guard their reputation for chastity. As a result, they are forced to play secret adulterous games in defiance of their husbands' openly double standard.

Although rape is not denounced in the novel, Le Guin shows that the sexual violation of women is common practice in a patriarchal society. Even an honest man like Shevek, after living awhile in the surroundings of sexual seduction and having a drop of wine, attempts to commit a rape and, for the first time, acquires a disgust for sex and feels moral guilt. Through the examples of Shevek's fall and Vea's total dehumanization, sexual seduction, and psychological distortion, Le Guin tries to convey the idea that, although men formulate all of patriarchal politics and ideology, patriarchy could not exist without women's collaboration.

Bai Hua and Le Guin, by using "sex" and "property," respectively, as metaphors, seem to focus their criticism on quite different aspects of patriarchy. These differences arise from the different social systems under which the two authors have lived. Before 1976, China was fairly egalitarian economically, but politically hierarchical. Bai Hua uses socialist China as the model for his dystopia. Although he ardently praises the Mosuo women and their matrilineality, he does not think that Chinese women are more repressed than Chinese men under the socialist system. His female characters, political leaders and doctors, are portrayed as more radical than men in following Chinese leftist politics and in abusing power. A female Red Guard named Xie Li audaciously produces legal marriage certificates and forces Gui Renzhong, a professor who has returned from America, to marry her. Examples of abuse of revolutionary laws and theories to satisfy personal gain pervade the entire novel. China's peculiar problem emerges from a proletarian dictatorship that has replaced "property" with "political capital," consolidating its new hierarchy amid a constant puritanical revolution against "sex," which is associated with the bourgeoisie.

Coming from a postindustrial world, Le Guin uses "property," the cornerstone of capitalism, as a metaphor to subvert propertarian authoritarianism in economic, intellectual, and political structures. Le Guin's criticism of the existing system in relation to women is more consciously feminist than that of Bai Hua, although she uses only one archetypal female character, Vea, to represent those who have adjusted themselves well to their victimized position in a male-dominated society. Bai Hua shares the contemporary Western feminist position in ascribing the evils of modern civilization to patriarchy. He states in his introduction that patriarchy brings violence to humankind and defines human relationships in terms of position, status, privilege, and money; patriarchy produces an entire ideological system to justify its oppression of men as well as women. Although Le Guin regards herself as a feminist, she accepts neither the radical feminist premise that "the root of all injustice, exploitation, and blind aggression is sexual injustice,"[34] nor the earlier feminist biological determinism that traces war, violence, and competition to the male nature.

Le Guin, like Li Ruzhen, shares Xun Zi's notion that "man's nature is evil; goodness is the result of conscious activity. The nature of man is such that he is born with a fondness for profit."[35] Shevek, at two years of age, wants to claim the light of the sun as his own. Even the birds occupy the newly leafed trees, singing: "This is my properteetee, this is my territoree, it belongs to mee, mee" (166). The only exit for humankind in our modern dilemma, therefore, is to dispossess ourselves through a constant battle against "egoism" and "privatism." Because Le Guin perceives capitalism giving a green light to egoism and privatism, she places her hope in a nonauthoritarian communism. Written from 1971 to 1974, *The Dispossessed* seems to have been influenced by China's Cultural Revolution, during which everyone acted as a rebel and "Being sceptical of everything and rebelling against all authorities" was the order of the day. The Revolution was marked by a pronounced lashing out at bureaucracy in the power structure and at privatism in the human soul, in accordance with Mao Zedong's theory of continuous revolution.[36] The syndicates and federatives on Anarres show the shadow of spontaneous mass organizations during that anarchist decade in China. If Le Guin had written her novel in the 1980s, she might, perhaps, have envisioned some way to deal with the consequences of an ongoing revolution that practically ripped China apart. Modern anarchism affected the Chinese youth in the 1920s. The internationally renowned writer Li Yaotang adopted Ba Jin as his pen name out of his respect for Bakunin and Kropotkin.

But in the 1980s he suggested setting up a special museum to warn future generations against the anarchist Cultural Revolution. Bai Hua perceived that the lawless, violent anarchism of the Cultural Revolution disguised a most hideous totalitarianism. In 1988, still smarting from the horrors of the Cultural Revolution, he expressed the Chinese people's reluctance to experience another social upheaval: "Many people believe that no war means peace. In the past thirty years, we have had no war but have never had a peaceful time. People who long for peace cannot have a moment of tranquility. Even the Mosuo Community by Lugu Lake suffered political encroachment. But because the Mosuonians refused to be involved in the fighting, no one could drag them into any strife."[37]

As a result, Bai Hua cherishes the well-ordered primitive community. That ideal order is sustained by a quasi-religious worship of the mother and an infant principle *(Ying'er Yuanze)*, as expounded in his novella, "Mom! Mom," published in 1980: "If the infant has any principle, the principle is the mother. Because mother is the whole universe for people at the infant stage, and this universe certainly includes the principle of humanity."[38] Through the story of a man who betrays his own mother and six foster mothers, who have raised him at the risk of their lives, Bai Hua ascribes human degeneration to the abandonment of this infant principle. In his introduction to *Country of Women*, Bai Hua further develops his notion of human relationships in the metaphor of mother and infant: "Man cannot live in separation from the mother. Man, either male or female, is born of the flesh of the mother. His soul also comes from the blessing of the mother. Only the mother can exercise the highest justice."[39] In his association of mother with universe, nurturing, and democratic humanism, Bai Hua comes very close to Lao Zi's notion of "mother of all things" *(Wanwu zhi mu)*.

In spite of their differences, Bai Hua and Le Guin both want to transform defective social systems by means of human idealism. They draw strength from a humanistic tradition, reducing life to its essentials and examining social systems in a real world. As Le Guin's character, Keng, says of Shevek: "You are like somebody from our own past, the old idealists, the visionaries of freedom; and yet I don't understand you, as if you were trying to tell me of future things; and yet, as you say, you are here, now!"[40] Bai Hua perceives the vitality of the matrilineal past in the present, while Le Guin reifies the anarchism of the future. Bai Hua's matrilineality and Le Guin's anarchism seem to share timeless values embodied by the female principle.

Matrilineality and the Female Principle

What is the female principle? According to Le Guin, "the 'female principle' is or at least historically has been, basically anarchic. It values order without constraint, rule by custom not by force. It has been the male who enforces order, who constructs power-structures, who makes, enforces, and breaks laws."[41] Classical utopias written by men from Plato, More, Campanella to Bellamy, including literary utopias such as *The Faerie Queene* and *Sanbao's Expedition to the Western Oceans*, are largely depictions of ideal city-states. The realization of their ideals demands law, hierarchy, and centralism. No matter what visions they create for women, their governing principle is based essentially on the male principle of law, class, and power centralization. As opposed to governance by the male principle, both real and fictionalized, feminist utopias of the twentieth century have visualized two basic social systems: matrilineality and anarchism. While *Herland*-type feminist utopias adhere to matrilineality, which can be regarded as a primitive model of anarchy, Le Guin's Anarres in *The Dispossessed* experiments with a higher form of anarchism. Bai Hua's utopian Mosuo Community in *Country of Women* manifests the basic principles in *Herland*-type quasi-matrilineality and contains the fundamental female principle on which Le Guin builds her ideal anarchism.

To some extent, the quasi-matrilineal utopia is a discourse of retrogress. Our lived experience of urban decay and blight under unnatural patriarchy rouses the feminist dream of coming home to the original model of human society. Bai Hua's Mosuo Community, Country of Women, embodies the reviving force of that model. Many nationalities have forgotten their ancient past, yet the Mosuo people still maintain a primordial matrilineality, which has eight prominent features: (1) an extended family structure; (2) rule by the mother; (3) the "sharing" principle; (4) worship of goddesses; (5) rituals; (6) female superiority; (7) sexual permissiveness and natural monogamy; and (8) circular time and cyclical process. Each of these features will be illustrated and compared with the general characteristics of Western feminist utopias written by women, and particularly with *The Dispossessed*.

The Mosuonians live in large, extended families. Old people and children reside in the *Yimei* (communal dormitory). A woman, from the age of thirteen until the time she is unwilling to receive *Axiao*, has a room of her own. Such families are women-centered: women are "hosts" and men are "guests."[42] A man of reproductive age, if not accepted by a woman, is homeless at night and often sleeps in a cowshed. A child in the Mosuo Community recognizes a relationship with his or her mother only. Sunamei says, "What is 'father'? What's his relationship with me? He neither feeds me nor works in the fields of our community. Isn't he a guest? He is only my mother's guest, and a night guest, too."[43]

The extended family of the Mosuo Community is formed naturally along the maternal line. The basic unit of social organization in most feminist eutopias resembles such an extended family. For instance, Herland is "like a pleasant family—an old, established, perfectly-run country place;"[44] the basic social unit on Le Guin's planet of Gethen is called a "hearth," which "intends to be communal, independent, and somewhat introverted."[45] These feminist utopias usually discard the biological basis in primitive communities: "People do not live together because they are related, but because they choose to be together;"[46] however, it is hard to say that "choosing" is more practical or better than the matrilineal formation. The former emphasizes individual choice; however, individual choice creates an instability caused by emotional fluctuations. The extended family structure of Bai Hua's Mosuo Community, being nonpolitical and nonpersonal, is purely a form of cooperation for survival: production, distribution, and communication. Le Guin gets closer to the essence of this type of cooperation in *The Dispossessed*. On Anarres, people live in small communities that still resemble extended families. They make few telephone calls to reach people outside the community and write almost no letters; they do not live together because of their emotional attachment but in order to follow their chosen form of work; sexual partners are often voluntarily separated because of their different choices of work based on social needs and intellectual interests; and they frequently change their residential communities because of work, which is tantamount to play.

The head of the Mosuo Community is the Mother. She is *Dabu* (the supreme authority), who wears all the keys of the community on her waist and safeguards their common property. Yet, her image is very much like a housekeeper who administers production and material distribution. Decisions concerning the community are reached by consensus. *Dabu*, as well as the community, exerts no political power over the individual will. When Sunamei chooses to go to the civilized world to become a dancer, Ami the *Dabu* lets her go in spite of her own unwillingness and the communal disapproval. Perhaps the function of the matrilineal system itself requires its ruler to be more a servant of her people than a tyrant. The administrative function of the *Dabu* resembles that of the PDC (Production and Distribution Coordination) in *The Dispossessed*.

In *Country of Women*, one trusts an impartial mother, whereas in *The Dispossessed*, one trusts an impersonal collective that operates through the individuals' voluntary cooperation. Decisions on Anarres are made democratically, as in the Mosuo Community: "There were no rules of parliamentary procedure at the meetings in PDC. Interruptions were sometimes more frequent than statements."[47] Although one often adjusts one's behavior according to public opinion and social conscience, an individual can choose to act against "the advice of the majority of the PDC."[48] Shevek, like Sunamei, goes to the dystopian world against the majority opinion of his society. Most Western feminist utopias advocate either collective female governance or anarchy, for they see the specter of patriarchal tyranny in a possible matriarchy. Le Guin warns us that when an ideal system goes wrong, the "bureaucratic machinery within PDC" will not be better than totalitarian dictatorship and even the social conscience can be "a machine, a power machine, controlled by bureaucrats!"[49] Therefore, an individual has to be an anarchist—to "accept no rule, to be the initiator of his own acts, to be responsible."[50]

The idea of sharing is stressed in nearly all feminist utopias. Class structure and private ownership do not exist in the Mosuo Community. Distribution of goods is strictly egalitarian; all people eat at the communal dining table, and children are treated as grown-ups. *Dabu*, who serves food, will not give her own daughter a mouthful more than any other person, even on her birthday. In Le Guin's *Dispossessed*, sharing is the core of Odonian education and philosophy. The baby is taught to understand: "Nothing is yours. It is to use. It is to share."[51] Because of sharing, people have "nothing but each other" and treat each other as equal human beings. "A child free from the guilt of ownership and the burden of economic competition will grow with the will to do what needs doing and the capacity for joy in doing it."[52] Moreover, the idea of sharing is not limited to material things. On Anarres, speech is "sharing—a cooperative art,"[53] as are ideas themselves, and brotherhood is based on shared suffering. Like Anarrestis, the Mosuonians share their labor, emotions, and love. Both communities act as one organic body to deal with the most basic human problem: "Survival. Species, group, individual."[54]

Rituals are essential to feminist utopias. The Mosuo Community, for example, has no laws. Its people live in perpetual peace and harmony without crime, violence, quarrels or even a sense of sin. They do, however, observe rites of passage. At the age of thirteen, girls and boys have a grand ceremony of changing clothes, indicating their entrance into adulthood. Before the age of thirteen, Mosuo girls and boys wear exactly the same kind of short gowns. At the ceremony the boy will change his gown for trousers, and the girl, hers for a skirt. As part of the ceremony, the girl will stand on *zhubiao* (preserved pork) and a sack of grain, signifying her nurturing power. Two other major rituals are ceremonies of death and birth.

Death in most feminist utopias is not a mournful event. To Shevek, in *The Dispossessed*, "to die is to lose the self and rejoin the rest."[55] As in Piercy's *Woman on the Edge of Time*, the funeral ceremony is a cheerful farewell where the dead are sent home to join their ancestors. The Mosuonians do not believe in immortality or incarnation. They think that the dead, who have had their share of everything in life, should be happy to relinquish their place on earth to the newly born. Birth rituals in the Mosuo Community involve worshipping goddesses and sacred mountains shaped like female breasts and male reproductive organs. New lives are as particularly treasured as they are in Gilman's eutopia. Although there is no selective pregnancy, as in Herland, the Mosuo children are particularly beautiful and healthy, because they are "products of free and pure sexual love, like two natural streams merging together, without any psychological and social pressure."[56]

Goddess worship is another feature of feminist utopias. The Mosuo people observe their most important festival on July 25 (the lunar calendar), the day they worship the Goddess Ganmu, who is personified by the highest mountain. The smaller mountains around her are said to be her *Axiao*. The goddess worshipped by Gilman's Herlanders is the Overmother, who represents infinite maternal love. Herlanders also have ceremonies and hymns resembling Christian religious services. The worship of the Goddess Ganmu is very much like a grand fair, attracting thousands of people to come in festive attire. After a solemn prayer to the goddess for good harvests and prosperity, men and women take the opportunity to look for *Axiao*. The Goddess Ganmu in their shrine is a young woman riding on a stag with a crown on her head, an arrow in one hand, and a lotus flower in the other. She also has an extra eye (the eye of wisdom) growing vertically in the middle of her forehead. This goddess embodies life, power, love, and wisdom. The mountain image of this goddess depicts her as naked, with the mountain valley symbolizing her vagina to demonstrate her sexual generosity. To some extent, Ganmu is a goddess of female independence and sexual freedom. In the Mosuo myth, she says to the jealous Warupula, who cuts off Zhezhi's penis and attempts to keep Ganmu in his possession, "If a woman is not willing to sleep with you, then stop your daydreaming. No matter how much gold and jewelry you have and how great is your strength, I am my own master."[57]

Although the Mosuonians practice strict egalitarianism in material distribution, the female is the center of their social attention and is superior to the male. The female sits in the place of honor, on the right side of the table, and the male sits on the left side. The Mosuo women do not court men, rather they choose among the men who court them. This is quite different from contemporary Western feminist utopias, portraying their female heroes as taking the sexual initiative. The Mosuo men are accustomed to respect and obey women: "If a Mosuo woman says 'Please leave,' any Mosuo man will go out of her room submissively."[58]

Bai Hua's Mosuo women are independent and never lose their own center in relationship to men, whereas in civilized China, a man becomes a woman's entire life. Sunamei tells Liang Rui that Mosuo women do not go out to look for men:

Do you think I would behave myself in such an inferior way as a Han woman? If her husband is not home by night, she searches the whole street; if the man does not want her any more, she cries as if the sky were falling. Once in town I met such a Han woman wailing. I asked her: Sister, why are you crying? She screamed: That man of mine, who deserves being butchered, abandons me! That heartless Beast! . . . Her curse was so much like singing. I told her: Sister, if he abandons you, why don't you abandon him? She was scared by my words. Blinking her eye for a moment . . . she wailed even louder: Oh, my Heaven! My Earth! My Life![59]

Women are superior in the Mosuo Community because they are the "models" (*Mo*) for their race, "the human beings who give birth to and bring up human beings."[60] Women keep the harmony of their

community through their virtues and their sense of equality and justice. A Mosuo man called Awuluku, who was cheated out of his money
by a prostitute in India, says, "In the whole world only Mosuo women
on the bank of the Mother Sea are women, not 'objects'; they are
women of flesh and blood, women of warmth and feelings, women of
gratitude and love, and women with souls."[61] Women's highest nobil-
ity in nurturing is fully manifested in motherhood. When Sunamei's
Ami (mother) becomes *Dabu*, she asks her lifelong night companion
to part from her so that she can move to the communal dormitory in
order to serve the community wholeheartedly. The serving power of
mother produces a discourse of maternal pantheism: the image of the
sun is Mother, and the sea is called Mother Sea.[62]

Either through sexual role reversal or by establishing an all-female
world, female superiority appears in most feminist utopias; but recent
feminist utopias such as Le Guin's *Dispossessed* reject the dualistic
hierarchy constructed from superiority/inferiority and ruler/ruled. In
The Dispossessed, sexual difference becomes "an unknown territory"
on Anarres,[63] though female superiority peeps out here and there.
Takver, the partner of Shevek, is more shrewd and decisive in dealing
with complicated political situations; she suggests that Shevek visit
Urras. Odo, who founded Anarres and established the female principle
behind its anarchism, is a woman; and so is Shevek's physics teacher.
To achieve a sexual balance in the narrative, we are informed that on
Anarres, only fifty percent of the scientists are women, and Shevek
is the originator of the Spontaneous Principle. The Mosuo women's
superiority and female superiority in Western feminist utopias are
largely based on a moral superiority completely different from that of
the male, which is based on oppression and exploitation of the other
sex.

The Mosuo Community has no marriage system, and members
enjoy complete sexual freedom. Men and women bathe in the same
pond. They make love in the fields and in the woods as well as in the
house. There is no jealousy between men or women. Sunamei first
enjoys sexual love with Longbu, then finds Yingzhi more attractive
with his tenderness and emotion. Longbu leaves Sunamei's place at
her slightest hint. The Mosuonians can never understand the absurdity of the civilized world, where "a man and a woman need one
stamped paper to sleep together and another to part from each other;
otherwise, they are caught as sinners or criminals."[64] They can never
accept marriage, which certifies a woman as man's property or a man
as woman's property.

Except for a few earlier feminist utopias like *Herland*, twentieth-century Western utopias by women advocate sexual permissiveness as an act of sharing love. Having experienced both homosexual and heterosexual love, Shevek finally establishes a lifelong partnership with Takver. Tom Moylan criticizes Le Guin for returning to monogamy. This monogamy, however, is not the product of a legalized institution but of personal choice. Le Guin believes that "despite our continuous sexuality and our intense self-domestication, (. . .) we are very seldom truly promiscuous."[65] The Mosuonians' practice fully supports Le Guin's belief. Mosuo men and women are free mates in love. There is absolutely no economic commitment between sexual partners. However, a woman will not make love with any man of her own community. A man sleeps at night with the woman who accepts him and goes out to work during the day for his own community. Although Mosuo women can change their lovers as frequently as they want, most of them, like Ami, prefer a stable, or even a lifelong, night companion. The Mosuonians believe that only by combining sex and love can true pleasure and friendship be produced.

The philosophy of life in Bai Hua's Mosuo Community and in Gilman's Herland are fundamentally rooted in Daoism. Instead of a temporally linear progress, their notion of time is circular—ongoing process. For over ten thousand years, Mosuo people have lived to share with others and have died to join their ancestors; they have never changed their matrilineal system and have been able to preserve it, because their matrilineality is not constructed like political machinery —it is purely nurturing, like a newly born baby's "consciousness, full of milk."[66]

The actual Mosuo people of China resist legal marriage and insist on their natural right to free love, because they have learned that the monogamous possession of women means the end of their matrilineality. In past centuries, they have been surrounded by patriarchal nationalities, such as the Han, the Li, and the Zang (Tibetan), and have lived under the governmental pressures extended by each dynasty. It seems miraculous that they have preserved their matrilineality and *Axiao* custom. During the Cultural Revolution, Jiang Qing, Zhang Chunqiao, and Yao Wenyuan regarded the Mosuo tribe as a shame to socialist China: "Only primitive men of ten thousand years ago lived like them—a child never knows who his father is!"[67] They took it as a great historical mission to "pull the Mosuo kinsmen from the time of antiquity to modern life, synchronizing with us!"[68] They forced the Mosuo people to marry and be bonded in monogamy; and they built a wall to separate women from men in bathing. Resisting these measures, most Mosuo villagers stopped making love rather than accept marriage. The few who were forced into marriage slipped back into their natural way of living as soon as the "civilized" authority left. At the end of *Country of Women*, Liang Rui, ardently praises this way of life:

> Here I witness a matrilineal society which is supposed to have only existed in antiquity. Yet it indeed exists. No outside pressure has power to change it. The Mosuo people live and love solemnly according to their own primitive way of existence. . . . Although modern men cannot appreciate their sexual permissiveness, nobody can deny the fact that among them there is no murder for love, no jealousy and hatred between mothers-in-law and daughters-in-law, between aunts and sisters, and not even any family quarrels. In their extended family there is no power struggle over inheritances and no selling of the body for money or position. On earth, only Mosuo women are their own masters. Only they have the right to love or not love, to want or not want, to accept or refuse. They are independent of men. In their world, there are no tied-up spouses, no lonely old men, no homeless orphans.[69]

Liang Rui's only reservation is that the austere Mosuo community does not have the comforts of modern civilization. Perhaps to emphasize the importance of cooperation for survival, most Western feminist eutopias are set in harsh conditions. Le Guin's Anarres, for example, is a desert. In spite of advanced technology, life on Anarres is deprived of bourgeois comfort. Odonianism insists that "Excess is excrement. . . . Excrement retained in the body is a poison."[70]

For Bai Hua, Nature is the mother who nurtures and holds a democratic impartiality, and human beings are related to it by the infant principle. His Mosuo Community acts as a metaphor for Nature, which treats men and women both as subjects in productive and reproductive activities. Mosuonian life, associated with woods and rivers, sun and stars, and mountains and sea, follows the Way of Nature. It is permissive, allowing a full development of masculine and feminine traits and the harmony between communal responsibility and personal psychology. It is pacific and may yield under pressure like water in a container, but it never compromises. This accounts for the survival of Mosuonian matrilineality under successive patriarchal brutalities. The image of modernized China, on the contrary, is a noisy truck or a machine gun with automated individuals as its parts. Most Western feminist utopias do not simply exclude technology as does Bai Hua's Mosuo community. As observed by Lyman Sargent in "A New Anarchism," they are ambivalent, rejecting the technology that produces pollution and reinforces patriarchal violence and oppression but respecting the technology that improves environment and human life. While Bai Hua stops short at the conflict between modernization and matrilineality, Western feminist utopian writers try to bridge them by technology conducive to a nurturing, democratic culture. Nevertheless, nearly all Western feminist utopias, like the Mosuo Community, take nature as their operative model and prefer an organic system. This system is, in fact, the female principle. It is in timeless female values that the Mosuo women, like Takver, are identified with and become an extension of Nature.[71]

The Mosuo Community, though more primitive than the civilized world and more extreme than most imaginary places in its female superiority, represents the essential values of an all-female world, which has dominated feminist utopian imaginations in the West since the end of the nineteenth century. These worlds are known as quasi-matrilineal societies, characterized as "classless, without government, ecologically minded, with a strong feeling for the natural world, quasi-tribal in feeling and quasi-family in structure," and "sexually permissive."[72] Though sharing the basic principles of the Mosuo matrilineal model, these Western utopias are quasi-matrilineal in their transforming of some matrilineal characteristics to conform with contemporary feminist ideology. Modern feminist utopias discard the biological basis for primitive matrilineality and are not really ruled by any individual mother. Their image of the overmother is very much a symbol of collective female rule. Furthermore, their sharing principle goes beyond material property to include all aspects of life. Although the Mosuo Community differs from modern feminist utopias in this area, it still represents the essential values of all-female societies and embodies the substance of the feminist notion of the female principle. Most readers regard *Herland*-type all-female worlds as mere fantasies of only symbolic significance; but the stubborn existence of the Mosuo community forces us to think about their plausibility. Talking about the destruction of our world by lethal weapons made and used by males, Robert Scholes says, "Maybe an all-female world is the only hope for the future of the human race."[73] If an all-female world is not possible, however, a new world operated by the female principle seems quite feasible.

Replacing North American Indian gentes under mother-right with the Mosuo Community as the original model of human society, Bai Hua continues Lewis H. Morgan's and Frederick Engels's reflection upon barbarism and civilization. The "civilization" that started with the overthrow of mother-right—"the world historical defeat of the female sex"—has proved itself a failure for humanity.[74] Bai Hua, as well as most Western feminists, agree with Morgan's projection of future as "a revival, in a higher form, of the liberty, equality and fraternity of the ancient gentes."[75] The Mosuo Community represents a past "more ancient than Yao and Shun (c. 2200 B.C.),[76] because during the era of Yao and Shun, women already were dependent upon men: E Huang and Nü Ying wailed for their lost husband: Oh, my Heaven! Their sky had fallen down."[77] Yet, this Mosuonian retention of a matrilineal past keeps alive our hope for the future.

Anarchism by the Female Principle

The ways in which modern feminist utopias surpass original matrilineality often drive them toward a new form of anarchism. A. Keinhorst observes: "The female principle has been the most repressed aspect of our lives in this rationalistic age; female authors of contemporary critical utopias reinstate the suppressed shadow. What happens in these novels [with quasimatrilineal utopias like Herland] can be described as 'creative regression'—the sojourn into the past becomes a projection into the future which in many ways surpasses the original model."[78] Among single-sex quasimatrilineal utopias, Joanna Russ's *Female Man* (1975) and Suzy McKee Charnas's *Motherlines* (1978) approach feminist anarchism and avoid the stasis of utopias like Gilman's Herland or Bai Hua's Mosuo Community by making the female principle dynamic. In the 1970s, there appeared several Western utopias that could be grouped into a category of feminist anarchism, including Le Guin's *The Dispossessed*, as well as Mary Staton's *From the Legend of Biel* (1975), Thea Plym Alexander's *2150 A.D.* (1971) and Marge Piercy's *Woman on the Edge of Time* (1976).[79]

The anarchism in Le Guin's *Dispossessed* is the most explicit. She declares a conscious departure from matrilineality:

> They [the communities on Anarres] would not regress to pre-urban, pre-technological tribalism. They knew that their anarchism was the product of a very high civilization, of a complex diversified culture, of a stable economy and a highly industrialized technology that could maintain high production and rapid transportation of goods. However vast the distances separating settlements, they held to the ideal of complex organicism.[80]

She also declares that Odonianism, the founding philosophy of Anarres in *The Dispossessed*, is "anarchism, as prefigured in early Daoist thought, and expounded by Shelley and Kropotkin, Goldman and Goodman. Anarchism's principal target is the authoritarian State (capitalist or socialist); its principal moral-practical theme is cooperation (solidarity, mutual aid)."[81] Le Guin's remarks invite three topics of immediate interest: (1) how Anarres departs from the primitive matrilineal or Mosuo model; (2) how Daoism relates to the female principle; and (3) how Le Guin's anarchism moves beyond the Daoist model.

As discussed earlier, although Anarres has its roots in the matrilineal past, it has outgrown feminist utopias of the matrilineal vein in nearly every respect. In social structure, the Anarresti communities are neither formed on a biological basis nor isolated in a primitive surrounding where "Dogs' barking and cocks' crowing can be heard from each side of the neighbors; and people never communicate till death."[82] Following Odo's idea of free cooperation, the individuals in each community are mobile. Movement is largely for the sake of work and research. Le Guin also appears to believe that work/play is as important as emotional life to communal survival and personal fulfillment. According to Odo's theory of decentralization, though:

> the natural limit to the size of a community lay in its dependence on its own immediate region for essential food and power . . . all communities [were] connected by communication and transportation networks, so that goods and ideas could get where they were wanted, and the administration of things might work with speed and ease, and no community should be set off from change and interchange. But the network was not to run from the top down.[83]

The social structure of Anarres reveals Le Guin's use of advanced communication and transportation for meeting the needs of a modern society characterized by speed and efficiency and for establishing a decentralized economic base to support the anarchist political structure.

As far as political structure is concerned, anarchism opposes the existence of oppressive rule and institutionalized authority. Le Guin's Anarres does not have government in our sense or any rule we might call matrilineal or female collective, as found in other feminist utopias. We may recall here that although the function of *Dabu* in the Mosuo Community is mainly administrative, *Dabu* is the supreme mother and cannot completely avoid personal authority. During Liang Rui's visit to the Mosuo Community, *Dabu* asks him and Sunamei to worship *Jizema* (female breasts) and *Jiumulu* (male productive organ). Although Liang Rui is a modern man who does not believe in such primitive images, he is obliged to consent: "Ami is *Dabu*, the supreme authority, I could not refuse to go. Moreover, I really love this host of the family, even with a little worship."[84] In Le Guin's Anarres, we find quite the opposite. There is only a computerized network for administration and management called "PDC, Production and Distribution Coordination. They are a coordinating system for all syndicates, federatives and individuals that do productive work."[85] This system only administers production and anounces the public opinion regarding the image of an individual in the social conscience; but it does not govern persons and has no authority over an individual.

PDC represents a nonpersonal administration, yet it can be manipulated by men like Sabul. Le Guin, therefore, provides two preventive methods to avoid the system's corruption. The first is the "cellular function" of the individual.[86] The real political power on Anarres is the power of moral choice in the hands of the individual; thus, an Anarresti might make a sacrifice for the communal good but should never compromise with any form of coercion or disguised authoritarianism. The second preventative is "permanent revolution."[87] Le Guin's idea of permanent revolution involves particularly a lasting vigilance against the dogmatizing of Odonianism or any revolutionary idea. Perhaps because of her association of original anarchy with an antiauthoritarian female principle, she makes an explicit protest against maternal authority. Her character Vea, acting as an observer, tells Shevek: "You've got a–a Queen Teaea inside you, right inside that hairy head of yours. And she orders you around just like the old tyrant did her serfs. She says, 'Do this!' and you do, and 'Don't!' and you don't."[88] Immediately after *The Dispossessed*, Le Guin wrote "The Day Before the Revolution"—an afterthought presented as foreground—portraying Odo, a woman of seventy-two with "a blood clot in a vein,"[89] at the moment of revolution that inspired the anarchists' settlement on the moon. It is not surprising that Le Guin uses Anarres to embody Odo's ideas and presents Odo as an old and decayed mother to warn people against the dangers of idolizing Odonian ideas as law or of mistaking them as absolute truth. By including and connecting the reality of the past, Shevek fights against the conservative, older Odonians represented by his own mother Rulag, who "only knows denial. How to deny the possibility of coming home."[90] Compared with the matrilineal power structure, the Anarresti political structure is obviously complex.

In terms of the sharing principle, Le Guin goes beyond material sharing to emphasize the sharing of suffering and ideas. Unlike most feminist utopists, who take the sharing of love as the core of sisterhood, Le Guin sees true cohesion in a spiritual cooperation that ensures survival. In Capital Square, Shevek proclaims: "It is our suffering that brings us together. It is not love. Love does not obey the mind, and turns to hate when forced. The bond that binds us is beyond choice. . . . We are brothers in what we share . . . in hunger, in poverty, in hope, we know our brotherhood."[91] The novel's structural theme develops on Le Guin's notion of spiritual sharing, as we see that Shevek's destiny is to break walls and share the idea of Anarres with all humankind. Interestingly, Le Guin's sophisticated sharing is more suitable for modern society, where people are less sentimental but more advanced in science and consciousness.

Le Guin deliberately tries to avoid notions of female superiority in *The Dispossessed*. Still, perhaps more than anything else, the existence of sexual equality on Anarres makes the novel a feminist utopia. Her successful creation of an equality between man and woman occurs on the level of language, as seen in the word used for sexual intercourse: "The usual verb, taking only a plural subject, can be translated only by a neutral word like copulate."[92] This stands in contrast to the more common English verbs, which suggest that one person is doing something to another person. Her utopia also does not have the concept of "bastard" or other sexually associated pejorative terms. Although Anarrestis still swear, they use only limited words such as "shit," "fart" and "Hell"; as we are told, "it is hard to swear when sex is not dirty and blasphemy does not exist."[93] By eliminating sexual differences embedded in words as well as in all other transactions of life, Le Guin avoids the male psychological repression hidden in most feminist utopias.

Ernst Bloch believes, "Humankind still lives in prehistory everywhere, indeed everything awaits the creation of the world as a genuine one. The real genesis is not at the beginning, but at the end, and it only begins when society and existence become radical, that is, grasp themselves at the root. The root of history, however, is the human being, working, producing, reforming, and surpassing the givens around him or her."[94] Consistent with Bloch's belief, Marcuse points out that a utopia of new direction must express an "instinctual basis for freedom" and must stress the quality of life—fulfilling human

needs like rebellion, sexual joy, and work pleasure—"in the infrastructure of man (itself a dimension of the infrastructure of society)."[95] It
would be wrong, therefore, to assume that socialist China from 1949
to 1972 was a model of utopia for having turned women into a productive social force and for largely socializing domestic work, when the
quality of life for both women and men was historically the worst in
terms of instinctual repression and totalitarian suppression. If Anarres
reflects the China of that period, as Moylan observes, it differs completely from China in liberating personal needs, especially the sexual
need. Anarres comes closest to Bai Hua's Mosuo Community in the
area of sexual freedom. Like Mosuonians, Anarrestis may have short
partnerships as well as lifelong ones. According to Le Guin, "Partnership was a voluntarily constituted federation like any other. So long as
it worked, it worked, and if it didn't work it stopped being. It was
not an institution but a function."[96] Earlier feminist utopists, as does
Gilman, deny sexual pleasure for the sake of women's autonomy. Le
Guin uses the figure of Odo to correct them: "Odo's femininity swayed
her . . . towards a refusal of real sexual freedom; here if nowhere else,
Odo did not write for men. As many women as men made this criticism, so it would appear that it was not masculinity that Odo failed to
understand, but a whole type of section of humanity, people to whom
experiment is the soul of sexual pleasure."[97] In its accommodation of
sexual experimentation and freedom for homosexuals and bisexuals,
Le Guin's anarchism obviously has been influenced by Western sexual
experimentation and the homosexual movements that have emerged
since the 1960s; her society surpasses the scope of sexual freedom
exhibited by Bai Hua's matrilineal model.[98]

    Le Guin distinguishes Anarres from primitive matrilineal utopias
by completely rejecting rituals and religions. She also tries to strike a
balance between linear time and circular time. In *Country of Women*,
Bai Hua emphasizes circular time by creating a utopia that has preserved the purity of its timeless matrilineality; in *The Dispossessed*, Le
Guin conceives a universe that combines linear time, evidenced by
an evolution that "includes creation and mortality," with circular
time, seen in the enduring nature of all things.[99] This view of time
forms what Nudelman has called the "spiral structure of a Le Guinian
Journey."[100]

    Le Guin's interest in Daoism is closely linked with her inclination
toward the female principle. By comparing Anarres's similarities to the
Mosuo Community, and its dissimilarities to the primitive matrilineal
model, it becomes clear that Le Guin's new anarchism, or social organicism, is an extension of the female principle, or is the female

principle made dynamic. The relation between Le Guin's anarchism and Daoist philosophy extends this further.

Daoism, founded by Lao Zi in the sixth century B.C., is a philosophy inspired by the ideals of prehistorical matrilineality. Dao is "the ancient name for an-animal-shaped world-mother" and Lao Zi's life-Dao "reproduces, sublimates images from earlier, matrilineal period in China."[101] Daoism, "the mother landscape of ruling and healing," claims the fullness of the inconspicuous, the strength of the weak, and triumph of the female over the male by its stillness.[102] Although Ernst Bloch and Joseph Needham agree about the matrilineal root of Daoism, Bloch takes Lao Zi as "the wandering hermit, hostile to custom, hostile to civilization, safe and secure only in the incomprehensible" and regards Daoism essentially as mysticism, unsuitable to ruling government.[103]

But Joseph Needham emphasizes Daoism as a resistance against the rise of civilization characterized by class division, private ownership, and man-made ethics. Bloch tends to blur the difference between Daoism and Confucianism, whereas Needham differentiates them by the female principle and the male principle and contrasts them. "The Confucian . . . social-ethical thought complex was masculine, managing, hard, dominating, aggressive, rational and donative—the Taoists broke with it radically and completely by emphasizing all that was feminine, tolerant, yielding, permissive, withdrawing, mystical and receptive."[104] Needham's interpretation of Daoism illuminates best the Daoist configurations in Le Guin's *Dispossessed*.[105] Le Guin's concept of the female principle, strengthened by Daoism, forms the principal philosophy of her anarchism. To show that the female principle operates on Anarres, Le Guin uses a woman philosopher, Odo, as the creator of her anarchism. (Le Guin seems to enjoy employing an outsider as the observer.) Astro from Urras, which is dominated by the male principle, criticizes Odonianism as "womanish" because it simply does not include the virile side of life: " 'Blood and steel, battle's brightness' . . . it doesn't understand courage—love of the flag."[106] Shevek, who is from Anarres, notes Urras' rejection of the female principle in the symbolic construction of their tables: "Apparently they, like the tables on the ship, contained a woman, a suppressed, silenced, bestialized woman, a fury in a cage."[107] In Le Guin's novel, the Western concept of the female principle and Daoism seem to join together in a conclusion that human individuals or society should follow the model of nature.

Daoism is indeed at the heart of Le Guin's literary imagination. In *City of Illusions* (1966), she creates Falk, a "turro-dowist" (a thorough

Daoist), as the novel's protagonist to convey the theme of "the Taoist ethic of balance."[108] In *The Left Hand of Darkness*, she uses Daoist androgyny to reinforce the theme of "unity through the creative tension of the opposites."[109] And in *The Lathe of the Heaven* (1970), she does "extensive investigations of Taoism in the development of the individual."[110] *The Dispossessed* reveals Le Guin's mature and more comprehensive understanding of Daoism in relation to political and social theories. The writings of Lao Zi and Zhuang Zi have influenced Le Guin's anarchist thought, especially by providing three natural principles: government through nonaction, nondifferentiation, and reversibility of the opposites.

Dao is "the governing force of the universe: the Mother, the One, the Way;"[111] but Dao governs through nonaction. Zhuang Zi says: "The silence of still water produces thunder; / Nature moves and Heaven follows; / With easiness and nonaction / All things float like dust on the wind."[112] Applying to human society this nonaction, connected with a kind of "co-ruling effectiveness" and resembling "secret working of eternally reigning nature."[113] Lao Zi suggests a minimal government.

> The more laws and orders are made
> The more thieves and robbers will rise
> Thus the Sage says:
> I take the way of nonaction
> And people will be naturally influenced
> I love peace
> And people will be naturally just
> I make no effort
> And people will be naturally affluent
> I have no desires
> And people will be naturally pure.[114]

Lao Zi's concept of minimal government through nonaction espouses the earliest form of anarchist thought. Lao Zi uses a sage who follows the model of nature as the paradigm for government, while Le Guin discards a human governing agent and takes advantage of highly developed technology to imagine an anarchist society operated only by a computerized administration, resembling the impersonal governing force of nature.

Daoist nondifferentiation includes the idea of equality of all beings and the relativity of truth. Lao Zi uses the natural law of nondifferentiation to oppose social hierarchy and legalized morality. He once advised Confucius: "If you indeed want the men of the world not to lose the qualities that are natural to them, you had best study how it is that Heaven and Earth maintain their eternal course, that the sun and moon maintain their light, the stars serried their ranks, the birds and nests their flocks, the trees and shrubs their station."[115] This well-ordered pattern offered by nature is the model for a nondifferentiated, nonoppressive society: "Just as there was no real greatness and smallness in Nature, so there should be none in human society. The accent should be on mutual service."[116] In a similar way, Le Guin eliminates the hierarchy between the superior and the inferior, and between men and women on Anarres, and puts accent on mutual aid and solidarity.

Lao Zi further uses the law of nondifferentiation to oppose moral judgments with artificial law: "If all under Heaven recognize beauty as beauty, / The idea of ugliness exists; / If all recognize virtue as virtue, / The conception of evil appears."[117] He also rejects so-called civilization burdened with ideologies and ethics: "When the great Dao declined, / The doctrine of humanity and righteousness arose; / When knowledge appeared, / There emerged great hypocrisy."[118] Similar to the Daoist idea of moral nondifferentiation, Le Guin visualizes an anarchist society free of legalized morality and conceptions of evil and crime; as Le Guin's philosopher Odo writes in her treatise, *The Social Organicism*, expressing her idea of anarchy and echoing Lao Zi: "To make a thief, make an owner; to create crime, create laws."[119]

Le Guin not only uses nondifferentiation to construct her utopian anarchy, but also applies its underlying principle—the relativity of truth—to the entire human world. Understandably, she calls *The Dispossessed* "an ambiguous utopia," because her Daoist tendency disallows any absolutist moral judgment, even in her own created world. When the protagonist Shevek declares "there is nothing on Urras that we Anarresti need" and calls Urras "Hell,"[120] the Terran Ambassador Keng, a woman of sixty or more, corrects his nondialectical view by telling him, "to me, and to all my fellow Terrans who have seen the planet, Urras is the kindliest, most various, most beautiful of all the inhabited worlds. It is the world that comes as close as any could to Paradise."[121] Shevek finally agrees with Keng that, despite all its evils, Urras is "full of good, of beauty, vitality, achievement" and alive with hope.[122] At this point, Shevek removes the final wall resisting the freedom of his own thought.

Shevek's personal transformation reflects a Daoist conception of eternal change, which is based on the constant reversibility of opposites, as Lao Zi says:

> Misfortune, good fortune leans against it;
> Good fortune, misfortune hides within it.
> Who knows where it ends?
> Is there no order?
> Normal can revert to abnormal;
> Good can revert to evil.[123]

The reversibility of opposites, or Odo's "causative reversibility,"[124] forms the core of Le Guin's theory of permanent revolution. Unlike Gilman's *Herland*, which attempts to present a perfect world inhabited by perfect people, Le Guin uses Anarres, a world inhabited by fallible, changing human beings, to probe problems that might occur during the decay of an ideal system and to explore ways of preventing this decay. Although Anarres appears to be Le Guin's utopia and Urras her dystopia, neither planet is purely so. Her utopia contains seeds of dystopia and conversely, her dystopia seeds of utopia. Although Anarres does not have private ownership, "devious ways of possessiveness, the labyrinths of love/hate" still exist.[125] In Bai Hua's *Country of Women*, the trust in the mother seems to have deprived Mosuonians of their instinct of scepticism or rebellion, which is regarded by Marcuse as in the biological nature of modern man.[126] Before *The Dispossessed*, Le Guin published a short story, "The Ones Who Walk Away from Omelas," in which mass happiness gains at the cost of a child's lonely torment. A "Featured Discussion" on the story, edited by Lyman Sargent, provides various interpretations of the child. Peter Fitting names it the outdated "Original Sin." In my opinion, the child embodies the spirit of scepticism in human nature that cannot be satisfied by material prosperity. The Odonians are the ones who walked away from Omelas or Urras and established a utopian anarchism on the moon. With the passage of 170 years, serious problems arise, such as intellectual truncation and ideological uniformity, and a group of men with ambitions like Sabul's attempt to seize personal power and exercise authoritarianism. Ironically, Tirin, a satirist and "a natural rebel," is driven insane and punished for his first free act by his Anarresti brothers, who have forgotten the very meaning of anarchism. This world suggests that a system, once established, inevitably develops in the opposite direction. Urras is Anarres' past and Anarres the hope and future of Urras, which also suggests that Urras could become the horrible future of Anarres. Such a political reversal, perhaps, can be managed by an understanding of the concept of permanent revolution, first realized within the individual and then transformed into group actions: "We'll make a new community. If our society is settling down into politics and power seeking, then we'll get out, we'll go make an Anarres beyond Anarres, a new beginning."[127]

The pattern of reversal in *The Dispossessed* carries with it a notion of returning that further resembles Daoist philosophy. In Daoism, the reversibility of opposites leads to an inevitable returning, as described by Lao Zi:

> Push far enough towards the void,
> Hold fast enough to Quietness,
> And of the ten thousand things none but can be worked on by you,
> I have beheld them, whither they go back,
> See, all things however they flourish
> Return to the root from which they grew.[128]

For Lao Zi, returning to the root means not only going back to the ahistorical primal beginning of all things but also gaining insight into the Way of Nature: "If, using one's brightness / One turns to insight / Life will be free of misfortune. / This is called learning the Absolute."[129] The Daoist return to insight seems to have influenced Le Guin's idea of returning, as inscribed on Odo's tombstone: "To be whole is to be part; / true voyage is return."[130] But, each return in Le Guin's novel is different, conforming even further with Daoism's "cyclically recurring differences."[131] When Shevek returns to his mother world of Urras, he gains instant insight; for him, the differences between Urras and Anarres were no more significant than "the differences between two grains of sand on the shore of the sea. There were no more abysses, no more walls. There was no more exile. He had seen the foundations of the universe, and they were solid."[132] Shevek's insight reveals Le Guin's faith in humanity. By returning to Anarres, Shevek perceives the importance of coming home to the original meaning of anarchism: "To shake up things, to stir up, to break some habits, to make people ask questions. To behave like anarchists!"[133]

Although Le Guin is strongly influenced by Daoism, she develops her own form of anarchism. *The Dispossessed* does not share Lao Zi's and Zhuang Zi's indiscriminate discarding of civilization and technology and their negation of human activism. Modern anarchist theories of Shelley and Kropotkin, Goldman and Goodman have helped Le Guin to develop the radical potentiality of Daoism and explore a higher form of anarchism.[134] Perhaps, the major difference between

Daoism and Le Guin's anarchism resides more in cognitive methods than in philosophy. Daoism emphasizes the importance of intuition, not rationality. Le Guin's multiple reliance on functional disruptions and features of communist and collective anarchism in her model planet, Anarres, demonstrates an intellectual mind that exercises itself on the edge of time and space simultaneously.[135] Indeed, Le Guin uses *The Dispossessed* as another scheme for her feminist thought-experiments. By using the "fundamental unity of the sequency and simultaneity" and "the concept of interval . . . to connect the static and the dynamic aspects of the universe,"[136] Le Guin brings past, future, and present at once into our consciousness for reflection. The very "means" used by Le Guin become, in a sense, the "end" of her book: to shake up things, to make people ask questions so that their minds cross cultural and ideological, as well as spatial and temporal, boundaries. In so doing, Le Guin again follows Daoism's Way of Nature.

> The supreme Tao, how it floods in every direction!
> This way and that, there is no place where it does not go.
> All things look to it for life, and it refuses none of them;
> Yet when its work is accomplished it possesses nothing.[137]

Drawing strength from the female principle, oriental Daoism, and Western anarchist thought, Le Guin attains a higher form of anarchism. As she repeatedly affirms in the novel, Anarres is an idea, and Shevek an idea made flesh, made possible by his society. Once her idea is shared with the reader, Le Guin like Dao, possesses nothing and starts anew.

—〰—

Bai Hua's matrilineality and Le Guin's anarchism seem to be two extremes of utopian imagination: the primitive and the postmodern. But because they are both rooted in the same female principle, they converge to show that the future of human society involves going home, or returning to a more natural state. In 1985, Le Guin wrote *Always Coming Home*, a novel that describes an anarchist community populated by the Kesh, a people who "might be going to have lived a long, long time from now in Northern California."[138] As in Bai Hua's *Country of Women*, the happy pastoral society is contrasted with a patriarchal, authoritarian Condor state that reflects our contemporary world. The small community of the Kesh, like the Mosuo Community, is remote, on the border of the world. The Kesh, like the Mosuonians, live and work closely with nature and enjoy the pleasures of life, rather than suffer the consequences of human politics.

Although *Always Coming Home*, with its nonlinear aesthetic form, is very different from *Country of Women*, it does have a journey plot, which, like a fable, reveals how Le Guin's utopian thought is similar to Bai Hua's. In Le Guin's novel, a young girl, North Owl, like Bai Hua's Sunamei, is fascinated by the patriarchal culture and warrior romanticism that exists outside the valley. She leaves the community and follows her father back to his world of religious conflict and war, where women are rigidly confined to their quarters and restricted in their activities as women were in old China. There she marries and has a child. Unable to tolerate male domination, she finally takes advantage of the Condor state's military defeat and escapes to the valley. She becomes a "Woman Coming Home," who represents all women, including men who want to follow her example. Her return symbolizes our nostalgic return to the original model of human society, whether we call it a Daoist anarchy or a quasi-matrilineal home; and with advanced technology, such as the planetary computer network in the community of the Kesh, our coming home will represent a new beginning.[139]

6

Influence, Decline, and Hope

In previous chapters, I have explored a preoccupation with female rule in feminist utopian literature of both East and West and I have sought to show cross-cultural parallels. I shall now address three independent but related topics: the significance of cross-cultural influence; the causes for the decline of feminist utopias in the West (including my opinions on some theoretical feminist controversies); and the complementariness of the three feminist visions of politics that I have identified.

Although the influences of Daoist philosophy and the Maoist theory of continuing revolution on Le Guin's *Dispossessed*, and of Western feminism on Bai Hua's *Remote Country of Women*, appear self-evident, no direct cross-cultural debts can be traced among the eight works I have studied. Zheng He's seven sea voyages in the fifteenth century opened China's vision to the world, yet Luo Maodeng was hopelessly lost in the idea of a cultural supremacy. The limited freedom for a woman in her time only allowed Chen Duansheng to produce a dream from seclusion. Li Ruzhen wrote *The Flowers in the Mirror* in 1820, forty-nine years earlier than John Stuart Mill's *Subjection of Women* (1869), five years ahead of William Thompson's *Appeal of one half of the human race, women, against the pretensions of the other half, men, to retain them in political, and thence in civil and domestic slavery* (1825), and only about thirty years later than Mary Wollstonecraft's *Vindication of the Rights of Woman* (1791). But, having died before the Opium War, Li did not have contact with modern Western thought, and his ideas of women's rights were entirely "indigenous."[1] Even though Bai Hua was influenced by Western feminism during his visits to West Germany and America in the 1980s, he did not read German or English, and no Chinese translations of feminist utopias were available. These works, then, are free of Western literary debts; however, this cannot be said of Qiu Jin's *Pebbles that Fill up the Sea*, which clearly demonstrates the strength of cross-cultural influences.

Qiu Jin's novel, written between 1905 and 1907, shows mixed traits of the Western-type modern utopia and the popular *tanci*. In a restrictive definition of utopia genre, Chang Huichuan insists that literary utopias in classical Chinese literature are "practically nonexistent."[2] Of course, according to his definition, few Western feminist utopias can fall into the genre of utopia. But he recognizes that, as an imported cultural phenomenon, "literary utopias are among the most pronounced genres" of the late Qing period.[3] Through studying abroad or reading Western works, such as Huxley's *Evolution and Ethics* and Bellamy's *Looking Backward*, Chinese writers started to speculate the future. There appeared novels such as *The Future World, Travels in Utopia, New China, New Universe, The Future of New China, The Roar of the Lion*, and *The New Year's Dream*. All these novels are set in the future, quite a departure from the traditional Chinese utopian imagination that always clings to an ideal moment in the past. They are known as political novels because of their concern with the fate of China and their transplanting of Western social and political theories. On the other hand, the traditional genre *tanci* was revitalized for disseminating new ideas, especially feminist ideas. Many *tanci* novels with modern feminist tendencies emerged, such as *Romance of Heroes and Heroines* (1902, by two unknown sisters), *Madame Roland, A French Heroine* (1904, by Wan Lan), *The History of Female Knights* (1905, by a woman named Yonglan), *The Civilization Beacon for Women of the Twentieth Century* (1912, by Xin Qing), *The Women's Chaibai Party* (1915, by Zhang Danfu), and *The Female Knights of Luoxiao* (1918, by Hu Huaichen). Except for Xin Qing's *tanci*, none of these works raise any theoretical arguments, such as those in Qiu Jin's *Pebbles that Fill up the Sea*,[4] which can be called both a political novel and a feminist *tanci*.

Qiu Jin's story is set in an oriental country called Huaxu Guo (Land of Chinese Descendents). The people of Huaxu Guo have been plagued by an overwhelming sleepiness and nearsightedness, and their state has deteriorated from generation to generation. This country has been vigorous in its oppression of women by depriving them of education and poisoning their minds with so-called feminine virtues. The Western Queen Mother dispatches female warriors from Chinese history and legend, such as Hua Mulan, Qin Liangyu, Shen Yunying, as well as male patriotic heroes, Yue Fei, Wen Tianxiang, and Zheng Chenggong, to rescue the women and save the country. Following her order, women who have not fulfilled their wishes in earlier life are reborn to destroy the old world and set up a new one.

These women of unfulfilled dreams, reborn in Huaxu Guo, suffer from unspeakable maltreatment and forced marriages. Huang Jurui, Liang Xiaoyu, and three other women gather together to lament the fate of the women and their nation. Then, the revolutionary wind from Europe and America reaches Huaxu Guo. By reading new novels, these four women learn that Westerners have observed the women of Huaxu Guo being treated as toys for men—as inferiors five-hundred ranks below men, ignorant of science and useful knowledge, trapped by a slave mentality, but versed in the art of pleasing men. These women then turn to Europe and America for new ideas; they come to believe that individual freedom, sexual equality, and human rights are endorsed by Heaven, indiscriminately to women and men. They realize that in Western countries, where everyone is talking about feminism, a woman may demand independence because the strength of a nation and the quality of its future generations rely on women. So, the women, with the help of Huang Jurui's teacher, escape abroad for a modern education. When they arrive at an island, Huang Jurui changes her name to Huang Hanxiong ("Huang" refers to Huangdi from whom the Chinese have descended; "Hanxiong" means the hero of the Han people). There she engages in revolutionary and feminist activities and gives public lectures, which forge her idiom of feminism and nationalism. Qin Jin had planned to write her utopia in twenty chapters, but her novel stops here, at Chapter 6, as she was executed on July 15, 1907, for organizing an armed rebellion against the Manchurian Government. According to the chapter titles left by her, we know the rest of the utopia would have incorporated Qiu Jin's autobiographical experience into her dream of emancipating women and saving China. Qiu Jin was not a mere dreamer but a doer, a feminist activist. She wrote a possible, immediate utopia. The success of sexual equality leads to the victory of national salvation. Her novel ends with a Great Republic of China founded at the overthrow of the Manchurian government. For her practical vision, Qin Jin is worthy of being termed a prophet of the Revolution of 1911.

Apparently, Qiu Jin, in her novel, combines Eastern and Western traditions. Like Chen Duansheng, she adopted the form of *tanci*, but not with the intention of producing a masterpiece. She claimed to have borrowed this popular form for the purpose of exposing patriar-chal evils and opening bright vistas for women, as did Dixie with her *Gloriana*. Following Li Ruzhen, Qiu Jin used the mythical Western Queen Mother to ordain the feminist mission as providential will; how-ever, neither Chen Duansheng nor Li Ruzhen had Western notions of sexual equality and human rights with which to theorize their thoughts. Qiu Jin has Westernized traditional Chinese utopian dis-course with an argumentative didacticism, expressing a modern Chi-nese consciousness influenced by Western humanism and feminism. Although she completed only six chapters, she expressed her feminist thoughts well in seven respects: (1) "*bu anming*," a woman should not submit herself to her "fate" as prescribed by a long patriarchal past; (2) "*chu zou*," a woman must leave her domestic cage; (3) "*qiu xue*," a woman must get a modern education, especially from abroad; (4) "*tu zili*," a woman must learn the necessary techniques or have a profes-sion in order to gain economic independence; (5) "*bai zimei*," women are encouraged to become sworn sisters since they have natural incli-nations toward women themselves and cooperate in their action and thinking;[5] (6) "*nannü pingquan, renquan tianfu*," both women and men have been endowed by heaven with equal political and human rights; and (7) "*nannü gongren*," women must share with men the responsibility of saving the country. Through these seven correlated aspects, Qiu Jin visualizes an integrated identity for a woman, whose individual self is harmoniously combined with other women and social obligations.

Qiu Jin had been an ordinary woman, restricted by a feudal mar-riage; but, when she moved to Beijing in 1903 at the age of 27, she gained access to Western feminism and utopianism through reading journals edited by Liang Qichao and books such as *The Biography of Madame Roland, Three Heroines of Italy, Outstanding Women of Eastern Europe*, and *The Future of New China*.[6] Western influences at the turn of the twentieth century indeed can account for Qiu Jin, a Chen Duansheng type of woman with suppressed masculine desires and a feminine poetic sensitivity, becoming overnight a feminist revo-lutionary. She poured her newly gained inspiration into popular songs, such as "I Admire the People of Europe and America" and "The Song of Women's Rights." Like Dixie, she often dressed in men's clothing and rode on horseback with a sword. A woman of adventure and action, she gave vehement public speeches on the topics of women's rights and national salvation, excelled in marksmanship, and involved herself in bomb-making and armed rebellion.[7] Her feminist ideas culminated in her utopia, *Pebbles that Fill up the Sea*, which, like Gilman's *Herland*, was written for a women's journal edited and published almost solely by herself.[8] The transformation of Qiu Jin and the vision of her utopia make one wonder why Western feminist utopias, since the 1970s, have not been properly introduced to China.

Although Western feminist criticism has led its Eastern sisters from the "image of women" criticism to the "female consciousness" criticism,[9] Chinese women writers have not used the genre of utopia as their theoretical expression. There are a few surmises as to why: (1) women writers in China are less concerned with theories than with critical practice; (2) Chinese writers and critics of today still value works of realism higher than speculative fiction;[10] (3) Western feminism, since the 1980s, has become very much of an elite intellectual movement, especially in the area of feminist utopias (some tending to polarize the differences between the sexes and substitute class struggle with sex struggle and ignore racial divergences in women's experience);[11] (4) assertions of sexual permissiveness and lesbian separatism, as well as metaphors of "killing man," or visions of an all-female world in Western texts, are hardly comprehensible to the Chinese reading public (though similar ideas have found their modest expression in stories written by Zhang Jie, Wang Anyi, and other women writers as utopian elements); or, perhaps, (5) the critical introduction of Western feminist utopias and translations of those works have made little progress in mainland China. Interestingly, in 1989, when I wrote to my colleagues in China about my proposal to compare Chinese and English feminist utopias, they frankly advised me not to choose such an insignificant subject, remarking that we have not done enough in comparing Shakespeare with the *Dream of the Red Chamber*.

—𝔪—

Although a strong Western interest in critical studies of feminist utopias has continued, speculative fiction in English since the 1980s appears to have declined from the high point of feminist utopianism of the 1970s.[12] There may be three causes contributing to this decline: a continuing intellectual battle between the sexes, a shift of theoretical interests in the 1980s, and a momentary confusion in feminist utopian exploration.

In cultural hegemonies, men have historically manipulated state romances and symbolic representations of women. It is not surprising that Edmund Spenser and Luo Maodeng, both enlightened men of the sixteenth century, distorted women's sexual and political power in order to stimulate men's spiritual transcendence and inspire the vision of a world-state utopia built on gender, class hierarchy, and power centralization. Their symbolic depictions of women as corruptive, emasculating, and alien forces further consolidate an ingrained historical denunciation of female government. Spenser's *Faerie Queene* and Luo Maodeng's *Sanbao's Expedition to the Western Ocean*, nevertheless, are not intentionally antifeminist. Reaction to feminist utopias of the 1970s and 1980s, however, resulted in a new wave of antifeminist utopias.[13] Works such as Parley J. Cooper's *Feminists* (1971), Edmund Cooper's *Gender Genocide* (1972), and Thomas Berger's *Regiment of Women* (1973), take feminist utopias as their satirical target. Some of them even liken the monstrosity of a feminist regiment to that of fascist totalitarianism. Moreover, the battle of the sexes in feminist utopias is readily observed in articles such as Joanna Russ's "*Amor Vincit Foeminam*" and Peter Fitting's "For Men Only." This sexual battle has affected the utopian optimism of feminist writers. Some of these writers, such as Zoë Fairbairns (*Benefits* 1979) and Margaret Atwood (*The Handmaid's Tale* 1985), have used the dystopian genre to warn readers about the possibility of reestablishment of a more brutal capitalist patriarchy and, even worse, of a legal deprivation of rights that women have won through decades of struggle.

A shift in theoretical interests in the 1980s may also account for the decline of feminist utopianism, for feminist utopias are directly related to feminist theory.[14] Recall how Gilman explicitly used *Herland* to convey ideas from *Women and Economics* and to expound upon her feminist-socialist idiom; and *The Dispossessed* is preoccupied with Le Guin's theory of a new anarchism. Since the 1980s, "the effect of the new theoretical discourse has been to suppress the memory of the vigorous and radically feminist criticism of the seventies."[15] Influenced by French feminist theory, which emphasizes the transformative power of language, Suzette Haden Elgin's *Native Tongue* (1984) and her *Native Tongue II: The Judas Rose* (1987) express the feminist utopian wish to subvert patriarchal society through the infiltration of a female language. While we recognize the importance of feminist rupture with the linguistic universe of the patriarchal establishment, we must be aware that power produces the dominant discourse.[16] Here, we may recall Foucault's insight that "the history which bears and determines us has the form of a war rather than that of a language: relations of power, not relations of meaning."[17]

The decline of feminist utopianism reflects a momentary confusion in feminist utopian exploration. This confusion, in my view, is caused by phobias, such as the fear of talking about female rule, the fear of biological determinism or feminist essentialism, the fear of falling into a trap of the old symbolic order, and so on. These phobias of the West suggest a double phenomenon. Women's cautiousness in regard to potential matriarchal tyranny or a reversed sexual dominance, as implied in earlier feminist utopias, leads to the anarchist ideal: "power for everyone; power over no one;"[18] yet it tends to deprive women of their newly gained power. In her discussion of "When Women Write of Women's Rule," Sarah Lefanu regards Marion Zimmer Bradley's *Ruins of Isis* (1980) as an antifeminist utopia and criticizes it for taking power away from women after giving it to them, under the pretext that "women can be just as bad as men."[19] Such simultaneous advocacy and undermining of a feminist alternative reveal that the utopian assertion of solidarity, or a common cause, among women as one group does not satisfy contemporary women's individualist feminism. To reimagine the strategies for female communitarian solidarity is a new task for feminist utopists.

Androcentric men and women have used biological determinism to categorize women as an inferior race. The feminist utopias I have discussed, except for Le Guin's *Dispossessed*, in one way or another, commit a reversed biological determinism—celebrating female superiority. Now women's own negation of biological determinism nullifies most feminist utopias and demonstrates, again, a female moral superiority, though politically to women's disadvantage.

Feminist essentialism has its historical function; the values represented by the female principle provide an alternative criterion for judging society and individuals. But a narrow feminist essentialism, such as arguing that feminist utopias can be written only by women, is naive and self-destructive. Charles Brockden Brown's *Alcuin* (1798) has been recognized as a pioneering Western feminist utopia, and it is no coincidence that most of the Chinese feminist utopias in this study are written by men. A rejection of feminist essentialism in postfeminism appears, oddly enough, as a feminism without women that is "actually engaged in negating the critiques and undermining the goals of feminism."[20] Ironically, the liberating theories of postmodernism have caught feminist writers and scholars in a snare of phobias, but the momentary confusion in feminist utopian exploration caused by these phobias, fortunately, reflects more an epistemological pause for progress rather than a real regress.

Although Western feminist utopianism has declined in more recent works, a few exceptions such as Le Guin's *Always Coming Home* and Joan Slonczewski's *A Door Into Ocean* have kept the fires burning. This decline, too, holds promise for a resurgent interest in the future. Peter Fitting, in "The Turn from Utopia in Recent Feminist Fiction," expresses many a reader's wish: "The utopian impulse at the heart of all science fiction, the awareness of the fundamental insufficiencies of the present, and the longing for a more just and humane world should not be denied."[21]

The scarcity of Chinese feminist utopias precludes any serious discussion of a rise or decline in their growth. Although these utopias do not stimulate a counter-tradition, antifeminist criticism has persisted. Moreover, the seed of an antifeminist utopia can be found as early as the seventeenth century, in the work of Fang Ruhao (c. 1635), where we find a community ruled by women called the "Town of Hens." The Town has laid down ten prohibitions for men: (1) whoring and gambling; (2) insulting and maltreating the mistress of the house; (3) taking concubines and mistresses (that is, having no children is better than taking more than one wife); (4) taking liberty with maids and male servants; (5) widowers remarrying; (6) husbands usurping their wives' authority; (7) excessive drinking and entertaining; (8) unexcused entry and exit (whenever a man goes out, he must seek permission from the mistress of the house as to his destination, activities, and companions); (9) greedy pursuit of wealth and fame; and (10) breaking any of the above prohibitions, which, like the law of state government, accord with heavenly principle and the human way.[22] One could say these ten prohibitions reflect a daring feminist utopian impulse in the late Ming Dynasty; yet, Fang Ruhao's Town of Hens appears a dystopia for men. Du Fuwei and Xue Ju, two main characters in the novel, defeat the head woman, the creator of this Town of Hens, by stripping off her clothes to expose her genitalia in public, and she suffers a providential punishment—an incurable ulcer continuously oozing black pus. This antifeminist episode betrays the truth that women have been defeated historically by men because of their biological body and sexuality. (This truth helps us appreciate the necessity of an open celebration of the female sexual body and the dashing of breasts at their enemies in the French feminist utopia, *Les Guérillères*, by Monique Wittig.)

Because of the shortage of contemporary Chinese feminist utopias, there seems no need for antifeminist utopias. Nevertheless, antifeminist criticism has been fierce, sniping at every feminist utopian element in Chinese women's writing in a misogynistic tongue that no longer dares to wag itself in the West.[23]

With the change in economic structure and the collapse in socialist ideology, there has been a rapid change in the status of women in China since 1980s. Instead of being desexualized aliens in the revolutionary machine, women and men find newly gained freedom to develop their distinctively feminine and masculine traits. The quality of a woman's emotional life is undoubtedly improved. Yet, women are faced with the loss of sexual equality in employment and politics. According to Qi Ming's reportage (1992), women are openly barred from some government jobs because of their biological "disadvantages," such as childbearing; the employment of female college students becomes a social problem; and a group of female college graduates were refused by a government unit simply because of their sex: the unit employs only males. The reportage comments sarcastically, "What an irony that the cradle of the women's liberation movement now refuses to liberate women."[24] Socialist China rescued women from the Old China, but fails to give them a qualitative life. Since the 1980s, China seems to be abandoning women, depriving them of the constitutional equal rights they had in the past. All the social structures they have experienced prove a failure for women's emancipation. Chinese women will be forced to break the closure of reality by imagination. They need to speculate a way out. The developing feminist consciousness in recent Chinese women's writing signals a promising future for feminist utopias.

The politics of female rule, as expressed in Chinese and English literature since the end of the sixteenth century, has undergone three significant transformations: from the negation of rule by women to rule by women through means of male impersonation; from rule by individual women to collective female rule; and from quasi-matrilineality to anarchism operating in accordance with the female principle. In an early stage of feminist struggle, women in society as well as in feminist utopias are driven to a gender subterfuge in order to obtain education, economic independence, and political position and dignity. Chen Duansheng's *Destiny of the Next Life* and Florence Dixie's *Gloriana; Or, The Revolution of 1900* best capture women's "fair-chance dream" of infiltrating into the patriarchal power structure. Charlotte Perkins Gilman's *Herland* rejects the male symbolic order by upholding a new civilization constituted purely by female values or maternalism. Although still confined by the old social structure, Li Ruzhen's *Flowers in the Mirror* is quite radical in playing the politics of separating from the existing world by sending new women to rule the Country of Women and by elevating them to Little Penglai for spiritual transcendence. Bai Hua's *Remote Country of Women*, like Gilman's *Herland*, fails to eliminate the opposition between masculinity and femininity in Bai Hua's extolment of matrilineal values, but it cherishes the female principle as the lifeline for future society, as does Le Guin's *Dispossessed*.

The three transformations correspond with the three tiers of feminist struggle described by Julia Kristeva in her "Women's Time": (1) women of liberal feminism demand equal access to the symbolic order; (2) women of radical feminism reject the male symbolic order in the name of difference and extoll femininity; and (3) women reject the dichotomy between masculine and feminine as metaphysical. In the late 1980s, three important critical books appeared that centered on feminist utopias—Eisler's *Chalice and the Blade: Our History, Our Future* (1987), Lefanu's *In the Chinks of the World Machine: Feminism and Science Fiction* (1988), and Bartkowski's *Feminist Utopias* (1989). Each of these studies may be correlated with a different tier of Kristeva's envisioned struggle: Lefanu's militancy still smacks of the first tier; Bartkowski's emphasis on the materiality of language does not differ much from the second tier; and Eisler's insistence on gylany for the future of humanity gives a theoretical foundation to the third tier. The utopian destruction of the opposition between masculinity and femininity in women's writings of the third tier, however, not only invalidates "matriarchy" but discards "women's government" or "female rule" as questionable objectives in feminist struggle. While Eisler's and other feminists' interpretation of female power as an affiliation, or linking, rather than ruling is prophetic,[25] one can easily argue that the first two tiers of the feminist struggle are still effective strategies for the present, because political and cultural structures in almost any place in the world are still patriarchal: Men hold the power and the majority of women are politically weak. To strengthen the intimate link between intellectual inquiry and women's struggle in society, Annette Kolodny vigorously proclaims that "theory devoid of activist politics isn't feminism but, rather, pedantry and moral abdication."[26]

The theme of female rule may seem to have run a full course, from Chen Duansheng's and Dixie's politics of competition with men, to Li Ruzhen's and Gilman's politics of separation from the patriarchal world, and finally to Bai Hua's and Le Guin's politics of the female principle for humanity; however, there is really no closure. Although the thematic diversity in feminist utopias indicates a growth in feminist consciousness, one cannot say that the types of feminist utopias emerging in the first or the second stage are out of date. What is most significant about these feminist utopias is that they offer us three visions of politics that coexist usefully in the current struggle against

patriarchy, illuminating the feminist utopian impulse in its inextrica-
ble complexity. Each of their political visions, in fact, is incomplete in
itself and complementary to the others. Chen Duansheng's and Dixie's
politics of competition cannot be disentangled from the existing political structure, while Li Ruzhen's proposed worldly detachment and
Gilman's imaginary all-female world reflect a retreat from contemporary politics.[27] Chen's and Dixie's political practicality still plays an
important part in the present, male-dominated world, and Li's and
Gilman's separation offers a more radical criticism of patriarchy by
inviting us to view women's problems and the world from an angle
unrestricted by established cultural and ideological conventions. As
a reaction to the atemporality and ideological uniformity implied in
Herland-type utopias, Le Guin visualizes a moving anarchism that
attempts to keep essential female values without ignoring individual
freedom, will, and natural desire—the constructive function of "dis-
functional music."[28]

As long as a social structure encourages male supremacy, each of
the three types of feminist utopia will recur but in new variations.
Chen Duansheng's and Dixie's concealment of sexual identity has
recurred in a more radical version of sex-role reversal in quite a few
feminist utopias of the 1970s; Gilman's all-female world has inspired
many separatist utopias no longer inhibited by a puritanical primness.
The disappearance of political, psychological, and even physiological
differences between male and female in Le Guin's utopias has pushed
feminist utopia to the wall of perfection.[29] As a result of this feminist
utopian standstill, we may see a turning to feminist dystopias or a
returning to matrilineal visions.

During the past four centuries, feminist consciousness has undergone significant metamorphoses, and the types of feminist utopias
found in these four phases form a "proliferation" like branches of a
tree.[30] As long as patriarchy exists, the three types of politics envisioned in those feminist utopias—reform within the existing structure;
autonomy outside the structure; and anarchism before/beyond the
structure—will continue to occur. But there is no repetition; feminist
utopias, which offer continually recurring differences, make critical
studies endlessly fascinating.

—〜〜—

To Le Guin, utopia is a thought experiment; that is to say, utopia
is a form to deliberate new ideas and a means to raise human consciousness. Feminist utopias have expressed individual women's

dreams, their desires for communitarian solidarity and collective action, and their struggle to regain individual identity for fear of tyrannical uniformity. Scholars of the twentieth century have come to recognize that utopias are unable to draw practical blueprints for future society but do allow the future to sit in judgment of the present. Feminist utopias remain a most effective way to criticize patriarchy. Because of their critique of patriarchy, they are often regarded as a discourse of vengeance from the wronged sex. Although their power in changing real world politics is feeble, feminist utopias continue creating visions for the individual woman, for women collectively, and for humanity. Their perseverance has won an independent arena both in speculative fiction and in utopian studies. As an illustration, I end with the myth of Jingwei Bird.

In the dark sky over the tyrannical sea, a bird, with the body of a crow but a patterned crest, white beak, and red claws, drops another pebble into an abyss below. This bird is the undying spirit of Nüwa, the daughter of Yan Di—the god, who taught human beings agriculture and tasted a hundred herbs to find cures for human disease, and the King, who earned his name for the Mountain of Flames. Nüwa had swum down to the eastern sea and was drowned by it. Her anger toward the sea was transformed into this bird, who has been carrying individually in her beak pebbles from the western mountains and dropping them into the eastern sea for thousands of years.[31] After each drop, she howls her own name: "Jingwei—Jingwei—" gathering her center and redoubling her strength. This bird of Jingwei is thus known as the Bird of the Wronged *(Yuanqin)*, the Bird of Vengeance *(Shiniao)*, and the Bird of Perseverance *(Zhiniao)*. Down through history, Jingwei Bird has been woven into the poetic imagination. Now, Qiu Jin discovers the important role of the pebbles and calls her utopia in Chinese *Jingwei Shi* (Jingwei Pebbles), not *Jingwei Niao* (Jingwei Bird). In Qiu Jin's utopian imagination, the bird symbolizes the mythical overmother, and every pebble she picks from the Mountain of Flames represents a wronged woman, ready to avenge herself against the sea. Although the strength of each pebble is feeble, and the sea seems a bottomless abyss, with perseverance, the gathered pebbles will prevail. Perhaps, this is the utopian belief that keeps women writing feminist utopias—the dreams of the wronged second sex, the voice of vengeance, the calling for Jingwei; their perseverance has moved men, and they have been writing, too.

Glossary
Notes
Bibliography
Index

Glossary

Axiao (a Mosuo term; a sleeping friend)	阿肖
Ami (a Mosuo term; mother)	阿咪
Bai Zimei (become sworn sisters)	拜姊妹
Bu Anming (not submit to one's fate)	不安命
Chu Zou (leave home)	出走
Dabu (the head of the Mosuo Community)	达布
Fufo (Negating Husband)	夫否
Huiwen Xuanjitu (palindrome)	回文璇玑图
Hundun (non-differentiated substance, chaos)	混沌
Jinshi (a successful candidate in the highest imperial examinations)	进士
Jingwei Niao (Jingwei Bird)	精卫鸟
Jingwei Shi (Jingwei pebbles)	精卫石
Jiumulu (a Mosuo term; male productive organ)	久木鲁
Jizema (a Mosuo term; female breast)	吉泽玛
Junjun Chenchen Zizi (the order of Emperor-Minister-Son)	君君臣臣子子
Kongxiang (wishful thinking)	空想
Lixiang Guo (ideal state, utopia)	理想国

Meng Lijun (a name) 孟丽君

Meng Lijun (a fair emperor in the dream) 梦丽君

Mingtang (an imperial hall) 明堂

Mo (a Mosuo term; daughter, model) 模

Nannü Pingquan, Renquan Tianfu (men and women are equal with human rights endowed by heaven) 男女平权. 人权天赋

Nannü Gongren (men and women share responsibility) 男女共任

Nü Zhuangyuan (the Female Number One Scholar at the highest imperial examination) 女状元

Nüquan (women's rights or power, feminist) 女权

Nüxing (women, feminine, femininity) 女性

Pingshi, Pingtan (tanci in the south) 评诗. 评弹

Qianyuan Dian (the Court of the Male Emperor) 乾元殿

Qiu Xue (seek education) 求学

Sancong Side (the Three Obediences and Four Virtues) 三从四德

Sanjiao Jiuliu (the Three Religions and the Nine Classes) 三教九流

Shengmu Shenhuang (Holy Mother-Providential Emperor) 圣母神皇

Shiniao (Bird of Vengeance) 誓鸟

Tanci (a literary form) 弹词

Taozhen (singing popular tales acompanied by string instruments for livelihood in the Song Dynasty 淘真

Tangchao Guizhong zhi Chen (Minister of the Tang Maidens) 唐朝闺中之臣

Tu Zili (gain economic independence) 图自立

Wanwu zhi Mu (mother of all things)   万物之母

Wenxue Shunü (the Virtuous Lady of Literature)   文学淑女

Wulun (the Five Principles of Confucian Ethics)   五伦

Wutuobang (nowhere, utopia)   乌托邦

Xiao (piety)   孝

Xiaoren (inferior men)   小人

Yang (male)   阳

Yi (justice or righteousness)   义

Yimei (a Mosuo term; the communal conference hall and dormitory)   一梅

Yin (female)   阴

Ying'er Yuanze (the infant principle)   婴儿原则

Yuanqin (Bird of the Wronged)   冤禽

Zaixiang (prime minister)   宰相

Zhengzhi Xiaoshuo (political fiction)   政治小说

Zhiniao (Bird of Perseverance)   志鸟

Zhong (loyalty)   忠

Zhuangyuan (Number One Scholar at the highest imperial examination)   状元

Zhubiao (a Mosuo term; preserved pork)   猪膘

Notes

1. Feminism in Literary Utopias

1. Vincent Geoghegan, *Utopianism and Marxism* (New York: Methuen, 1987), 106.

2. Michel Foucault, *Power/Knowledge: Selected Interviews and Other Writings, 1972–1977* (New York: Pantheon, 1980), 114.

3. Ibid., 142. Foucault sets the notion of power free from its narrow conception of state, sovereign, and sovereignty and defines it as "a multiform of production of relations of domination," that is, a force interwoven with relations of production, kinship, family, and sexuality.

4. For all Chinese names, the family name appears first; with the exception of long, adopted terms and names in quotations, modern Chinese phonetics are used. In the text, all titles and quotations that originally appeared in Chinese are rendered only in English. Transliterated Chinese titles are given in the Notes and in the Bibliography.

5. Krishan Kumar, *Utopia and Anti-utopia in Modern Times* (New York: Basil Blackwell, 1987) does not even mention the genre of feminist utopia.

6. Carol Farley Kessler, ed., *Daring to Dream* (Boston: Pandora, 1984), 8.

7. Rokeya Sakhawat Hossian, *Sultana's Dream, and Selections from the Secluded Ones* (New York: Feminist, 1988). Unlike the indigenous Chinese feminist utopias discussed here, *Sultana's Dream* is not only written in English but is also directly influenced by the West.

8. *Xinhua Cidian* (New Chinese dictionary) (Beijing: Shangwu, 1985), 884. According to the dictionary, *wutuobang*, of Greek origin, means "no place" (*wu* means "no" and *tuobang* means "place"). Derived from the title of More's *Utopia*, it is now used as a synonym for fantasy or daydream. In contemporary usage, the Greek meaning of "good place" in the concept of utopia is forgotten.

9. Yang Yi, *Zhongguo Xiandai Xiaoshuo Shi* (History of modern Chinese fiction) (Beijing: Renmin Wenxue, 1986), 1:24. Except where noted, all quotations from Chinese texts are my translations.

10. Gerda Lerner, *The Creation of Patriarchy* (Oxford: Oxford Univ. Press, 1986), 212–29.

11. Concerning Chinese patriarchy in theory and practice, see Judith Stacey, *Pa-*

171

triarchy and Socialist Revolution in China (Berkeley: Univ. of California Press, 1983); Esther S. Lee Yao, *Chinese Women: Past and Present* (Mesquite, Tex.: Ide House, 1983); Richard W. Guisso and Stanley Johannesen, eds., *Women in China* (Youngstown, N.Y.: Philo, 1981); and Li Youning and Zhang Yufa, eds., *Jindai Zhongguo Nüquan Yundong Shiliao: 1842–1911* (Documents on the Feminist Movements in Modern China: 1842–1911) (Taibei: Zhuanji Wenxue, 1976) 1:1–167.

12. *The Four Books for Women*, which includes the *Nüjie*, the *Nü Lunyu*, the *Neixun*, and the *Nüfan Jielu* (written over the course of one thousand years from the Han to the Ming dynasties), are feudal commands ranging from aspects of female obedience and filial piety to details on a woman's daily activities.

13. See Howard S. Levy, *Chinese Footbinding: The History of a Curious Erotic Custom* (London: Neville Spearman, 1966); Yao, 93–96; and Patricia Buckley Ebrey, *The Inner Quarters: Marriage and the Lives of Chinese Women in the Sung Period* (Berkeley: Univ. of California Press, 1993), 269. I disagree with Ebrey's view that "Footbinding was associated with the prusuit of beauty, not self-control or sexual segregation."

14. In *Dissent in Early Modern China: Ju-lin wai-shih and Ch'ing Social Criticism* (Ann Arbor: Univ. of Michigan Press, 1981), 120, Paul S. Ropp observes that the values and institutions reinforcing the subordination of women were "never stronger than during the Ch'ing dynasty."

15. The Lienü tradition starts with the *Biographies of Women* in the Western Han Dynasty (206 B.C.–A.D. 8). Although its author Liu Xiang (77–6 B.C.) categorized his female subjects into seven types: Model Mothers, the Noble, the Intelligent, the Good and Wise, the Chaste and Righteous, the Perspicacious, and the Evil and Depraved, the Lienü tradition emphasizes female chastity and encourages women's suicide. For discussion of the historical development of the Lienü, see Andrew C. K. Hsien and Johnathan D. Spence, "Suicide and the Family in Pre-modern Chinese Society," in *Normal and Abnormal Behavior in Chinese Culture*, ed. Arthur Kleinman and Tsung-yi Lin (Boston: D. Reidel, 1981), 29–48; Marina H. Sung, "The Chinese Lieh-nü Tradition," in *Women in China*, ed. Richard W. Guisso and Stanley Johannesen (Youngstown, N.Y.: Philo, 1981), 63–74.

16. Riane Eisler, *The Chalice and the Blade: Our History, Our Future* (San Francisco: Harper & Row, 1987), 25.

17. Ibid., xvii.

18. Ibid., 105.

19. Anne K. Mellor, "On Feminist Utopias," *Women's Studies* 9 (1982): 243.

20. The fact that a matrilineal society existed in the China of remote antiquity before the establishment of the Shang Dynasty is generally accepted in China and is supported by Western scholars, such as Marcel Granet, *Chinese Civilization* (London: Kegan Paul, Trech, Trubner, 1930); Harrlee Glessner Creel, *The Birth of China* (New York: John Day, 1954); and Richard Wilhelm, *A Short History of Chinese Civilization* (New York: Kennikat, 1970).

21. Two books about this matrilineal community were published in the 1980s in China: Zhan Chengxue et al., *Yongning Naxi Zu de Azhu Hunyin he Muxi Jiating* (Yongning Naxi's Azhu marriage and matrilineal family) (Shanghai: Renmin, 1980); Yan Ruxian and Song Zhaolin, *Yongning Naxi Zu de Muxi Zhi* (Yongning Naxi's matrilineality) (Yunnan: Renmin, 1983). Bai Hua's novel is based on this actual model.

22. Yao, 28.

23. Yuan Ke, comp., *Gu Shenhua Xuanshi* (Ancient myths of China) (Beijing:

Renmin Wenxue, 1979); Zhang Zhenli, *Zhongyuan Gudian Shenhua Liubian Lunkao* (On the transformations of ancient myths in the Central Plains) (Shanghai: Wenyi, 1991), 43–44. According to Zhang Zhenli, the myth of Nüwa as the sky-mender, sky-supporter, flood-conqueror, and disease-curer appeared much earlier than the myth of Pangu.

24. Abby Wettan Kleinbaum, *The War Against the Amazons* (New York: McGraw-Hill, 1983), 1.

25. The story of Hua Mulan is best recounted in the ballad, "Mulan Shi." It was first written by an unknown author in the Northern Wei Dynasty (A.D. 386–534) and became popular in the Tang Dynasty.

26. The tale of the Women Warriors of the Yang Family comes from the novel, *Warriors of the Yang Family*, which is believed to have been written by Xiong Damu of the Ming Dynasty.

27. Yao, 63–64.

28. Hu Ji, *Wu Zetian Benzhuan* (Biography of Wu Zetian) (Xi'an: Sanqin, 1986), 33–46.

29. *Tanci* is largely a poetic narrative. See chap. 3.

30. Zhao Jingshen, "Zhongguo Gudian Jiangchang Wenxue Congshu Xu" (Preface: the classical telling and singing literature in China) in Chen Duansheng, *Zaisheng Yuan* (The destiny of the next life) (Henan: Zhongzhou Shuhua, 1982), 3.

31. Guisso, 60. However, Chinese literature offers a rich portrayal of shrewish wives and henpecked husbands. I discuss the "Town of Hens" by Fang Ruhao of the Ming Dynasty as an example of Chinese misogyny in my chap. 6.

32. Because writing is a deviation from so-called feminine virtues, women are often forced to hide their writings as something shameful and indecent, or to simply burn them. Lady Sun of the Tang Dynasty burned the manuscript of poems she wrote for her husband's examination, saying, "Intellect should not be a faculty for women" (*Quan Tangshi*). Sun Huilan of the Yuan Dynasty also burned her own poems, saying, "A woman should weave and do her duty of piety; letters and poems are not her business" (*Yuanshi Xuan: Lüchuang Yigao*). See Su Zhecong, *Zhongguo Lidai Funü Zuopin Xuan* (Selected writings of Chinese women in history) (Shanghai: Guji, 1987), 4–5.

33. Sue Fawn Chung offers a defense for Ci Xi in "The Much Maligned Empress Dowager: A Revisionist Study of the Empress Dowager Tz'u-Hsi (1835–1908)," *Modern Asian Studies* (Great Britain) 13, no. 2 (1979): 177–96.

34. Ku Yen, "Chiang Ch'ing's Wolfish Ambition in Publicizing 'Matriarchal Society,'" *Chinese Studies in History* 12, no. 3 (1979): 75–79. Ku Yen argues that history reveals no basis for Jiang Qing's pro-matriarchy activities.

35. Gerard Budok, *Sir Thomas More and His Utopia* (Amsterdam: Firma A. H. Kruyt, 1923), 19.

36. See Ellen Widmer, *The Margins to Utopia: Shui-hu hou-chuan and the Literature of Ming Loyalism* (Cambridge: Harvard Univ. Press, 1987); and dissertations such as Pi-twan H. Wang, "Utopian Imagination in Traditional Chinese Fiction" (Ph. D. diss., Univ. of Wisconsin, 1981); Chang Hui-chuan, "Literary Utopia and Chinese Utopian Literature: A Generic Appraisal" (Ph. D. diss., Univ. of Michigan, 1986); and Koon-ki T. Ho, "Why Utopias Fall: A Comparative Study of the Modern Anti-Utopian Traditions in Chinese, English and Japanese Literature" (Ph. D. diss., Univ. of Illinois, 1987).

37. A discussion comparing these three utopian thoughts with Western utopian traditions will be provided in chap. 2.

38. Kumar insists that the modern utopia appears "only in the West," 19. Chang Hui-chuan also denies the existence of the Thomas More-type of utopian genre in traditional Chinese literature.

39. According to Confucius, a woman does not have a home until she gets married; thus, having a home means being married off to a man.

40. In the 1970s, a number of articles published in the West treated China as a utopia. See Henry Jacoby, "China as Utopia," *Schweizer Monatshefte* (Switzerland) 54, no. 2 (1974): 90–94; Maurice Meisner, "Maoist Utopianism and the Future of Chinese Society," *International Journal* (Canada) 26, no. 3 (1971): 535–55.

41. Ho, "Why Utopias Fall," 98.

42. Ono Kazuko, *Chinese Women in a Century of Revolution, 1850–1950*, ed. Joshua A. Fogel (Stanford: Stanford Univ. Press, 1989). Ono provides an excellent account of women's liberation in the Heavenly Kingdom of Great Peace.

43. Fan Wenlan, *Zhongguo Jindai Shi* (Modern Chinese history) (Beijing: Renmin, 1952), 1:135.

44. Ono, 89.

45. Stacey, 266.

46. Ibid., 262–6

47. Suzanne Pepper, "Review Articles: Liberation and Understanding: New Books on the Uncertain Status of Women in the Chinese Revolution," *China Quarterly* 108 (1986): 704–18. Pepper points out that current economic policies have strengthened the family and weakened the position of women.

48. Ernst Bloch, *The Principle of Hope*, trans. Nevile Plaice, Stephen Plaice, and Paul Knight. (Cambridge, Mass.: MIT, 1986), 595. Geoghegan points out that by "postponed," Bloch means that "women have a utopian dimension to contribute to future socialist society, a contribution defined in terms of 'special qualities' of women," 94.

49. Kleinbaum says: "For nearly three millennia, generation after generation of men in the West, champions all, have enlisted in the war against the Amazons. The opponents are mythical, but the battles are nonetheless real," 1.

50. Barbara Brandon Schnorrenberg, "A Paradise Like Eve's: Three Eighteenth Century English Female Utopias," *Women's Studies* 9 (1982): 204. According to Schnorrenberg, Mary Astell has been designated as the first eighteenth-century English feminist. She envisaged a utopian "Monastery" or a "Happy Retreat" for women to rebuild a paradise like Eve's.

51. In early utopias by men, women appear merely as one of the authors' many concerns. Moreover, sexual egalitarianism is often abstractly posited, then rejected in detail. For instance, in his *Republic* (c. 380 B.C.), Plato first argues against sexual difference in nature and division of labor and agrees that women can hold office as men; but women in his utopia are soon portrayed as hounds following their masters to war. A retrogression occurs in More's *Utopia*, where women and children have to kneel in front of the patriarch of the family to confess their sins. In *The City of the Sun* (1623), Tommaso Campanella insists even more vigorously on the differences in men's and women's nature and on the division of labor.

52. As Elizabeth Cleghorn Gaskell declares at the very beginning of *Cranford* (1863), "Cranford is in possession of the Amazons." *Cranford* is indeed a utopia of spinsters, which reflects the spirit of the women's utopia in Gaskell's age; a community of women experiment in the female management of business, in political independence at the sacrifice of sexual love, and voluntarily reliquish power for moral superiority.

53. See Lyman Tower Sargent, "English and American Utopias: Similarities and

Differences," *Journal of General Education* 28, no. 1 (1976): 16–22; also Nan Bowman Albinski's introduction to *Women's Utopias in British and American Fiction* (New York: Routledge, 1988).

54. Albinski, *Women's Utopias*, 38.

55. In the Chinese imperial court system, the highest position beneath the emperor is called *Zaixiang*. Its power and position are similar to that of a prime minister. Because the position of emperor is inherited, *Zaixiang* is the highest position of state power one can reach; I use its conventional translation, "prime minister," in this study. In fact, China did not have a parliamentary system until the 1911 revolution.

56. Mary E. Bradley Lane's *Mizora: A Prophecy* (1889) provides a prototype for an all-female world. It is a transitional feminist utopia that inherits the spirit of educational and economic reforms of the eighteenth and nineteenth century feminist impulse but starts to claim women's autonomous political power. It unfortunately retains class distinction and private ownership—e.g., salary.

57. Kessler, 18.

58. "Future Visions: Todays Politics: Feminist Utopias in Review," in *Women in Search of Utopia: Mavericks and Mythmakers*, ed. Ruby Rohrlich and Elaine Hoffman Baruch. (New York: New York Press, 1984), 309.

59. Kessler, 7.

60. Albinski, *Women's Utopias*, 134.

61. Angela Carter, *The Sadeian Woman: an Exercise in Cultural History* (London: Virago, 1979).

62. Ursula K. Le Guin, "Is Gender Necessary?" in *Aurora: Beyond Equality*, ed. Vonda N. McIntyre and Susan Janice Anderson. (Greenwich: Fawcett, 1976), 134.

63. Herbert Marcuse, *Five Lectures* (Boston: Beacon, 1970), 63.

64. Ursula K. Le Guin *The Language of the Night*, rev. ed. (New York: Harper Collins, 1992), 156–59.

65. Kobo Abé, *Inter Ice Age 4*, trans. E. Dale Saunders (Tokyo: Turtle, 1971), 226.

66. "Micropower" is a term used by Foucault in his *Power/Knowledge*.

2. Monstrous or Natural:
The Faerie Queene and Sanbao's Expedition to the Western Ocean

1. Kleinbaum, 39, 46.

2. Edmund Spenser, *The Faerie Queene*, ed. A. C. Hamilton (New York: Longman, 1977).

3. In her "Female Reigns: *The Faerie Queene* and *The Journey to the West*," *Comparative Literature* 39, no. 3 (1987): 218–35, Dore J. Levy traces allegorical parallels between the Amazon country of women in Book V of *The Faerie Queene* and the Women's Kingdom of Western Liang in *The Journey to the West*. The Women's Kingdom of Western Liang is, however, a simple allegory of sexual temptation, whereas the militant Amazons give Spenser's realm of women a political complexity; and in ignoring this essential difference, Levy's article fails to discuss the political dimensions of the female reign and its function within the overall intention of *The Faerie Queene*.

4. Luo Maodeng, *Sanbao Taijian Xiyang Ji Tongsu Yanyi* (Sanbao's expedition to the western ocean) (Shanghai: Guji, 1982).

5. World-state is a term used by Northrop Frye, who says: "the utopia, as a literary genre, should be retrieved at the time of Renaissance, the period in which the medieval social order was breaking down again into city-state units or nations governed

from a capital city." "Varieties of Literary Utopias," in *Utopian Thought in the Western World,* ed. Frank E. Manuel and F. P. Manuel (Cambridge, Mass.: Belknap, 1979), 27.

6. Virginia Woolf, *A Room of One's Own* (1929; reprint, London: Hogarth, 1967), 66.

7. It appears that no scholars have formally claimed *The Faerie Queene* as a utopia. Frye regards *The Faerie Queene* as "belong[ing] peripherally to the utopian tradition;" but he mentions only its education myth and features in the genre of courtier-literature and ignores the myth of the Golden Age. Critics such as Harry Levin, C. S. Lewis, and Frederich Charles Osenburg have treated the myth of the Golden Age in *The Faerie Queene.* Judith E. Boss thinks that Spenser uses the three utopian traditions merely "for the purpose of saying something about the nature of man and the nature of reality."

The Faerie Queene is seldom treated by scholars as a utopian work because of its use of allegory, its epic form, and its camouflage of "an historical fiction"; however, the genre of utopia, with its divisions of eutopia, dystopia, satirical utopia, and antiutopia, is always defined in terms of its social and political imagination rather than its narrative mode. Its function is "to provoke a fruitful bewilderment, and to jar the mind into some heightened but unconceptualized consciousness of its own powers, functions, aims, and structural limits;" therefore, one cannot exclude *The Faerie Queene* from the category of utopia because of its allegorical devices and epic form. Neither does Spenser's historical fiction run counter to utopian representation; instead it enables him to borrow the image of Arthur and benefit from the Arthurian literary tradtion in constructing his utopian dream. Combining historical fiction with elaborate allegory, therefore, *The Faerie Queene* is a literary utopia with a highly refined aesthetic style. Frye, "Varieties," 38; Harry Levin, *The Myth of the Golden Age in the Renaissance* (Bloomington: Indiana Univ. Press, 1969); C. S. Lewis, *English Literature in the Sixteenth Century Excluding Drama* (Oxford: Clarendon, 1954); Frederich Charles Osenburg, "The Idea of the Golden Age and the Decay of the World in the English Renaissance," (Ph. D. diss., Univ. of Illinois, 1939); Judith E. Boss, "The Golden Age, Cockaigne and Utopia in *The Faerie Queene* and *The Tempest*," *The Georgia Review* 26 (1972): 145–55.

8. Spenser (1552–1599) composed *The Faerie Queene* while in Ireland, indeed a "fallen land," and the landscape of his epic even resembles Ireland of his day. Moreover, he held several government posts in Ireland during a period of insurrection that posed serious threats to the Anglo-Irish and English. As an official, he was involved in efforts to dominate and colonize that country.

9. "Letter to Raleigh," in Spenser, 737.

10. Chastity as a political virtue in Book III is discussed by Bruce Thomas Boehrer in his " 'Carelesse Modestee': Chastity as Politics in Book 3 of *The Faerie Queene*," *ELH* 55, no. 3 (1988): 555–73.

11. In "Spenser's Mutabilitie Cantos and the End of the *Faerie Queene*," *Southern Review* 15 (1982): 46, Marion Campbell says that "more recent opinion seems to favor the notion that the Mutabilitie Cantos form a coherent whole which Spenser appended as a fitting conclusion to the epic he saw he could never complete."

12. For a detailed study of these three traditions, see Kumar 2–19.

13. Kumar, 7.

14. Boss, 149.

15. Ibid., 146.

16. Spenser, V.Pr.9.

17. Ibid., V.Pr.2.

18. Levin, 101–2.

19. The influences of European masters, such as Virgil, Ariosto, and Tasso, on Spenser's *Faerie Queene* have been amply discussed elsewhere.

20. Book VII, "The Mutabilitie Cantos," was first published in 1609. Little is known about Luo Maodeng; he is believed to have lived during the Wanli period (1573–1619) of the Ming Dynasty. The original preface of the novel was signed "Luo Maodeng of the Ernanli."

21. Classical Chinese literature adopts a highly aristocratic, literary language; the use of vernacular or daily language in long fiction begins with the Ming Dynasty. As a result, the genre of novel had been disparaged in Chinese literary history.

22. No previous scholars have analyzed the utopian dimensions of Luo Maodeng's novel.

23. Some Chinese scholars such as Lu Xun have criticized its textual roughness and its imitation of *The Journey to the West*, while others, such as Yu Yue, a literary critic of the Qing Dynasty, have regarded it as a masterpiece superior to *Fengshen Yanyi* and *The Journey to the West*. In my view, although *The Western Ocean* lacks allegorical as well as textual refinement, it does reveal an effective combination of the fantastic with the real. It has its own vernacular charm and draws strength from history, mythology, and cultural tradition.

Fengshen Yanyi is a popular novel, also known as *Fengshen Bang*. Its author is believed to have been either Xu Zhongling or Lu Xixing. This fantastic novel of war among gods and demons has one hundred chapters and blends the story of King Wu punishing King Zou with Chinese mythology, legends, and folk tales.

24. The western oceans actually refer to the west of east meridian line 110°. It includes the South Ocean (the Malay Archipelago, the Malay Peninsula, and Indonesia, etc.) and the Indian Ocean. In about a thirty-year period, Zheng He made seven voyages, visiting seventeen countries in Asia and Africa. Liu Zhi'e, in his *Zheng He*, provides a concise historical account of Zheng He and his voyages to those western ocean regions.

25. *Yingya Shenlan*, by Ma Huan, and *Xingcha Shenlan*, by Fei Xin, are both records of Zheng He's sea expeditions. Zhao Jingshen compares the novel with these two books in detail in his "Sanbao Taijian Xiyang Ji" (On Sanbao's expedition to the western ocean), in Luo, 1298–1328.

26. This brings to mind the quest for the Holy Grail in Arthurian legend.

27. "Peach Blossom Springs," in *Gleanings from Tao Yuan-ming*, trans. Fang Zhong (Shanghai: Foreign Language Education, 1984), 156–61. Tao Yuan-ming (Tao Qian A.D. 365–427.) lived as a Daoist utopian poet. He declined official posts and tilled land with his wife. In living a plain life with pastoral freedom, he established his spiritual "Taohuayuan."

28. Ho, "Why Utopias Fall," 92. Christian utopianism, which advocates the perfectibility of man and a vision of the New Jerusalem, also works as an underpinning in *The Faerie Queene*.

29. Stevie, Davies, *The Feminine Reclaimed: The Idea of Woman in Spenser, Shakespeare and Milton* (Lexington: Univ. Press of Kentucky, 1986), 414.

30. The utopianism of Datong culminates in Kang Youwei's *Book of Datong (One World Philosophy)*, which blends traditional Daoist utopianism with Confucian Datong and resembles the Western world-state utopianism represented by Bellamy's *Looking Backward*. See N. T. Shatin, "In and Out of Utopia: K'ang Yu-wei's Social Thought, 2: Road to Utopia," *The Chung Chi Journal* (Hong Kong) 7 (1968): 101–149.

178 / Notes to Pages 25-33

31. In *Utopia*, 7, Kumar believes that the Cokaygne utopia is to "be found in practically all folk cultures." It indeed exists in Chinese stories such as "The Dream of Millet" or "The Dream of Nanke"; however, the Chinese emphasize the transiency and emptiness of such wish-fulfillment and seldom regard it as utopia.

32. Luo, 644.

33. Ibid., 1110. Although Luo Maodeng mentions Islamism, he never gives it any special attention. Zheng He (Sanbao) came from an Islamic family.

34. Luo Maodeng's pessimism is mentioned by Lu Xun, *A Brief History of Chinese Fiction* (Beijing: Foreign Languages, 1976); Zhao Jingshen, "Sanbao;" and Xiang Da, "Lun Luo Maodeng Zhu *Sanbao Taijian Xiyang Ji Tongsu Yanyi*," in Luo, 1291–97.

35. Luo, 1286.

36. Michelle Carbone Loris, "Images of Women in Books III and IV of Spenser's *Faerie Queene*," *Mid-Hudson Languages Studies* 8 (1985) 11–13. Loris discusses Florimell as "an object of prey, an object to win, possess, and overpower."

37. Spenser, III.i.18.

38. On Spenser's treatment of female sexual power, see Susan Hannah, "Womb(an) Power: Or a Faerie Tale of the Good, the Bad, and the Ugly," *RE: Artes Liberales* 5 (1978): 27–35; and Water Kendrick, "Earth of Flesh, Flesh of Earth: Mother Earth in the *Faerie Queene*," *Renaissance Quarterly* 27 (1974): 533–48.

39. Spenser, V.iv.31.

40. Ibid., V.v.22.

41. Ibid., V.v.23.

42. James E. Phillips, Jr., "The Woman Ruler in Spenser's *Faerie Queene*," *Huntington Library Quarterly* 5 (1942): 211.

43. Ibid.

44. *Lords Journals* I: 453; quoted in James E. Phillips, Jr., "The Background of Spenser's Attitude Toward Women Rulers," *Huntington Library Quarterly* 5 (1942): 8.

45. Phillips, "The Women," 234.

46. Spenser, V.v.25.

47. Mihoko Suzuki, *Metamorphoses of Helen: Authority, Difference, and the Epic*. (Ithaca: Cornell Univ. Press, 1990), 208.

48. Spenser, V.iv.36.

49. Luo, 439.

50. As historical phenomena, it is recorded in *Zhoushu: Yiyu Zhuan* (Book of Chou: stories of the foreign land) and *Suishu: Xiyu Zhuan* (Book of Sui: stories of Xiyu). See Song Zhaolin, *Gongfu Zhi yu Gongqi Zhi* (Polyandry and polygamy) (Shanghai: Shanghai Shudian, 1990), 122.

51. Luo, 315.

52. According to Liu Zhi'e, *Zheng He* (Jiangsu: Guji, 1984), Zheng He was born into an Islamic family in Yunnan. He was captured and castrated by the Ming Troops when he was twelve years old and later became an imperial eunuch. His castration in the novel has triple significance in the way it signifies chastity, impotence, and sympathy. At the Ming Court, he is the only person who dares to take on the task of the expedition. In the Country of Women, his castration enables him to sympathize with the sexual starvation suffered in an all-female world, though he is unable to be tempted. The angry Queen attempts to execute him for his impotence.

53. Luo, 598. In "Qianyan" (Foreword), in Luo, 6–18, Lu Shulun and Zhu Shaohua warn the reader against vulgarity in Luo's description of the Country of

Women. The sentence quoted here serves as an example. At the beginning of the chapter, Sanbao's scouts see that everything in the Country of Women resembles the men's world except that women squat to urinate. The only difference between men and women, therefore, is their sex.

54. Although Luo borrows the metaphors of the Reflecting Bridge and the Mother-child River from earlier writings, he is very inventive in using three princesses to guard the spring. Compared with the Women's Kingdom of Liang in *The Journey to the West*, Luo's militant Country of Women is no longer a simple allegory of temptation.

55. Luo, 610.

56. Louis Adrian Montrose, "The Elizabethan Subject and the Spenserian Text," in *Literary Theory / Renaissance Texts*, ed. Patricia Parker and David Quit (Baltimore: Johns Hopkins Univ. Press, 1986), 329.

57. Thomas K. Dunseath, *Spenser's Allegory of Justice in Book V of The Faerie Queene* (Princeton: Princeton Univ. Press, 1968), 50.

58. Apart from Robin Hedlam Wells, who regards *The Faerie Queene* as a glorification of the ideal ruler Elizabeth, other critics, such as Harry Berger and Lauren Silberman, consider Britomart a new type of woman or feminist heroine. To Berger, Britomart is the conqueror of the male imagination embodied by Busirane. Silberman believes that Spenser genuinely revises the marginalization of women that had become conventional in Petrarchan and Platonic traditions. In 1986, feminist critics Margaret W. Ferguson, Maureen Quilligan, and Nancy J. Vickers, in *Rewriting the Renaissance: The Discourses of Sexual Differences in Early Modern Europe* (Chicago: Univ. of Chicago Press, 1986), chose Spenser as the only male author who wrote on behalf of women during the Renaissance and placed Silberman's article on Spenser, "Singing Unsung Heroines," in a section entitled "The Works of Women: Some Exceptions to the Rule of Patriarchy."

59. Pamela J. Benson, "Rule, Virginia: Protestant Theories of Female Regiment in *The Faerie Queene*," *English Literary Renaissance* 15 (1985): 285.

60. James W. Broaddus, "Renaissance Psychology and Britomart's Adventures in *Faerie Queene* III," *English Literary Renaissance* 17, no. 2 (1987): 190.

61. Linda Woodbridge, *Women and the English Renaissance: Literature and the Nature of Womankind, 1540–1620* (Chicago: Univ. of Illinois Press, 1984), 135–36 n.4.

62. Harry Berger, Jr., "Busirane and the War Between the Sexes: An Interpretation of *The Faerie Queene* III.xi–xii," *English Literary Renaissance* 1 (1971): 99–100.

63. In ibid., 117, Berger explains "too bold" as "too violently inhibit her 'true femininitee' and 'goodly womanhood." Spenser, III.xi.54.

64. Ibid., III.vi.51.

65. Critics have given the Hermaphrodite various interpretations. Northrop Frye and Thomas P. Roche see it as an emblem of Christian marriage. A. R. Cirillo regards it as a sign of the higher union of souls. Kathleen Williams emphasizes "the necessary concord of opposites" symbolized in the Hermaphrodite image, whereas Donald Cheney stresses Britomart's or an onlooker's divided consciousness in watching the oneness of the "faire Hermaphrodite."

66. Lauren Silberman, "The Hermaphrodite and the Metamorphosis of Spenserian Allegory." *English Literary Renaissance* 17 (1987): 212.

67. Spenser, 1590, III.xii.45.

68. Woodbridge, 184.

69. Eric Sterling, "Spenser's *Faerie Queene*," *Explicator* 46, no. 3 (1988): 10. In "King Lear and *The Faerie Queene*," *Notes and Queries* 31 (1984): 207, Martin Coyle

points out that when Shakespeare was writing *King Lear* he had Spenser's Malbecco in mind because of "the simple fact that both Malbecco and Lear are driven mad by the cruelty of womankind." Obviously, Sterling surpasses Shakespeare in the male-centeredness of his reading of *The Faerie Queene*.

70. Woodbridge, 268.

71. Spenser, III.ix.28.

72. Ibid., III.ix.6.

73. Ibid., III.x.36.

74. There are some interesting parallels between the scene of Hellenore, the May-Queene, among the Satyres, and of Una among the Satyres. Richard Douglas Jordan points out that when Una's veil was snatched from her face, the response of the pagan Sansloy is lust, whereas the Satyres' response is to worship her beauty. He mentions the Satyres' double worship of Una and of the ass. Perhaps, to Spenser's Satyres, truth and sex are of equal beauty.

75. Spenser, III.x.44.

76. Ibid., III.x.48.

77. Ibid., III.x.51.

78. Harry Berger, Jr., "The Discarding of Malbecco: Conspicuous Allusion and Cultural Exhaustion in *The Faerie Queene* III ix–x," *Studies in Philology* 96 (1969): 144.

79. Woodbridge, 134.

80. Suzuki, 35, 67.

81. Jacob Burckhardt, *The Civilization of the Renaissance in Italy* (1860; reprint trans. S. G. C. Middlemore, New York: Albert and Charles Boni, 1935). Ferguson, Quilligan, and Vickers begin their "Introduction" to *Rewriting the Renaissance* by refuting Burckhardt's view.

82. R. Valerie Lucas. "Hic Mulier: The Female Transvestite in Early Modern England," *Renaissance and Reformation* 12, no. 1 (1988): 68–69.

83. Lucas, 65.

84. Elizabeth Bieman, "Britomart in Book V of the *Faerie Queene*," *University of Toronto Quarterly* 37 (1968): 165.

85. Judith Anderson, " 'Nor Man It Is:' The Knight of Justice in Book V of Spenser's *Faerie Queene*," *PMLA* 85 (1970): 65.

86. Bieman, 162.

87. "Spinsters and Seamstresses: Women in Cloth and Clothing Production," in Ferguson, 194.

88. Ferguson, xix.

89. Lillian S. Robinson, *Monstrous Regiment: The Lady Knight in Sixteenth-Century Epic* (New York: Garland, 1985), 341.

90. Anderson calls Britomart "a humanizer of Justice," 70. Bieman says that in his fall "the austere Artegall becomes a more human character," 163.

91. Lucas, 80.

92. For a detailed discussion, see Woodbridge, 145.

93. Lucas, 73.

94. Book III suggests Spenser's awareness of men's jealousy and fear of accomplished women, but Book V reveals that male jealousy and fear have influenced his own representation of Britomart and Radigund.

95. Spenser, V.vii.34.

96. See Carol Gilligan, *In a Different Voice: Psychological Theory and Women's Development* (Cambridge: Harvard Univ. Press, 1982), 69 n. 17.

97. Spenser, V.vii.42.
98. In "Shaping Fantasies," 77, Montrose says, "the engulfing Amazon and the nursing Virgin are two archetypes of Elizabethan culture."
99. Ruth Kelso, *Doctrine for the Lady of the Renaissance* (1956; reprint, Urbana: Univ. of Illinois Press, 1978), 3.
100. Celeste Turne Wright, "The Amazons in Elizabeth Literature," *Studies in Philology* 37 (1940): 433.
101. Spenser, V.vii.30.
102. Ibid., V.vii.32.
103. Bieman, 170.
104. Spenser, V.vii.34.
105. A. C. Hamilton, *The Structure of Allegory in the Faerie Queene* (Oxford: Oxford Univ. Press, 1961), 159.
106. Humphrey Tonkin, "Spenser's Garden of Adonis and Britomart's Quest," *PMLA* 88 (1973): 414.
107. Ferguson, xx.
108. Spenser, "Letter to Raleigh," 737.
109. Quilligan, 163.
110. Montrose, 309.
111. William Camden, *The History and Annals of Elizabeth, Queen of England,* trans. Richard Norton (London, 1963), Book 1, 28–29.
112. Hamilton, 172.
113. Montrose, "Shaping Fantasies," 76.
114. Luo, 1150.
115. Ibid., 1157.
116. Ibid., 860.
117. Ibid., 314.
118. Ibid., 1153.
119. Ibid., 647.
120. Ibid., 1012.
121. Kleinbaum, 94, 98.

3. As Women's Destiny: *The Destiny of the Next Life* and *Gloriana; Or, The Revolution of 1900*

1. Chen Duansheng, *Zaisheng Yuan* (The destiny of the next life), ed. Liu Chongyi (Henan: Zhongzhou Shuhua, 1982), 106.
2. Ibid., 924.
3. See Zhang Dejun, "Chen Duansheng de Muqin Dui Ta zai Wenxue Shang de Yingxiang" (The influence of Chen Duansheng's mother on her literary career,) *Guangming Ribao,* 25 July 1961.
4. Chen Duansheng, 925.
5. It is traditionally believed that Chen Duansheng wrote *The Next Life* to express her feeling of sadness caused by the separation from her husband and that she would not complete the story till her husband came back from exile. This belief is unreliable; there are controversies among Chinese historians about the identity of Chen Duansheng's husband. Moreover, Chen Duansheng wrote the first sixteen books long before she knew her husband. After a twelve-year interruption, she wrote Book Seventeen, which does not show any sign of weakening in her literary sensitivity but has a

stronger tone of rebellion. At the beginning of Book Seventeen, she wrote: "I scratch my head to question the Heaven / whether there is a heavenly path to return." After Book Seventeen, Chen Duansheng lived another seven years without finishing the epic.

6. "Ci" means words and "tan" playing the string instrument. Thus, *tanci*, composed of alternating prose and verse, is the word for telling and singing. Although *The Next Life* represents a refined type of *tanci* fiction for reading, it retains some performing features. The origin of *tanci* is controversial. Some scholars believe that it originates from the bianwen of the Tang Dynasty (618–907); others insist that it develops directly from Gongdiao of the Song and Jin Dynasties. Nevertheless, *tanci* becomes popular in the middle of the Ming Dynasty (1368–1643). For discussion on the technical features of *tanci* see chap. 1 of Toyoko Yoshida, "Women in Confusian Society: A Study of Three T'an-Tz'u Narratives" (Ph. D. diss., Columbia Univ., 1974); also, Marina Hsiu-wen Sung, "The Narrative Art of 'Tsai-sheng-yuan': A Feminist Vision in Traditional Confucian Society" (Ph. D. diss., Univ of Wisconsin, 1988).

7. Zhao Jingshen provides a concise discussion of telling-singing literature in his "Zhongguo Gudian," 1–4.

8. In the Song Dynasty, the blind, particularly girls, sang popular tales accompanied by string instruments for livelihood. Their profession is known as *taozhen*. See Tan Zhengbi and Tan Xun, comp., *Pingtan Tongkao* (Historical comments on *Pingtan*) (Beijing: Zhongguo Quyi, 1985), 397–98.

9. In "On the Literature Written by Chinese Women Prior to 1917," *Asian and African Studies* 15 (1979): 65–99, Marian Galick makes two mistakes about women writers of *tanci*. First, she stresses that women's *tanci* lags at least one hundred years behind that of men, without noting generic contributions and transformations made by women; second, she draws hasty generalizations without discussing specific features of women's *tanci*. Consequently, she echoes traditional views on Chen Duansheng's *Next Life* and other women's works. *Tanci* fiction as a genre for women will be treated in a separate study.

10. Zheng Zhenduo, *Zhongguo Suwenxue Shi* (History of Chinese popular literature) (Shanghai: Shanghai Shudian, 1984), Vol. 2, 353–54.

11. Chen Yinke, "Lun *Zaishen Yuan*" (On *the destiny of the next life*), *Hanliu-tang Ji* (Shanghai: Guji, 1980), 62.

12. Chen Duansheng, 1.

13. Ibid., 733.

14. Ibid., 793, 733. Chen Duansheng's poetry collection, *Huiyingge*, unfortunately has been lost.

15. Ibid., 1.

16. Chapter 31 of the novel begins with the line: "Daughter composes new lines with a purple brush, while Mother weaves magic words with jade threads." It is the earliest known *tanci* in the south perhaps written at the beginning of the Qing Dynasty. See Tan Zhengbi, *Zhongguo Nüxing Wenxue Shihua* (History of Chinese women's literature) (Tianjin: Baihua Wenyi, 1984), 400–401. The version titled *Xinke Yuchuan Yuan Quanzhuan* (24 vols., 1842) is existant, with a preface by Xihu Jushi.

17. Traditional *tanci* focuses on the successes of male heroes in war and courtly life, with women as their rewards. In *Anbangzhi*, Shaoqing becomes Prime Minister, having nine wives; in *Dingguozhi*, he becomes the Lord of Dingguo, having twelve wives. Similar to those *tanci* tales, *The Destiny of the Jade Bracelet* portrays Xie Yuhui as a paradigm of loyalty and fidelity. He climbs to the position of Lord Guangping, with six wives (including Princess Minghua and General Li Zhenqing captured from war).

18. Chen Duansheng, 925.

19. Ibid., 106.

20. *Jinguijie* did not have a good reception because Hou Zhi cut off too much of Chen Duansheng's original text in her process of editing and adapting. See Liu Chongyi, "Youxu" (Introduction), in *Zaisheng Yuan* (The destiny of the next life), by Chen Duansheng (Henan: Zhongzhou shuhua, 1982), 10–11.

21. See Tan, *Zhongguo*, 353–56. The birth date of Wang Yun is unknown. But she completed *Fanhua Meng* (A dream of splendor) by 1718 with the prefatory poem I quoted.

22. *Zai Zaotian* (The re-creation of the heaven) employs the myth of Nüwa and the legend of Wu Zetian to satirize the patriarchal notion that stupidity is a woman's virtue and that a talented woman in power is monstrous. Its female protagonist is again defeated by Shaohua, defender of the feudal order. *Bi Sheng Hua* (Flowers from the brush) was written by Qui Xinru whose husband was intellectually inferior. Her protagonist, Jiang Dehua, in male guise realizes her dream of passing all levels of examinations and reaching the position of prime minister. The revealing sexual crisis carries a strong gender protest: "Since I inherited Old Father's talent, why can't I be treated like a man rather than a woman? Through efforts I gained my achievements. Now who knows, all my glory is gone to the dust. What's the use of a woman's exceptional talent? [Once she is discovered a woman] she is expelled from whatever high positions?" (chap. 22). However, the author's imagination is confined by the feudal ethic of chastity, and her protagonist compromises to her fate of marriage eventually, as in the ending of *The Next Life*, written by Liang Desheng.

23. *Yujing Tai* (The jade dresser) has only one book of five chapters published. In *Zhongguo*, 468, Tan Zhengbi calls it "the rearguard of the golden age of women's *tanci*.

24. Tan, *Zhongguo*, 388.

25. Brian Roberts, *Ladies in the Veld* (London: John Murray, 1965), 81.

26. Ibid.

27. Ibid., 180.

28. Nan Bowman Albinski, "Female Cross-dressing in the Novels of Lady Florence Dixie," *Macquarie Conference Papers 1989*, ed. Catherine Waters and Helen Yardly (Sydney: Macquarie Univ., 1989), 9.

29. For her biography, see Roberts, *Ladies in the Veld*, 178–80; for information on her entire family, see Roberts, *The Mad Bad Line* (London: Hamish Hamilton, 1981).

30. Florence Caroline Dixie, "Women's Position," *The Modern Review* 1, no. 3 (1890): 227.

31. Ibid., 228.

32. Florence Caroline Dixie wrote several travel books and three novels. In addition to *Gloriana, Or, the Revolution of 1900* (London: Henry, 1890), she wrote *Aniwee, Or, The Warrior Queen: A Tale of the Araucanian Indians*, (London: Richard Henry, 1890) and *Izra, Or A Child of Solitude* (London: John Lang, 1906).

33. *The Woman's Herald*, 14 June 1890.

34. Dixie gave an account of this experience in "Modernities," *Modern Review* 3, no. 1 (1893): 32–33.

35. Traditionally a Chinese man adopts a style name that conveys the meaning of his personal name.

36. Hu Ji, 79.

37. Dixie, *Gloriana* 348.

38. A brief review of the fourth edition of *Gloriana* is carried in *Modern Review* 1, no. 2 (1890): 193.

39. There is one manuscript copy, and eighteen editions of *The Next Life* exist. For its textual history, see Sung, "The Narrative Art" 14–17. Since the 1970s, with a revived interest in singing-telling literature, Chen Duansheng's *Next Life* and its performed version adapted by Qin Jiwen, have been both available in print. Feminist reevaluation of women's *tanci* headed by Chen Yinke, Guo Moruo, Zhao Jingshen, and Tan Zhengbi become more influential than ever before. Toyoko Yoshida Chen devotes a chapter of her dissertation (1972) to an analysis of Chen Duansheng's *Next Life*. Although she recognizes Chen Duansheng as being more radical in feminist thinking than any other women writers of *tanci*, she fails to grasp the essential vision and spirit of *The Next Life*. She does not even mention Meng Lijun's poem written at the moment she discarded her female attire and put on the male guise, a poem that serves as a key to the book. Sung's dissertation (1988) seems to have overemphasized Meng Lijun's internal conflict between her love for a man and her desire to succeed as a man. Meng Lijun is never really tormented by her love for man or the duty of a proper wife, or piety to parents, but by the fixed order of *yang* over *yin* that deprives a woman of equal rights with men. Because Chen Duansheng could not express her rebellious thoughts in a straighforward way at that time, she resorts to subversive irony.

40. Chen Duansheng, 135.

41. Dixie, *Gloriana*, viii.

42. Michael R. Booth, *English Melodrama* (London: Herbert Jenkins, 1965), 13–14. For a discussion of *Gloriana* as a melodrama, see Nan Bowman Albinski, " 'The Law of Justice, of Nature, and of Right:' Victorian Feminist Utopias," in *Feminism, Utopia, and Narrative*, ed. Libby Falk Jones and Sarah Webster Goodwin (Knoxville: Univ. of Tennessee Press, 1990), 50–68.

43. Dixie, *Gloriana*, x.

44. Rachel Blau DuPlessis, "The Feminist Apologues of Lessing, Piercy, and Russ," *Frontiers: A Journal of Women Studies* 4, no. 1 (1979): 1.

45. *Auchendolly*, 21 May 1890.

46. *Women's Herald*, 9 June 1890.

47. Ibid., 5 Mar. 1890.

48. *The Atheneum*, 17 May 1890: 638.

49. Chen Yinke, 4.

50. A comparison of *The Destiny of The Next Life*, as a satirical epic, with Byron's *Don Juan* deserves an independent study. Interestingly, *The Next Life* is about one woman in a world of men, while *Don Juan* is about one man in a world of women.

51. Liu Chongyi, "Youxu" (Introduction), in Chen Duansheng, 19.

52. Guo Moruo, "Xu *Zaisheng Yuan* Qian Shiqi Juan Jiaoding Ben" (Preface to the edited seventeen books of *The Destiny of the Next Life*), *Guangming Ribao*, 7 Aug. 1961.

53. Hu Shi, Lin Yutang, and other critics consider *The Flowers in the Mirror*, by Li Ruzhen (1830), the first feminist utopia in China. They have neglected *The Next Life*.

54. N. P. Ricci, "The End/s of Woman," *Canadian Journal of Political and Social Theory* (French Fantasies) 11, no. 3 (1987), 12.

55. The story of Liang Shanbo and Zhu Yingtai originated in the Tang Dynasty. It developed in many versions and spread to Japan, Korea, and other Asian countries. See Lu Gong, ed., *Liang Shanbai he Zhu Yingtai Yanchang Gushi Ji* (A collection of

Liang Shanbai and Zhu Yingtai's tales in ballad form) (Shanghai: Guji, 1985). About Hua Mulan, see my introduction.

56. The tale of Hua Mulan is used in Maxine Hong Kingston's *The Woman Warrior* (New York: Knopf, 1976). But its narrator finally unravels the mother's confused message about the warrior-wife-slave and becomes a true feminist warrior through a painful separation from her mother.

57. For a detailed discussion about the significance of the utopia of outlaws in China, see Widmer, 157–82.

58. Chen Duansheng, 109.

59. See Wang Jianhui and Yi Xuejin, eds., *Zhongguo Wenhua Zhishi* (The essentials of Chinese culture) (Hubei: Renmin, 1989), 309–10.

60. In Chinese literary tradition, concealing sexual identity tends to be more political than comical. Compared with the Country of Women imagined by Luo Maodeng and Li Ruzhen, *The Next Life*'s elements of comedy produced by sexual inversion are less significant. A brilliant comedy of sexual inversion in Asian literature was written between 1196 and 1202 by an unknown Japanese woman, *The Changelings: A Classical Court Tale*, trans. Rosette F. Willig (Stanford: Stanford Univ. Press, 1983). For a comparative analysis of *The Next Life* and *The Changelings*, see Qingyun Wu, "Feminist Potentialities and Dilemmas: *The Changelings* and *The Destiny of the Next Life*," in *Proceeding of the Thirteenth International Symposium of Asian Studies* (Hong Kong: Asian Research Service, 1991), 211–21.

61. Liu Qingyun is the granddaughter of Liu Mengmei and Du Liniang, the fictional characters in *The Peony Pavilion*, a famous play by Tang Xianzu (1550–1617). Du Liniang falls in love with Liu Mengmei in a dream and dies of love for him; Liu Mengmei falls in love with Du Liniang when he picks up her portrait left before her death under the Peony Pavilion. Their love conquers death, and Du Liniang comes to life to marry Liu Mengmei.

62. Virginia Woolf, *Orlando* (New York: Harcourt Brace Jovanovich, 1956), 64.

63. Ibid., 188.

64. Ibid.

65. Albinski, "Female Cross-dressing," 4–5.

66. "Woman's Position," 232.

67. Chen Duansheng, 481.

68. Ibid., 955–96..

69. In "Thunder over the Lake" in *Women in China*, 60, Guisso observes, "Thus, in every age of Chinese history where Confucianism was exalted, the woman who survived, the woman who had age and the wisdom and experience which accompanied it, was revered, obeyed, and respected . . . even if her son were an emperor."

70. Chen Duansheng, 268.

71. Ibid., 670.

72. "Woman's Position," 226.

73. Dixie, *Gloriana*, 160.

74. Ibid., 160.

75. Ibid., 161.

76. "Women's Position," 228.

77. Thomas O. Beebee, "Going Clarissa's Will: Samuel Richardson's Legal Genres," *International Journal for the Semiotics of Law* 2, no. 5 (1989): 173.

78. Dixie, *Gloriana*, 24–31.

79. The quoted phrases are from Le Guin, 155–59.

80. Dixie, *Gloriana*, 3.

81. Ibid., x.

82. Ibid., 175.

83. Ibid., 181.

84. Simone de Beauvoir, *The Second Sex*, trans. H. M. Parshley (New York: Knopf, 1953), xix.

85. Chen Duansheng, 973.

86. The version edited by Liu Chongyi contains the three sequel books written by Liang Desheng. Liang provides a happy ending of marriage and birth. Her ending is obviously subversive to Chen Duansheng's utopia, enabling *The Next Life* to have been popular for so long without threatening any real social structures.

87. Guo Moruo, "*Zaisheng Yuan* Qian Shiqi Juan he Tade Zuozhe Chen Duansheng" (The first seventeen books of *The Destiny of the Next Life* and its author Chen Duansheng), *Guangming Ribao*, 4 May 1961.

88. Albinski, "Female Cross-dressing" 8–9.

89. Dixie, *Gloriana*, 128.

90. Ibid., 338.

91. Ibid., 136.

92. Ibid., 284.

93. Chen Duansheng, 514.

94. Ibid., 986.

95. Ibid., 1088.

96. Ibid., 817.

97. In Charlotte Perkins Gilman, *Herland* (1915; reprint, New York: Pantheon, 1979), 67, the character Jeff says, "Women are the natural cooperators, not men!"

98. Albinski, "The Law of Justice," 63.

99. Ricci, 11.

100. *The Women's Herald* 3 May 1890.

101. Dixie, *Gloriana*, ix.

102. Ibid., 293.

103. Helen Diner, *Mothers and Amazons: the First Feminine History of Culture*, ed. John Philip Lundin (New York: Julian, 1965), 128.

104. Dixie, *Gloriana*, 92.

105. Ibid., vii.

106. Ibid., 139.

107. Carol S. Pearson, "Beyond Governance: Anarchist Feminism in the Utopian Novels of Dorothy Bryant, Marge Piercy and Mary Staton," *Alternative Futures* 4, no. 1 (1981): 126.

108. Kessler, 13.

109. Jean Pfaelzer, *The Utopian Novel in America 1886–1896: the Politics of Form* (Pittsburgh: Univ. of Pittsburgh Press, 1984), 158.

110. Albinski, *Women's Utopias*, 16.

111. Guo Moruo, "*Zaisheng Yuan* Qian Shiqi Juan." *The Next Life* is an extremely subtle book that requires careful reading to perceive an intentional nature in its discrepancies. Though Guo Moruo is right to point out Chen's ideological restrictions, he misses ironical and satirical intentions in attacking a system by upholding its doctrines.

112. Dixie, *Gloriana*, 180, 204.

113. Florence Caroline Dixie, Interview, *Women's Penny Paper*, 12 Apr. 1890. This was the only English paper conducted, written, and published by women at that time.

114. *Personal Rights Journal* (June 1890): 61.
115. Dixie, *Gloriana*, 4.

4. Separation from the Patriarchal World:
The Destiny of the Flowers in the Mirror and *Herland*

1. Li Ruzhen, *Jinghua Yuan* (The destiny of the flowers in the mirror), ed. Zhangyou he, 2 vols. (Beijing: Renmin Wenxue, 1955). Li Ruzhen is known in English as Li Ju-chen, and an adapted translation of his novel is *The Flowers in the Mirror*, trans. Lin Tai-yi (Berkeley: Univ. of California Press, 1965).

2. Steven Goldberg, "The Universality of Patriarchy," in *Gender Sanity*, ed. Nicholas Davison (New York: Univ. Press of America, 1989): 136.

3. "Xiucai" is one who passes the imperial examination at the county level in the Ming and Qing dynasties.

4. The publication history of *The Flowers* proves that it has been a popular novel in both premodern and modern China. When first completed, it was circulated in manuscript. Meanwhile, Li carefully revised it until its publication in a wood block edition in 1828. In 1829, it was reprinted in Guangdong with 108 illustrations. In 1888, a lithographic edition appeared with new illustrations and a preface by Wang Tao. In 1923, a punctuated edition with a long introduction by Hu Shi was printed by Yadong Shuju. In 1955, a Beijing edition was published by the Renmin Wenxue. In 1983, a Taiwan edition was published by the Sanmin Shudian, with an introduction by You Xinxiong. I have used largely the Beijing edition for its academic quality. For more background information about Li Ruzhen and his novel, see Sun Jiaxun, *Jiahua Yuan Gong'an Bianyi* (Controversies on *The Flowers in the Mirror*) (Jinan: Qilu Shushe, 1984).

5. Nancy J. F. Evans, "Social Criticism in the Ch'ing: The Novel of *Ching-hua yuan*," *Papers on China* 13 (1970): 64.

6. The quotation is from Sun Zhichang's (Li Ruzhen's close friend) "Prefatory Poem" in the 1828 edition of *The Flowers*.

7. Li Ruzhen, 3.

8. See James J. Y. Liu, *Chinese Theories of Literature* (Chicago: Univ. of Chicago Press, 1975), 133. Liu quotes Hu Yinglin's words: "To draw an analogy with the flower in the mirror and the moon reflected in water: formal style and musical tone are the water and the mirror; inspired imagery and personal airs or spirit are [the reflections of] the moon and the flower."

9. Li Ruzhen, 772.

10. Ibid., 9.

11. Tang Ao, originally a Xiucai, achieves the title of Tanhua at the imperial examination. Because he is a friend of the loyalists who are against Wu Zetian, Wu Zetian deprives him of his Tanhua title. Ironically, the two Chinese characters of Tanhua literally mean "search for flowers"; Wu Zetian's punishment sends Tang Ao on his path to search for flowers abroad.

12. Frederick P. Brandauer, "Women in the *Ching-hua yuan*: Emancipation Towards a Confucian Ideal," *Journal of Asian Studies* 36 (1977): 684.

13. Lin Tai-yi, 6.

14. According to You Xinxiong, Li poses the conflict between the loyalists and Wu Zetian as a disguised conflict between the Manchu government and those who opposed the suppression of Confucian scholars, because Li intends to incite the oppressed Han people into overthrowing the Manchu dictatorship. *The Flowers'* sophisti-

cated allegory and theme of spiritual quest invite comparisons with Spenser's *Faerie Queene*. See H. C. Chang, *Allegory and Courtesy in Spenser: A Chinese View* (Edinburgh: Edinburgh Univ. Press, 1955). Also, Li Ruchen's lengthy discussions of phonetics, medicine, mathematics, chess, and other sciences have led to the treatment of *The Flowers* as a scholarly novel obsessed with a display of erudition, a characteristic of the premodern Chinese period as well as the Middle Ages in the West. In 1991, Mark Elvin published an analysis of Chinese life in Li's time, "The Inner World of 1830," *Daedalus* 120 (1991): 33–61.

15. Hu Shi, "*Jinghua Yuan* de Yinlun" (An Introduction to *The Flowers in the Mirror*), in *Hu Shi Wencun* (Works of Hu Shi) vol. 3, bk. 2 (Taibei: Yuandong Tushu, 1965), 433.

16. Lin Tai-yi, 7.

17. Evans, 63.

18. Brandauer, 660.

19. Hsia, C. T., "The Scholar-Novelist and Chinese Culture: A Reappraisal of *Ching hua yuan*," in *Chinese Narrative: Critical and Theoretical Essays*, ed. Andrew Plaks (Princeton: Princeton Univ. Press, 1977), 266–305. Hsia's interpretation influenced Hsin-sheng C. Kao's *Li Ju-chen* (Boston: Twayne, 1981), which provides a summary argument against the feminist reading of *The Flowers*, 93–101.

20. You Xinxiong, ed., *Jinghua Yuan* (The flowers in the mirror), by Li Ruzhen (Taiwan: Sanmin Shuju, 1983), 2.

21. In *Li Ju-chen* 16, Kao observes "The School of Han Learning, as it is referred to by Liang Ch'i-ch'ao and other Ch'ing scholars, derives its name from its emphasis on the study of the classics of Han (206 B.C.–A.D. 220), as well as Confucian canons, textual analysis, historical and exegetical studies, philology, epistemology, and phonetics. It is a reaction against the School of Mind and the late Ming dynasty, also known as the School of Lu Chiu-yuan (1139–1193) and Wang Shou-jen (1472–1529)."

22. "*Jinghua Yuan* de Yinlun," 433.

23. Mary A. Hill, *The Making of a Radical Feminist: 1860–1896* (Philadelphia: Temple Univ. Press, 1980), 14.

24. Ibid., 17.

25. See Dianne Hunter, "Hysteria, Psychoanalysis, and Feminism: The Case of Anna O," in *The (M)other Tongue*, ed. Shirley Nelson Garner et al. (Ithaca: Cornell Univ. Press, 1985), 89–115. The real name of Anna O, the inventor of the "talking cure," is Bertha Pappenheim. Like Gilman, Bertha possessed a powerful intellect and suffered hysteria when her potential career was threatened. She cured herself by talking about feminism and participating in the struggle for social reforms focused on women's liberation.

26. Correa Moylan Walsh, *Feminism* (New York: Harper and Row, 1962), 74.

27. Mary A. Hill, "Charlotte Perkins Gilman: A Feminist Struggle with Womanhood," *The Massachusetts Review* 21 (1980): 503.

28. Hill, *The Making*, xxxvii.

29. This is from the social settlement reformer Florence Kelley's letter to Charlotte Stetson on July 26, 1898, quoted in Hill, "Charlotte," 503.

30. Introduction, *Herland*, xii.

31. Albinski, *Women's Utopias*, 68.

32. "A Lost Feminist Utopian Novel" is the subtitle of *Herland* as published in book form in 1979.

33. Carol Pearson includes Marge Piercy's *Woman on the Edge of Time* and Le Guin's *Dispossessed* in her *Herland*-pattern.

34. Pearson found a *Herland*-pattern in seemingly divergent feminist utopias in her "Women's Fantasies and Feminist Utopias," *Frontiers* 1, no. 3 (1977), two years before *Herland* was republished.

35. Peter Fitting wrote several articles on feminist utopias. Among them is "For Men Only: a Guide to Reading Single-Sex Worlds," *Women's Studies* 14 (1987): 101–17.

36. Joanna Russ, "Recent Feminist Utopias," in *Future Female: A Critical Anthology*, ed. Marleen S. Barr (Bowling Green: Bowling Green State Univ. Popular Press, 1981), 72.

37. Ibid., 76. Russ summarizes the main features of contemporary feminist utopias as follows: "Classless, without government, ecologically minded, with a strong feeling for the natural world, quasi-tribal in feeling and quasi-family in structure, the societies of these stories are sexually permissive."

38. Libby Falk Jones and Sarah Webster Goodwin, ed., *Feminism, Utopia, and Narrative* (Knoxville: Univ. of Tennessee Press, 1990), 119.

39. Ann J. Lane, "Introduction," *The Charlotte Perkins Gilman Reader*, (New York: Pantheon, 1980), xvi.

40. Frances Bartkowski, *Feminist Utopias* (Lincoln: Univ. of Nebraska Press, 1989), 28.

41. Christopher P. Wilson, "Charlotte Perkins Gilman's Steady Burgers: the Terrain of Herland," *Women's Studies* 12 (1986): 271–92.

42. Hoda M. Zaki, "Utopia and Ideology in *Daughters of a Coral Dawn* and Contemporary Feminist Utopias," *Women's Studies* 14, no 2 (1987): 129.

43. In Chinese history, only the Heavenly Kingdom of Great Peace (1851–1864) held examinations for women.

44. Li Ruzhen, 284.

45. Ibid., 426.

46. After the historical Wu Zetian died in November of the same year she was dethroned, the patriarchal court took away her title of emperor and only recognized her as "Zetian, Holy Dowager." See Sima Guang, *Zizhi Tongjian* (Comprehensive mirror for aid in government) (Shanghai: Feiying Guan, 1888), chap. 208.

47. Li Ruzhen, 771.

48. Ibid., 231.

49. Ibid., 232.

50. See Chunfeng Wenyi, ed., *Caizi Jiaren Xiaoshuo Shulin* (Essays on the novels of scholars and beauties) (Shenyang: Chunfeng Wenyi, 1985).

51. Li Ruzhen, 373; Lin Yutang's translation in "Feminist Thought in Ancient China," *Tien Hsia Monthly* 1, no. 2 (1935), 150.

52. See Gao Shiyu, "Cong Tangdai Nüxing de Shehui Mianmao Tan Wu Zetian Chengdi" (Wu Zetian's throne and the social conditions for women in the Tang Dynasty); Niu Zhiping, "Wu Zetian he Tangdai Funü" (Wu Zetian and the Tang women), in *Wu Zetian yu Qianling*, ed. Zhang Yuliang and Hu Ji (Wu Zetian and Qianling tombs) (Shanxi: Sanqin, n.d.), 27–37, 38–46.

53. Li Ruzhen, 764–65.

54. Ibid., 78.

55. Ibid., 113.

56. Nearly all argument against feminist readings of *The Flowers* is based on the assumption that Li advocates Ban Zhao's Four Virtues for Women; therefore, I provide a more detailed discussion in this area.

57. Ban Zhao, "Nüjie," in *Zhongguo Lidai Funü Zuopin Xuan* (Selected writings of Chinese women in history), ed. Su Zhecong (Shanghai Guji, 1987), 479.

58. Ibid., 480.

59. Li Ruzhen, 525.

60. Ibid., 232.

61. Ibid., 241.

62. Yan Zixiao resembles Supergirl in Western science fiction; she follows Tang Guichen to Little Penglai.

63. Li Ruzhen, 1.

64. Ibid. 717–18.

65. Gilman, *Herland*, 25.

66. Margaret Miller, "The Ideal Woman in Two Feminist Science-Fiction Utopias," *Science-Fiction Studies* 10 (1983): 192.

67. Ibid.

68. Gilman, *Herland*, 67.

69. Gilman, *With Her in Ourland*, 323.

70. S. M. Gearhart, "Future Visions: Today's Politics: Feminist Utopias in Review," in *Women in Search of Utopia: Mavericks and Mythmakers*, ed. Ruby Rohrlich and Elaine Hoffman Baruch (New York: York Press, 1984), 297.

71. Gilman, *Herland*, 121.

72. Ibid., 132.

73. Ibid.

74. Ibid., 137.

75. Ibid., 128.

76. Ibid., 15.

77. Ibid., 98.

78. Ibid., 59.

79. Ibid., 137.

80. Ibid., 89.

81. In Gilman's novel, "our world" refers to the whole world that we live in, not just Asia.

82. Gilman, *With Her in Ourland*, 94.

83. Ibid., 73.

84. Ibid.

85. Ibid., 137.

86. Ibid., 323.

87. Ibid., 325.

88. Luo Hongju and her mother escaped from China in fear of Wu Zetian's persecution, while Yin Ruohua came to China to escape the persecution of her mother King's concubines. Tang Ao rescued Yao Zhixin when she was surrounded by male merchants who wanted to kill her because she taught local women silk culture and harmed their kapok trade. Men's resentment at women's participation in productivity is brought to light here. It seems that women's health was a big problem in Li's time. Apart from the case of Lan Yin, illness caused about ten talented girls to fail to attend the court examination on time.

89. Hu Shi, "A Chinese 'Gulliver' on Woman's Rights," *The People's Tribune*, n.s., 7, no. 2 (1934): 126.

90. Li Ruzhen, 525.

91. Sung, "The Chinese," 68.

92. Li Ruzhen, 13.

93. Ibid., 26.

94. Ibid.

95. The old Confucian rituals demanded that the son observe three years of funeral rites for the father but only one year for the mother. Wu Zetian challenged its gender unfairness. From the hardship of bringing up a child, Wu Zetian appealed to the court for equal respect for the mother and succeeded. See Niu, 41.

96. Hu Ji, 45.

97. Su Hui's palindrome (huwen xuanjitu) woven on a tapestry is not a gesture of compromise or exaltation of Ban Zhao's feminine ideal, as suggested by Kao and Brandauer. Su wove this tapestry when she refused to follow her husband with his concubine to his new post. The content of the poems tells of Su's poetic pleasure in solitude, gives political advice to her husband, and shows her true feelings for him, with not a word of pleading or seduction. Her effort is aimed at achieving a certain communication between man and woman. In *The Flowers*, Wu Zetian distributed Su's palindrome all over the country with a preface by herself. Shi Youtan discovered a way to get two hundred poems out of the palindrome, and Ai Qunfang read another hundred poems by viewing it from a different angle.

98. Li Ruzhen, 356.

99. Ibid., 308–9; translated by Hu Shi, "A Chinese 'Gulliver,' " 127.

100. Gilman, *Herland*, 111–12.

101. Ibid., 112–13.

102. Ibid., 115.

103. Ibid., 104.

104. Ibid., 105.

105. Ibid., 106.

106. Ibid., 104.

107. Patricia Huckle, "Women in Utopias," in *The Utopian Vision: Seven Essays on the Quincentennial of Sir Thomas More*, ed. E.D.S. Sullivan (San Diego: San Diego State Univ. Press, 1983), 118.

108. Van observes: " 'We' and 'we' and 'we'—it was so hard to get her [Ellador] to be personal." Later, Ellador explains that "she had to 'think in we's' " *Herland*, 126, 129.

109. Ibid., 68.

110. In her *Conflicting Stories: American Women Writers at the Turn into the Twentieth Century* (New York: Oxford Univ. Press, 1991), 34, Elizabeth Ammons says, "Gilman, an unreflecting racist, put gender first." In *Herland*, Gilman imagines a new race produced from one mother in order to set up a civilization uncontaminated by the known male-dominated civilization. She emphasizes the elimination of women who have known men, as well as men. Her use of "pure stalk" to describe this new race seems to be out of her paramount gender concern. However, it may betray her unconscious racism. For the issue of Gilman's racism, see Susan S. Lanser, "Feminist Criticism, 'The Yellow Wallpaper,' and the Politics of Color in America," *Feminist Studies* 15, no. 3 (1989): 415–42.

111. Li Ruzhen, 78.

112. Ibid., 504.

113. Ibid., 109.

114. Ibid., 131. On the other side of the fan is Su Hui's palindrome, as copied by Tingting of her own accord.

115. Liu Zaifu, and Lin Gang, *Chuantong yu Zhongguoren* (Tradition and the Chinese) (Hong Kong: Sanlian, 1988), 35.

116. Li Ruzhen, 760.

117. Kao, 68.

118. The Three Religions refer to Daoism, Confucianism, and Buddhism. The Nine Classes restrictively refer to the nine schools of thought (the Confucians, the Daoists, the Yin-Yang, the Legalists, the Logicians, the Mohists, the Political Strategists, the Eclectics, and the Agriculturists) and broadly represents all sorts of people.

119. Kao, 100.

120. Sandra M. Gilbert and Susan Gubar, No Man's Land: The Place of the Woman Writer in the Twentieth Century (New Haven: Yale Univ. Press, 1989), 74.

121. Ann J. Lane, xiv.

122. Gilman, Herland, 94.

123. Frederick Engels, The Origin of the Family, Private Property and the State (New York: International Publishers, 1972), 121–23.

124. Lao Tzu (Lao Zi), The Tao of Power (Dao De Jing), trans. R. L. Wing (New York: Dolphin, 1986), Chap. 80

125. Forest Lin, "Utopias East and West: The Relationship Between Ancient and Modern Chinese Ideals," Alternative Futures 3, no. 3 (1980): 16.

126. S. B. Knoll, "Form or Content? Reflections and the Concept of Utopia in Asian and West European Thought," Alternative Futures 3, no. 3 (1980): 12.

127. Ho, "Why Utopias Fall," 93.

128. Li Ruzhen, 106–8.

129. Gilman, Herland, 59.

130. Gearhart, "Future Visions," 305.

131. Barr uses the term "feminist fabulation" to group contemporary feminist utopias in the genre of science fiction. These utopias are "replete with visions which are disconcerting to the patriarchy (planets populated by lesbian separatists, for example)." See Marleen S. Barr, "Food for Postmodern Thought: Isak Dinesen's Female Artists as Precursors to Contemporary Feminist Fabulators," in Feminism, Utopia, and Narrative, ed. Libby Falk Jones and Sarah Webster Goodwin (Knoxville: Univ. of Tennessee Press, 1990), 21; Barr, Feminist Fabulation: Space/Postmodern Fiction (Iowa: Univ. of Iowa, 1992), 22–24.

132. Frye, "Varieties," 38.

133. Gearhart, "Future Visions," 300–301.

134. Ann J. Lane, xiv.

135. Lesbian separatism in feminist utopias does not refer to the limited, genital, or clinical definitions of lesbianism. It is rather a female worldview or female consciousness that holds radical politics of marginality with equal "strength, independence and resistance to patriarchy." Bonnie Zimmerman, "What Has Never Been: An Overview of Lesbian Feminist Criticism," in Making a Difference: Feminist Literary Criticism, ed. Gayle Greene and Coppélia Kahn (New York: Methuen, 1985), 184.

136. Ann J. Lane, xi.

5. From Matrilineality to Anarchism:
The Remote Country of Women and The Dispossessed

1. Bai Hua, "My Footprints," Chinese Literature 2 (1989): 118.

2. Bai Hua, Yuanfang Youge Nü'er Guo (The remote country of women) (Beijing: Renmin Wenxue, 1988); (Taiwan: Sanmin, 1988). This book has used the text of the Beijing edition and Bai Hua's "Zixu" in the Taiwan edition. The Taiwan edition also contains a map of the Country of Women, some photos of the Mosuo Community (on

which the novel is based), a brief biography of Bai Hua, and a bibliography of his works. See also its English version, *The Remote Country of Women*, trans. Qingyun Wu and Thomas O. Beebee (Honolulu: Univ. of Hawaii Press, 1994).

3. Jiang Qing, Zhang Chunqiao, Yao Wenyuan, and Wang Hongwen are known as "the Gang of Four," the clique who attempted to seize state power during the Cultural Revolution.

4. Bai Hua, "Zixu," 1.

5. Inspired by the matrilineal model, Bai Hua made two trips to a Mosuo Community along the Lugu Lake in 1985 and 1986; in fact, the Taiwan edition of *Country of Women* carries color photos of his visits. In December 1987, I wrote to Bai Hua to ask him why he wrote a feminist utopia. In his reply, he refused to call *Country of Women* a utopia (perhaps because of traditional disparagement of the utopian genre in China), insisting that he is a realist writer and that the Country of Women that he wrote about actually exists. Nevertheless, comparing the two books of scientific investigation with Bai Hua's novel demonstrates that Bai Hua's Country of Women has been idealized. Although he presents the Mosuo myths, rituals, and customs truthfully, he omits, through artful selection, some unfavorable elements that might endanger his fictional utopia. According to the two investigations, the Mosuo Community experiences problems with the overworking of women and the psychological repression of men. A part of its Naxi ethnic group has already been converted to modern monogamy.

6. Bai hua, "Zixu," 2.

7. Joe Debolt, ed., *Ursula K. Le Guin: Voyager to Inner Lands and to Outer Space* (London: Kennikat, 1979), 15.

8. About her relationship with her husband, Le Guin says:

It wasn't like he would say, "Well, I feel good today so I stay with the kids." I'd say, "I've got to finish the story"; and he'd say, "Okay, I'll take them." That kind of thing is very important and I don't think you can make it work with marriage contracts. Your heart has got to be in it. One person cannot do two full-time jobs, and we had three of them: my writing, his teaching and writing, and mothering. But two persons can do three full-time jobs. They really can. That's why I'm so strong on partnership. It can be a great thing.

See Win McCormack and Anne Mendel, "Creating Realistic Utopias: The Obvious Trouble with Anarchism Is Neighbors," *Seven Days*, 11 April 1977, 40.

9. Jewell Parker Rhodes, "Ursula Le Guin's *Left Hand of Darkness*: Androgyny and the Feminist Utopia," in *Women and Utopia*, ed. Marleen S. Barr and Nicholas D. Smith (Lanham: Univ. Press of America, 1983), 108.

10. Tom Moylan, *Demand the Impossible: Science Fiction and the Utopian Imagination* (New York: Methuen, 1986), 113.

11. John Fekete, "The Dispossessed and Triston: Act and System in Utopian Science Fiction," *Science-Fiction Studies* 18 (1979): 131.

12. Moylan, 114.

13. Moylan's criticism of Le Guin is largely based on John Fekete's view. In "Le Guin's Science Fiction Fantasies Defended," in *Inventing the Future: Science Fiction in the Context of Cultural History and Literary Theory*, ed. Ib Johansen and Peter Ronnov-Jessen (Aarhus, Denmark: Univ. of Aarhus, 1985), 59–72, Christen Kold Thomsen, using the theory developed in Rosemary Jackson's *Fantasy: The Literature of*

Subversion (New York: Methuen, 1981), attributes Fekete's interpretation to his confinement to reading conventions as well as his ignorance of Le Guin's intentions.

14. Daphne Patai, "Beyond Defensiveness: Feminist Research Strategies," in *Women and Utopia*, ed. Marleen S. Barr and Nicholas D. Smith (Lanham, Md.: Univ. Press of America, 1983), 156, 159.

15. Le Guin, *The Language*, 155.

16. Ibid., 95–96.

17. Women critics, such as Pearson, Russ, Mellor, and Keinhorst, have all discussed *The Dispossessed* as a feminist utopia.

18. Bai Hua, *Country of Women*, 10.

19. Ibid., 9.

20. Ibid., 27.

21. Ibid., 64.

22. Ibid., 340.

23. Talking about the formation of her concept of anarchism, Le Guin admitted to the influence of Engels and Marx. See *The Language*, 95.

24. Le Guin, *The Dispossessed*, 173.

25. Ibid., 14.

26. Ibid., 173

27. Ibid., 59, 60.

28. Ibid., 181.

29. Ibid., 173.

30. Ibid., 236.

31. Marcuse argues, in *An Essay on Liberation* (Boston: Beacon, 1969), 3–4, that "What is denounced as 'utopia' is no longer that which has 'no place' and cannot have any place in the historical universe, but rather that which is blocked from coming about by the power of the established societies."

32. Le Guin, *The Dispossessed*, 171.

33. Ibid., 171–72.

34. Le Guin, *The Language*, 137.

35. Hsun Tzu (Xu Zi), *Hsun Tzu*, trans, Burton Watson, (New York: Columbia Univ. Press, 1963), 156.

36. Although the Chinese Cultural Revolution was defeated by the political cliques's rivalry for the state power, it stimulated the radical thoughts, including Western feminism, which were channelled into a genuine cultural revolution of the 1980s.

37. Bai Hua, "Zixu," 3.

38. Bai Hua, "Mama ya! Mama" (Mom! Mom), *Shouhuo* 4 (1980): 6.

39. Bai Hua, "Zixu," 3.

40. Le Guin, *The Dispossessed*, 281. Peter Fitting reads Le Guin's "The Ones Who Walk Away from Omelas" as an attack "on the utopian ideal itself and on those who believe in the possibility of social change." See, "Readers and Responsibilities: A Reply to Kenneth M. Roemer," *Utopian Studies* 2, no. 1–2 (1991): 28. Le Guin's story is a prelude to "The Day Before the Revolution," which is a prelude to *The Dispossessed*. The Odonians are the walkers, and Keng's comment on Shevek proves that Le Guin is just like Fitting—a human utopist and a believer in social change.

41. Le Guin, *The Language*, 163–64. In 1987 Le Guin revised her definition of the female principle, "The 'female principle' has historically been anarchic; that is, anarchy has historically been identified as female. The domain allotted to women—'the family,' for example—is the area of order without coercion, rule by custom not by force.

Men have reserved the structures of social power to themselves (and those few women whom they admit to it on male terms, such as queens and prime ministers); men make the wars and peaces, men make, enforce, and break the laws." See Le Guin's *Dancing at the Edge of the World: Thoughts of Words, Women, Places* (New York: Grove, 1989), 11–12.

42. Bai Hua, *Country of Women*, 52.

43. Ibid., 5.

44. Gilman, *Herland*, 238.

45. Le Guin, *The Language*, 162.

46. Pearson, "Beyond Governance," 126.

47. Le Guin, *The Dispossessed*, 283.

48. Ibid., 285.

49. Ibid., 135.

50. Ibid., 288.

51. Ibid., 22.

52. Ibid., 199.

53. Ibid., 24.

54. Ibid., 183.

55. Ibid., 5.

56. Bai Hua, *Country of Women*, 208. Mosuonians have a taboo about intercourse within the same community; but it seems that a mother and daughter's having an affair with the same man is permissible.

57. Ibid., 80.

58. Ibid., 333.

59. Ibid., 334.

60. Ibid., 56.

61. Ibid., 240.

62. Ibid., 336.

63. Le Guin, *The Dispossessed*, 14.

64. Bai Hua, *Country of Women*, 10.

65. Le Guin, *The Language*, 165–66.

66. Bai Hua, *Country of Women*, 341.

67. Ibid., 8–9.

68. Ibid., 9.

69. Ibid., 337–38.

70. Le Guin, *The Dispossessed*, 80.

71. Ibid., 150.

72. Russ, "Recent Feminist Utopias," 71.

73. Robert Scholes, "A Footnote to Russ's Recent Feminist Utopias," in *Future Females: A Critical Anthology*, ed. Marleen S. Barr (Bowling Green: Bowling Green State Univ. Popular Press, 1981), 87.

74. Engels, 120.

75. Ibid., 237.

76. Yao and Shun were the first rulers of Chinese society, over four thousand years ago. According to a Chinese legend, E Huang and Nü Ying were Shun's wives. When Shun died on the path of inspection to the south, E Huang and Nü Ying ran to the Xiang River and wailed along its edge. They both jumped into the river and drowned themselves.

77. Bai Hua, *Country of Women*, 60.

78. Annette Keinhorst, "Emancipatory Projection: an Introduction to Women's Critical Utopias." *Women's Studies* 14 (1987): 92.

79. For an analytic study of anarchist feminism, see Pearson, "Beyond Governance"; Lyman Tower Sargent, "A New Anarchism: Social and Political Ideas in Some Recent Feminist Eutopias," in *Women and Utopia*, ed. Marleen S. Barr and Nicholas D. Smith (New York: Univ. Press of America, 1983), 3–33. Sargent includes studies of utopias by Le Guin, Alexander, Russ, and Charnas.

80. Le Guin, *The Dispossessed*, 77–78.

81. Le Guin, *The Wind's Twelve Quarters* (New York: Harper & Row, 1975), 285.

82. Lao Zi, chap. 80. This quotation from Lao Zi has become a well-known expression in China today; it indicates isolation or extreme lack of communication.

83. Le Guin, *The Dispossessed*, 77.

84. Bai Hua, *Country of Women*, 327.

85. Le Guin, *The Dispossessed*, 61.

86. Ibid., 267.

87. Ibid.

88. Ibid., 177.

89. Ursula Le Guin, "The Day Before the Revolution," in *The Wind's Twelve Quarters* (New York: Harper & Row, 1975), 275.

90. Ibid., 303.

91. Ibid., 241.

92. Ibid., 42–43.

93. Ibid., 208.

94. Jack Zipes, *Breaking the Magic Spell: Radical Theories of Folk and Fairy Tales* (London: Heinemann, 1979), 129.

95. Marcuse, *An Essay*, 4.

96. Le Guin, *The Dispossessed*, 197.

97. Ibid.

98. The demand for sex and food as basic human rights is exceptionally high in post-Mao fiction, as a reaction to the previous puritanical politics. However, most Chinese writers, like Bai Hua, reject homosexuality as unnatural. Bai Hua's Mosuo Community shows no sign of homosexual relationships.

99. Le Guin, *The Dispossessed*, 179.

100. Rafail Nudelman, "An Approach to the Structure of Le Guin's SF," *Science-Fiction Studies* 2 (1975): 219.

101. Bloch, 1228.

102. Ibid.

103. Ibid., 1225.

104. Joseph Needham, *Science and Civilization in China* (Cambridge: Cambridge Univ. Press, 1956), 2: 59.

105. See Elizabeth Cummins Cogell, "Taoist Configurations: *The Dispossessed*," in *Ursula K. Le Guin: Voyager to Inner Lands and to Outer Space*, ed. Joe DeBolt (London: Kennikat, 1979), 153–79.

106. Le Guin, *The Dispossessed*, 230.

107. Ibid., 60.

108. Charlotte Spivack, *Ursula Le Guin* (Boston: Twayne, 1984), 25.

109. Ibid., 50.

110. Cogell, 154.

111. Dena C. Bain, "The *Tao Te Ching* as Background to the Novels of Ursula K. Le Guin," in *Ursula Le Guin*, ed. Herald Bloom (New York: Chelsea House, 1986), 212.

112. Zhuang Zi, "Zaiyou," *Zhuang Zi* (Taibei: Taiwan Shangwu, 1968).
113. Bloch, 1228, 1230.
114. Lao Zi, chap. 57.
115. Arthur Waley, *Three Ways of Thought in Ancient China* (Garden City: Doubleday, 1956), 13–14.
116. Needham, 103.
117. Lao Zi, chap. 2.
118. Lao Zi, chap. 18.
119. Le Guin, *The Dispossessed*, 112.
120. Ibid., 278.
121. Ibid., 279.
122. Ibid.
123. Lao Zi, chap. 58.
124. Le Guin, *The Dispossessed*, 37.
125. Ibid., 212.
126. Marcuse, *An Essay*, 5.
127. Le Guin, *The Dispossessed*, 304–305.
128. Holmes Welch, *Taoism: The Parting of the Way* (Boston: Beacon, 1966), 65.
129. Lao Zi, chap. 52.
130. Le Guin, *The Dispossessed*, 68.
131. Needlam, 75.
132. Le Guin, *The Dispossessed*, 226.
133. Ibid., 309.
134. Peter Kropotkin influenced her with communist anarchism, and Paul Goodman with the concept of an integrated community. Emma Goldman is the model for Odo, her anarchist woman leader. For a detailed discussion, see Kingsley Widmer's "The Dialectics of Utopianism: Le Guin's The Dispossessed," *Liberal and Fine Arts Review* 3, no. 1–2 (1983): 1–11; Victor Urbanowicz, "Personal and Political in *The Dispossessed*," in *Ursula Le Guin*, ed. Herald Bloom (New York: Chelsea House, 1986), 145–54. Also, in his "New Anarchism," Sargent offers a concise discussion of historical anarchist theories and feminist utopian anarchism.
135. Bain, 211. I agree with Bain's observation: "The Chinese sages taught through poetic paradox, not through the rational dualism of analysis and synthesis, and the importance of Ursula Le Guin's contribution to science fiction lies in her ability to use a distinctly Western art form to communicate the essence that is Tao."
136. Le Guin, *The Dispossessed*, 225.
137. Lao Zi, quoted from Needham, 37.
138. Ursula K. Le Guin, *Always Coming Home* (New York: Harper & Row, 1985), ix.
139. After the June 4 incident in 1989, a writer under the pen name of Bao Mi wrote a three-volume dystopia, *Huang Huo* (Yellow peril) (Port Credit, Ontario: Canada Mirror Books, 1991). It predicts the total distruction of China and the rest of the world by energy crisis, population explosion, power struggle, and nuclear wars and foresees the birth of a new civilization that is based on a green philosophy, underlined by Daoism.

6. Influence, Decline, and Hope

1. Bao Jialin. "Li Ruzhen de Nannü Pingdeng Sixiang" (Li Ruzhen's ideas of equality between men and women), *Shihuo Yuekan Fukan* 1, no. 12 (1972): 12–19.

2. Chang Hui-chuan, 201.

3. Ibid.

4. Qin Jin, *Jingwei Shi* (Pebbles that fill up the sea), in *Qiu Jin Ji* (Works of Qiu Jin) (Hongkong: Changfeng Tushu, 1974), 117–60.

5. Qiu Jin's married life was very unhappy. Although she was closely associated with many male revolutionaries after she deserted her home, she never sought love with men; instead, her close relationships with several women were quite noticeable. The day she changed into male dress, she gave her wedding shirt and shoes to her sworn sister Wu Zhiying, in a bold lesbian gesture. In *The Next Life*, Chen Duansheng imagined a woman marrying a woman and used four pages to describe Meng Lijun's attraction to Su Yingxue's beauty. In *The Pebbles*, Qiu Jin's portrayal of the love between Liang Xiaoyu and Huang Jurui involves emotion, physical appearance, and political fate.

6. Guo Yanli, ed. *Qiu Jin Yanjiu Ziliao* (Research references on Qiu Jin) (Jinan: Shandong Jiaoyu, 1987), 24–25.

7. For more information, see Mary Backus Rankin, "The Emergence of Women at the End of the Ch'ing: The Case of Ch'iu Jin," in *Women in Chinese Society*, ed. Margery Wolf and Roxane Witke (Stanford: Standford Univ. Press, 1975), 39–66.

8. Qiu Jin sponsored, edited, and published *Journal of the Chinese Women* in 1907. *Pebbles that Fill up the Sea* was written for the journal. Its first six chapters were believed to be carried in Volume 3; the Qiu Jin Museum in Zhejiang has only the first two volumes.

9. In the 1980s, there appeared feminist criticism of Chinese texts akin to the Western "Images of Women" approach. This kind of critical interest is unbated. In 1990, there appeared a new kind of feminist criticism, which might be classified as "Female Consciousness" or Chinese gynocritics. The "Images of Women" criticism deals largely with women in works by men, while the "Feminist Consciousness" criticism approaches exclusively women's works.

10. Nearly all Western feminist utopias of the twentieth century are written in the form of science fiction. In China, science fiction, an alien flower transplanted from the Western soil, is "in the bud, and has not reached its growth period." It has been treated either as nonserious, or juvenile literature, or as a kind of popular science writing, whose authors should be scientists and whose readers must have scientific knowledge. However, there are writers of science fiction like Zheng Wenguang, who gradually realized that "all science fiction is about the present" and "the focus of these works is the present, contemporary men's and women's nature and weaknesses." Although the editor in chief of *Science-Fiction World*, the only magazine of science fiction in China today, is a woman, a genre seems to have not been employed for feminist purposes. See Yang Xiao, "From SF World to World SF in China," *LOCUS* 28, no., 1 (1992): 43; Zheng Wenguang, "Speech by Zheng Wenguang," *LOCUS* 28, no. 1 (1992): 43.

11. There are women utopian writers like Marge Piercy, author of *Woman on the Edge of Time*, who treat gender as the product of society and culture and whose speculative imagination embraces a larger and more complex social reality.

12. See Peter Fitting, "The Turn from Utopia in Recent Feminist Fiction," in *Feminism, Utopia, and Narrative*, ed. Libby Falk Jones, and Sarah Webster Goodwin (Knoxville: Univ. of Tennessee Press, 1990), 141–58; Fitting, "Reconsiderations of the Separatist Paradigm in Recent Feminist Science Fiction," *Science-Fiction Studies* 19, no. 1 (1992): 32–48. In my correspondence with Lyman T. Sargent, I learned that

feminist utopias presently are "still one of the largest, if not still the largest category of utopias." Nevertheless, feminist utopias are a barometer of the changing feminism at large in society. Fitting's observation of the decline in the production of feminist utopias since 1985, and his warning against rejection of feminist utopianism or "backing away from the utopian hopes and dreams of the 1970s," are in accord with the general situation of postfeminism.

13. Antifeminist utopia in the West followed in the wake of feminist utopia. Pfaelzer, in *The Utopian Novel*, discusses three anti-feminist-utopias of the 19th century. Albinski, in her *Women's Utopias*, extends the discussion of antifeminist utopias, especially by women, into the twentieth century, though her discussion is scattered and lacks a systematic analysis. In *"Amor Vincit Foeminam:* The Battle of the Sexes in Science Fiction," *Science Fiction Studies* 7 (1980): 2–15, Joanna Russ covers ten antifeminist utopias by male writers of the 1920s, 1960s, and 1970s. The border between a feminist utopia and an antifeminist utopia in the 1980s sometimes becomes blurred. For instance, Bradley's *Ruin of Isis* and Pamela Sargent's *Shore of Women* are criticized as antifeminist utopias by Sarah Lefanu and Fitting, respectively, while they are received as feminist utopias by some other critics.

14. In *Future Females*, xi, Barr describes the correlation between feminist utopian writing and feminist theory: "As soon as her lips part, two fiery steeds, a dark horse named Speculative Fiction and an energetic mare named Feminist Theory, also appear. Feminist Theory is tied to her right wrist; Speculative Fiction to her right."

15. Carol Thomas Neely, "Constructing the Subject: Feminist Practice and the New Renaissance Discourses," *English Literary Renaissance* 18 (1988): 14.

16. Women in Jiangyong County, located in the southern part of Hunan Province in China, have used a language of their own in writing for generations; but their social structure remains patriarchal.

17. Foucault, 114.

18. Pearson, "Beyond," 126.

19. Jones and Goodwin, 121. *The Ruins of Isis* is not consciously antifeminist. In fact, critics such as Libby Falk Jones consider it a feminist utopia with an ambiguous nature that attempts to "puncture the facade of male/female equality in the unity" through the characters' relationships, actions, and responses. Bradley invents Isis, however, as a matriarchal society whose male oppression imitates present-day female oppression. This type of role reversal in feminist utopias is problematic.

20. Tania Modleski, *Feminism Without Women: Culture and Criticism in a "Postfeminist" Age* (New York: Routledge, 1991), 3.

21. Fitting, "The Turn," 156.

22. Fang Ruhao, 315–19. For a more detailed translation of the ten prohibitions, see Keith McMahon, *Causality and Containment in Seventeenth-Century Chinese Fiction* (T'ong Pao) (New York: E. J. Brill, 1988), 114–15.

23. During Barbara Hendrishke's visit to China in 1982, she found the comments on women writers by Liu Xicheng, a coeditor of an anthology of women's literature, to possess "a rather shocking similarity to the narrow framework through which Western male literary criticism has for a long time approached works written by women," remarking further that "the expectations of the Chinese public towards women's literature do not encourage feminist writing." See Barbara Hendrischke, "Feminism in Contemporary Chinese Women's Literature," in *Women and Literature in China*, edited by Anna Gerstlacher, Ruth Keen, Wolfang Kubin, Margit Miosga and Jenny Schon (Bochum: Studienverlag, 1985), 403, 404. With the vigorous growth of feminist literature in

China, antifeminist criticism has become quite aggressive since the late 1980s. I have cited numerous examples of misogynous criticism of women writers, such as Zhang Jie, Wang Anyi, and Zhang Kangkang, in my paper "Validity of Western Feminist Theories in Interpreting Chinese Texts," presented at the Second Conference of the American Association of Chinese Comparative Literature (Univ. of California, Los Angeles) in 1992. Although Chinese women writers and critics try to avoid offending men by an overt feminist spearatism, Chinese male readers already feel threatened and offended. In "Nüxing Wenxue Tengqi Hou de Shiluo" (The pitfalls after the rise of feminist literature), *Wenxue Pinglunjia* (Jinan) 3 (1990), 25, Li Xiaofeng expresses a general antifeminist sentiment: "Right from its birth, feministm of the New Period [1979–1989] has been influenced by Western Feminist theories and Freud's theories on sexual drive and it has gone astray because of transplanting those theories through superficial inter-pretations. . . . In order to 'save themselves,' the awakening women all take fictive anti-men as their starting point."

24. Qi Ming, "Nüren de Jiazhi: Gongguan zai Zhongguo" (The value of women: ladies of public relations in China), *Zhongguo Zuojia* 44, no. 2 (1992): 45.

25. Eisler, 193.

26. Kolodny, 464–65.

27. For detailed discussion, see Jan Relf, "Women in Retreat: The Politics of separatism in Women's Literary Utopias," *Utopian Studies* 2, no. 1–2 (1991): 131–46.

28. Le Guin, *The Dispossessed*, 141.

29. In order to speculate upon what is "simply human," Le Guin creates a world devoid of sex distinction. If the Herland-type utopias show a retreat from the real world politics, Le Guin's utopia, devoid of sex distinction, reveals a shunning from the real problems of women. This perhaps sheds light on Le Guin's turn to matrilineal visions in *Always Coming Home*, when she became more radical in feminist thinking in the 1980s.

30. I thank Carol F. Kessler for this simile.

31. "Beishan Jing," in *Shan Hai Jing* (The wonders of the mountains and rivers), ed. Yuan Ke (Shanghai: Guji, 1985), 69.

Bibliography

Abé, Kobo. *Inter Ice Age 4*. Translated by E. Dale Saunders. Tokyo: Turtle, 1971.

Adkins, E. C. S. "*Ching Hua Yuan*–China's *Gulliver's Travels*." *China Society Annual* (1954): 34–37.

Albinski, Nan Bowman. "Female Cross-dressing in the Novels of Lady Florence Dixie." In *Macquarie Conference Papers 1989*, edited by Catherine Waters and Helen Yardley, 3–10. Sydney: Macquarie Univ., 1989.

———. " 'The Laws of Justice, of Nature, and of Right:' Victorian Feminist Utopias." In *Feminism, Utopia, and Narrative*, edited by Libby Falk Jones and Sarah Webster Goodwin, 50–68. Knoxville: Univ. of Tennessee Press, 1990.

———. *Women's Utopias in British and American Fiction*. New York: Routledge, 1988.

Aldridge, A. Owen. "Utopianism in World Literature." *Tamkang Review* 14, no. 1–4 (Aug. 1983–Sum 1984): 11–21.

Alexander, Thea Plym. *2150 A. D.* Tempe: Macro, 1971.

Allen, Jeffner. "An Introduction to Patriarchal Existentialism: A Proposal for a Way Out of Existential Patriarchy." In *The Thinking Muse*, edited by Jeffner Allen and Iris Marion Young, 71–84. Bloomington: Indiana Univ. Press, 1989.

Ammons, Elizabeth. *Conflicting Stories: American Women Writers at the Turn into the Twentieth Century*. New York: Oxford Univ. Press, 1991.

Anderson, Judith. " 'Nor Man It Is:' The Knight of Justice in Book V of Spenser's Faerie Queene." *PMLA* 85 (1970): 65–77.

Andors, Phyllis. *The Unfinished Liberation of Chinese Women*. Bloomington: Indiana Univ. Press, 1983.

Appleton, Jane Sophia. "Sequel to 'The Vision of Bangor in the Twentieth Century.' " 1848. Reprint. In *American Utopias: Selected Short Fiction*, edited by Arthur O. Lewis. New York: Arno, 1971.

Aristophanes. *Ecclesiazusae*, edited by R. G. Ussher. Oxford: Claredon, 1973.

Astell, Mary. *A Serious Proposal to the Ladies for the Advancement of Their True and Greatest Interests*. London: British Library, 1694.

Atheneum, The, 17 May 1890, 638.

Atwood, Margaret. *The Handmaid's Tale*. Toronto: McClelland and Stewart, 1985.

Auchendolly, 1890.

Bai Hua. "Kulian" (Unrequited love). In *Zai Bai Hua de Kulian Shijie Li* (In Bai Hua's world of unrequited love), edited by Ye Hongsheng, 212–306. Taibei: Caifeng, 1982.

―――. "Mama ya! Mama" (Mom! Mom). *Shouhuo* 4 (1980): 4-99.

―――."My Footprints." *Chinese Literature* 2 (1989): 117–120.

―――. *The Remote Country of Women*. Translated by Qingyun Wu and Thomas O. Beebee. Honolulu: Univ. of Hawaii Press, 1994.

―――. *Yuanfang Youge Nü'er Guo* (The remote country of women). Beijing: Renmin Wenxue, 1988.

―――. "Zixu" (Preface). In *Yuanfang Youge Nü'er Guo*, 1–4. Taiwan: Sanmin, 1988.

Bain, Dena C. "The *Tao Te Ching* as Background to the Novels of Ursula K. Le Guin." In *Ursula Le Guin*, edited by Herald Bloom, 211–24. New York: Chelsea House, 1986.

Ban Zhao. "Nüjie" (Commandments for women). In *Zhongguo Lidai Funü Zuopin Xuan* (Selected writings of Chinese women in history), edited by Su Zhecong, 478–81. Shanghai: Guji, 1987.

Bao Jialin. "Li Ruzhen de Nannü Pingdeng Sixiang" (Li Ruzhen's ideas of equality between men and women). *Shihuo Yuekan Fukan* 1, no. 12 (1972): 12–21.

Bao Mi. *Huang Huo* (Yellow peril). Port Credit, Ontario: Canada Mirror Books, 1991.

Barr, Marleen S. *Alien to Femininity: Speculative Fiction and Feminist Theory*. New York: Greenwood, 1987.

―――. *Feminist Fabulation: Space/Postmodern Fiction*. Iowa: Univ. of Iowa Press, 1992.

―――. "Food for Postmodern Thought: Isak Dinesen's Female Artists as Precursors to Contemporary Feminist Fabulators." In *Feminism, Utopia, and Narrative*, edited by Libby Falk Jones and Sarah Webster Goodwin, 21–33. Knoxville: Univ. of Tennessee Press, 1990.

―――, ed. *Future Females: A Critical Anthology*. Bowling Green: Bowling Green State Univ. Popular Press, 1981.

Barr, Marleen S., and Nicholas D. Smith, eds. *Women and Utopia*. Lanham: Univ. Press of America, 1983.

Bartkowski, Frances. *Feminist Utopias*. Lincoln: Univ. of Nebraska Press, 1989.

Bauer, Wolfgang. *China and the Search for Happiness: Recurring Themes in Four Thousand Years of Chinese Cultural History*. Translated by Michael Shaw. New York: Seabury, 1976.

Beauchamp, Gorman. "How America Could Become Utopia." *Canadian Review of American Studies* 18, no. 2 (1987): 273–78.

Beauvoir, Simone de. *The Second Sex*. Translated by H. M. Parshley. New York: Knopf, 1953.

Beebee, Thomas O. "Going Clarissa's Will: Samuel Richardson's Legal Genres." *International Journal for the Semiotics of Law* 2, no. 5 (1989): 159–82.

Bellamy, Edward. *Looking Backward: 2000–1887*. 1887. Reprint. New York: Modern Library, 1917.

Benson, Pamela J. "Rule, Virginia: Protestant Theories of Female Regiment in *The Faerie Queene*." *English Literary Renaissance* 15 (1985): 277–92.

Berger, Harry, Jr. "Busirane and the War Between the Sexes: An Interpretation of *The Faerie Queene* III. xi–xii." *English Literary Renaissance* 1 (1971): 99–121.

———. "The Discarding of Malbecco: Conspicuous Allusion and Cultural Exhaustion in *The Faerie Queene* III. ix–x." *Studies in Philology* 96 (1969): 135–54.

Berger, Thomas. *Regiment of Women*. New York: Simon & Schuster, 1973.

Bieman, Elizabeth. "Britomart in Book V of the *Faerie Queene*." *University of Toronto Quarterly* 37 (1968): 156–74.

Birch, Cyril. "In the Country of Women." In *Anthology of Chinese Literature II*, 187–189. New York: Grove, 1972.

Bishop, Donald H. "Universalism in Chinese Thought, Mo Tzu and Kang Yu Wei," *Chinese Culture* 42 (1976): 79–92.

Bittner, James W. "Cheonosophy, Aesthetics, and Ethics in Le Guin's *The Dispossessed: An Ambiguous Utopia*." In *No Place Else*, edited by Eric S. Rabin, Martin H. Greenberg, and Joseph D. Olander, 244–70. Carbondale: Southern Illinois Univ. Press, 1983.

Bloch, Ernst. *The Principle of Hope*. Translated by Nevile Plaice, Stephen Plaice, and Paul Knight. Cambridge, Mass.: MIT, 1986.

Boehrer, Bruce Thomas. " 'Carelesse Modestee': Chastity as Politics in Book 3 of *The Fairie Queene*." *ELH* 55, no.3 (1988): 555–73.

Booth, Michael R. *English Melodrama*. London: Herbert Jenkins, 1965.

Boss, Judith E. "The Golden Age, Cockaigne, and Utopia in *The Faerie Queene* and *The Tempest*." *The Georgia Review* 26 (1972): 145–55.

Bradley, Marion Zimmer. *The Ruins of Isis*. Norfolk: Donning/Starblaze, 1978; London: Arrow, 1980.

Brandauer, Frederick P. "Women in the *Ching-hua yuan*: Emancipation Towards a Confusion Ideal." *Journal of Asian Studies* 36 (1977): 647–60.

Broaddus, James W. "Renaissance Psychology and Britomart's Adventures in Faerie Queene III." *English Literary Renaissance* 17, no. 2 (1987): 186–206.

Brown, Charles Brockden. *Alcuin*. 1798; New York: Gehenna, 1970.

Bryant, Dorothy. *The Kin of Ata Are Waiting for You*. New York: Random House, 1976. Originally published as *The Comforter*. Berkeley: Moon Books, 1971.

Bucknall, Barbara J. *Ursula K. Le Guin*. New York: Frederick Ungar, 1981.

Budok, Gerard. *Sir Thomas More and His Utopia*. Amsterdam: Firma A. H. Kruyt, 1923.

Burckhardt, Jacob. *The Civilization of the Renaissance in Italy*. 1860. Reprint. Translated by S. G. C. Middlemore. New York: Albert and Charles Boni, 1935.

Cai Yuanpei. *Xinnian Meng* (New Year's dream). 1904. Reprint. In *Cai Yuanpei Quanji* (Complete works of Cai Yuanpei) edited by Gao Pinshou, 1:230–41. Beijing: Zhonghua Shuju, 1984.

Camden, William. *The History and Annals of Elizabeth, Queen of England*. Translated by Richard Norton. London, 1963.

Campanella, Tommaso. *The City of the Sun*. 1623. Reprint. Berkeley: Univ. of California Press, 1981.

Campbell, Marion. "Spenser's Mutabilitie Cantos and the End of The Faerie Queene." *Southern Review* 15 (1982): 46–59.

Carter, Angela. *The Sadeian Woman: An Exercise in Cultural History*. London: Virago, 1979.

Cavendish, Margaret. *The Description of a New World, Called the Blazing World*. London: J. Maxwell, 1666.

Chang, H. C. *Allegory and Courtesy in Spenser: A Chinese View*. Edinburgh: Edinburgh Univ. Press, 1955.

———. "The Women's Kingdom." In *Chinese Literature: Popular Fiction and Drama*, 405–66. Edinburgh: Edinburgh Univ. Press, 1973.

Chang, Hui-chuan. "Literary Utopia and Chinese Utopian Literature: A Generic Appraisal." Ph.D. diss., Univ. of Michigan, 1986.

Charnas, Suzy Mckee. *Motherlines*. New York: Berkeley, 1978.

Chen Dongyuan. *Zhongguo Funü Shenghuo Shi* (The history of Chinese women's life). Taibei: Taiwan Shangwu, 1966.

Chen Duansheng. *Zaisheng Yuan* (The destiny of the next life). Henan: Zhongzhou Shuhua, 1982.

Chen Tianhua. *Shizi Hou* (The roar of the lion). 1904–1905. Reprint. In *Chen Tianhua Ji* (Complete works of Chen Tianhua), 103–215. Shanghai: Minzhi Shudian, 1928.

Chen, Toyoko Yoshida. "Women in Confucian Society: A Study of Three T'an-Tz'u Narratives." Ph.D. diss., Columbia Univ., 1974.

Chen Yinke. "Lun *Zaisheng Yuan*" (On *The Destiny of the Next Life*). In *Hanliutang Ji*, 1–96. Shanghai: Guji, 1980.

Cheney, Donald. "Spenser's Hermaphrodite and the 1590 *Faerie Queene*." *PMLA* 87 (1972): 192–200.

Cheney, Patrick. " 'And Doubted Her to Deeme an Earthly Wight': Male Neoplatonic 'Magic' and the Problem of Female Identity in Spenser's Allegory of the Two Florimells." *Studies in Philology* 86, no. 3 (1989): 310–40.

Chesneaunx, Jean. "Egalitarian and Utopian Traditions in the East." *Diogenes* 62 (1968): 76–102.

Ching, Julia. "Neo-Confucian Utopian Theories and Political Ethics." *Monumenta Serica* 30 (1972): 1–56.

Chun Hui Ge, Preface. *Anbang Zhi.* Shanghai: Dada Tushu, 1936.

———. Preface. *Dingguo Zhi.* Shanghai: Dada Tushu, 1936.

———. Preface. *Fenghuang Shan.* Shanghai: Dada Tushu, 1936.

Chunfeng Wenyi, ed. *Caizi Jiaren Xiaoshuo Shulin* (Essays on the novels of scholars and beauties). Shenyang: Chunfeng Wenyi, 1985.

Chung, Sue Fawn. "The Much Maligned Empress Dowager: A Revisionist Study of the Empress Dowager Tz'u-Hsi (1835–1908)." *Modern Asian Studies* (Great Britain) 13, no.2 (1979): 177–96.

Cirillo, Albert R. "The Fair Hermaphrodite: Love-Union in the Poetry of Donne and Spenser." *Studies in English Literature, 1500–1900* 9 (1969): 81–95.

Cogell, Elizabeth Cummins. "Taoist Configurations: *The Dispossessed.*" In *Ursula K. Le Guin: Voyager to Inner Lands and to Outer Space,* edited by Joe DeBolt, 153–79. London: Kennikat, 1979.

Cooper, Edmund. *Gender Genocide.* New York: Ace Books, 1972.

Corbett, Elizabeth Burgoyne. *New Amazonia: A Foretaste of the Future.* London: Tower, 1889.

Coyle, Martin. "King Lear and *The Faerie Queene.*" *Notes and Queries* 31 (1984): 205–7.

Creel, Harrlee Glessner. *The Birth of China.* New York: John Day, 1954.

Cummins, Elizabeth. "The Land-Lady's Homebirth: Revisiting Ursula K. Le Guin's Worlds." *Science-Fiction Studies* 17, no. 2 (1990): 153–66.

Dardess, John W. "The Transformation of Messianic Revolt and the Founding of the Ming Dynasty." *Journal of Asian Studies* 29 (1970): 539–58.

Davies, Stevie. *The Feminine Reclaimed: The Idea of Woman in Spenser, Shakespeare and Milton.* Lexington: Univ. Press of Kentucky, 1986.

DeBolt, Joe, ed. *Ursula K. Le Guin: Voyager to Inner Lands and to Outer Space.* London: Kennikat, 1979.

Diamond, Irene, and Lee Quinby, eds. *Feminism and Foucault.* Boston: Northeastern Univ. Press, 1988.

Diner, Helen. *Mothers and Amazons: the First Feminine History of Culture.* Translated by John Philip Lundin. New York: Julian, 1965.

Dixie, Florence Caroline. *Aniwee; Or, the Warrior Queen: A Tale of the Araucanian Indians.* London: Richard Henry, 1890.

———. *Gloriana; Or, the Revolution of 1900.* London: Henry, 1890.

———. Interview. *Women's Penny Paper* 12 Apr. 1890.

———. *Izra, A Child of Solitude.* London: John Lang, 1906.

———. "Lady F. Dixie and Lord Salisbury." *The Woman's Herald,* 28 Feb. 1891.

———. "Modernities." *The Modern Review* 3, no. 1 (1893): 32–33.

———. "Short Papers on Woman's Position." *Women's Penny Paper,* 26 Apr. 1890.

———. "Woman's Position." *The Modern Review* 1, no. 3 (1890): 224–236.

Donaldson, Laura E. "The Eve of De-struction: Charlotte Perkins Gilman and the Feminist Re-creation of Paradise." *Women's Studies* 16 (1989): 373–87.

Du Bois, Page. *Centaurs and Amazons: Women and the Prehistory of the Great Chain of Being.* Ann Arbor: Univ. of Michigan Press, 1982.

Dunseath, Thomas K. *Spenser's Allegory of Justice in Book V of The Faerie Queene.* Princeton: Princeton Univ. Press, 1968.

DuPlessis, Rachel Blau. "The Feminist Apologues of Lessing, Piercy, and Russ." *Frontiers: A Journal of Women Studies* 4, no. 1 (1979): 1–8.

Duyvendak, J. J. L. *A Chinese "Divinia Commedia".* Leiden: E. J. Brill, 1952.

Ebrey, Patricia Buckley. *The Inner Quarters: Marriage and the Lives of Chinese Women in the Sung Period.* (Berkeley: Univ. of California Press, 1993.

Eisler, Riane. *The Chalice and the Blade: Our History, Our Future.* San Francisco: Harper & Row, 1987.

Eisenstein, Hester. *Contemporary Feminist Thought.* London: Unwin Paperbacks, 1984.

Elgin, Suzette Haden. *Native Tongue.* New York: Daw, 1984.

———. *Native Tongue II: The Judas Rose.* New York: Daw, 1987.

Elvin, Mark. "Female Virtue and the State in China." *Past and Present* 104 (1980): 111–52.

———. "The Inner World of 1830." *Daedalus* 120 (1991): 33–62.

Engels, Frederick. *The Origin of the Family, Private Property and the State.* New York: International Publishers, 1972.

Evans, Nancy J. F. "Social Criticism in the Ch'ing: The Novel of Ching-hua yuan." *Papers on China* 13 (1970): 52–66.

Fairbairns, Zoë. *Benefits.* London: Virago, 1979.

Fan Wenlan. *Zhongguo Jindai Shi* (Modern Chinese history). Beijing: Renmin, 1952.

Fang, Edith Kuang-Lo. "Utopian Tradition: East and West." *Tamkang Review* 6, nos. 2 & 7, no. 3 (1975-1976): 187–96.

Fang Ruhao (Qingxi Daoren). *Tanzhen Yishi* (Lost tales of the True Way). Jinan: Qilu Shushe, 1986.

Fang Zhong, trans. *Tao Yuanming Shiwen Xuanyi* (Gleanings from Tao Yuan-ming). Shanghai: Foreign Language Education, 1984.

Fekete, John. "The Dispossessed and Triston: Act and System in Utopian Science Fiction." *Science-Fiction Studies* 18 (1979): 129–43.

Ferguson, Margaret W., Maureen Quilligan, and Nancy J. Vickers, eds. *Rewriting the Renaissance: The Discourses of Sexual Differences in Early Modern Europe.* Chicago: Univ. of Chicago Press, 1986.

Fitting, Peter. "For Men Only: A Guide to Reading Single-Sex Worlds." *Women's Studies* 14 (1987): 101–117.

———. "Readers and Responsibilities: A Reply to Kenneth M. Roemer." *Utopian Studies* 2, no. 1–2 (1991): 24–29.

———. "Reconsiderations of the Separatist Paradigm in Recent Feminist Science Fiction." *Science-Fiction Studies* 19, no. 1 (1992): 32–48.

———. "The Turn from Utopia in Recent Feminist Fiction." In *Feminism,*

Utopia, and Narrative, edited by Libby Falk Jones and Sarah Webster Goodwin, 141–58. Knoxville: Univ. of Tennessee Press, 1990.

Foucault, Michel. *Power/Knowledge: Selected Interviews and Other Writings, 1972–1977.* New York: Pantheon, 1980.

Fox, Alice. " 'What Right Have I, a Woman?': Virginia Woolf's Reading Notes on Sidney and Spenser." In *Virginia Woolf: Centennial Essays,* edited by Elaine K. Ginsberg and Laura Moss Gottlieb, 249–56. Troy: Whitston, 1983.

Freibert, L. M. "World Views in Utopian Novels by Women." In *Women and Utopia,* edited by Marleen S. Barr and Nicholas D. Smith, 67-84. Lanham, Md.: Univ. Press of America, 1983.

Frye, Northrop. "The Structure of Imagery in *The Faerie Queene.*" *University of Toronto Quarterly* 30 (1961): 109–127.

———. "Varieties of Literary Utopias." In *Utopias and Utopian Thought,* edited by Frank E. Manuel, 25–49. Boston: Beacon, 1965.

Galik, Marian. "On the Literature Written By Chinese Women Prior to 1917." *Asian and African Studies* 15 (1979): 65–99.

Gao Dalun and Fan Yong, eds. *Zhongguo Nüxing Shi 1851–1958* (The history of Chinese feminists: 1851–1958). Chengdu: Sichuan Univ. Press, 1987.

Gao Shiyu. "Cong Tangdai Nüxing de Shehui Mianmao Tan Wu Zetian Chengdi" (Wu Zetian's throne and the social conditions for women in the Tang Dynasty). In *Wu Zetian yu Qianling* (Wu Zetian and Qianling tombs), edited by Zhang Yuliang and Hu Ji, 27–37. Shanxi: Sanqin, n.d.

Gaskell, Elizabeth Cleghorn. *Cranford.* 1863. Reprint. New York: Dutton, 1969.

Gearhart, S. M. "Future Visions: Today's Politics: Feminist Utopias in Review." In *Women in Search of Utopia: Mavericks and Mythmakers,* edited by Ruby Rohrlich and Elaine Hoffman Baruch, 296–309. New York: New York Press, 1984.

———. *The Wanderground.* Watertown: Persephone, 1978.

Geoghegan, Vincent. *Utopianism and Marxism.* New York: Methuen, 1987.

Gilbert, Sandra M., and Susan Gubar. *No Man's Land: The Place of the Woman Writer in the Twentieth Century.* New Haven: Yale Univ. Press, 1989.

Gilligan, Carol. *In a Different Voice: Psychological Theory and Women's Development.* Cambridge: Harvard Univ. Press, 1982.

Gilman, Charlotte Perkins. *Herland.* 1915. Reprint. New York: Pantheon, 1979.

———. *The Living of Charlotte Perkins Gilman.* New York: Harper & Row, 1975.

———. *Moving the Mountain.* 1911. Reprint. Westport, Conn.: Greenwood, 1968.

———. *With Her in Ourland. The Forerunner* 1–12 (1916): 6–11, 38–44, 67–73, 93–98, 123–128, 152–157, 179–185, 208–213, 237–243, 263–269, 291–297, 318–325. Reprint. Westport, Conn.: Greenwood, 1968.

———. *Women and Economics*. New York: Harper & Row, 1966.

———. "The Yellow Wallpaper." *The Charlotte Perkins Gilman Reader*. New York: Pantheon, 1980.

Goldberg, Steven. "The Universality of Patriarchy." In *Gender Sanity*, edited by Nicholas Davison, 129–45. Lanham, Md.: Univ. Press of America, 1989.

Goodman, Paul, and Percival Goodman. "Paradigm II." *Communitas*. New York: Vintage-Knopf, 1960.

Graham, A. C. "The Nung-chia 'School of the Tillers' and the Origins of Peasant Utopianism in China." *Bulletin of the School of Oriental and African Studies* 42 (1979): 66–100.

Granet, Marcel. *Chinese Civilization*. London: Kegan Paul, Trech, Trubner, 1930.

Gray, Elizabeth Dodson. *Patriarchy as a Conceptual Trap*. Wellesley: Round-table, 1982.

Griffith, Mary. *Three Hundred Years Hence*. 1836. Reprint. Boston: G. K. Hall, 1975.

Guisso, Richard W. *Wu Tse-tien and the Politics of Legitimation in T'ang China*. Bellingham: Western Washington, 1978.

Guisso, Richard W. and Stanley Johannesen, eds. *Women in China*. Youngstown, N.Y.: Philo, 1981.

Guo, Jianzhong. "SF in China." *LOCUS: The Newspaper of the Science Fiction World* 28, no. 1 (1992): 44.

Guo Moruo. "Xu *Zaisheng Yuan* Qian Shiqi Juan Jiaoding Ben" (Preface to the edited seventeen books of *The Destiny of the Next Life*). *Guangming Ribao*, 7 Aug. 1961.

———. "*Zaisheng Yuan* Qian Shiqi Juan he Tade Zuozhe Chen Duansheng" (The first seventeen books of *The Destiny of the Next Life* and its author Chen Duansheng). *Guangming Ribao*, 4 May 1961.

Guo Yanli, ed. *Qiu Jin Yanjiu Ziliao* (Research references on Qiu Jin). Jinan: Shandong Jiaoyu, 1987.

Hamilton, A. C. *The Structure of Allegory in the Faerie Queene*. Oxford: Oxford Univ. Press, 1961.

Hannah, Susan, "Womb(an) Power: Or a Faerie Tale of the Good, the Bad, and the Ugly." *RE: Artes Liberales* 5 (1978): 27–35.

Hartley, C. Gasquoine. *The Age of Mother-Power*. New York: Dodd, Mead, 1914.

He Yanxia and Wang Runsheng, eds. *Shi'er Guafu Chuzheng* (Twelve widows' expedition to the west). Henan: Henan Renmin, 1984.

Hendrischke, Barbara. "Feminism in Contemporary Chinese Women's Literature." In *Women and Literature in China*, edited by Anna Gerstlacher, Ruth Keen, Wolfang Kubin, Margit Miosga, and Jenny Schon, 397–428. Bochum: Studienverlag, 1985.

Hill, Mary A. "Charlotte Perkins Gilman: A Feminist Struggle with Womanhood." *The Massachusetts Review* 21 (1980): 503–526.

———. *The Making of a Radical Feminist: 1860–1896.* Philadelphia: Temple Univ. Press, 1980.

Ho, Koon-ki T. "Utopianism: A Unique Theme in Western Literature?—A Short Survey on Chinese Utopianism." *Tamkang Review* 13, no.1 (1982): 87–108.

———. "Why Utopias Fall: A Comparative Study of the Modern Anti-Utopian Traditions in Chinese, English, and Japanese Literature." Ph.D. diss., Univ. of Illinois, 1987.

Hossian, Rokeya Sakhawat. *Sultana's Dream, and Selections from the Secluded Ones.* New York: Feminist, 1988.

Hou Xiangye (Hou Zhi). *Zaizao Tian* (The re-creation of the heaven). Xiangye Ge edition, 1831.

Hsiao, Kung-chuan. "In and Out of Utopia: K'ang Yu-wei's Social Thought, 2: Road to Utopia." *The Chung Chi Journal* 7 (1968): 101–149.

Hsia, C. T. "The Scholarly-Novelist and Chinese Culture: A Reappraisal of *Ching hua yuan.*" In *Chinese Narrative: Critical and Theoretical Essays,* edited by Andrew Plaks, 266–305. Princeton: Princeton Univ. Press, 1977.

Hsien, Andrew C. K., and Jonathan D. Spence. "Suicide and the Family in Pre-Modern Chinese Society." In *Normal and Abnormal Behavior in Chinese Culture,* edited by Arthur Kleinman and Tsung-yi Lin, 29–47. Boston: D. Reidel, 1981.

Hsun Tzu (Xun Zi). *Hsun Tzu.* Translated by Burton Watson. New York: Columbia Univ. Press, 1963.

Hu Ji. *Wu Zetian Benzhuan* (Biography of Wu Zetian). Xi'an: Sanqin, 1986.

Hu Shi (Hu Shih). "A Chinese Declaration of the Rights of Women." *The Chinese Social and Political Science Review* 8, no. 2 (1924): 105–7. Also under the title, "A Chinese 'Gulliver' on Woman's Rights," *The People's Tribune.* New Series, 7, no. 2 (1934): 121–27

———. "Guanyu *Jinghua Yuan* de Tongxin" (Correspondence concerning *The Flowers in the Mirror*). In *Works of Hu Shih,* Vol. 3, Book 3, 580. Taibei: Yuandong Tushu, 1965.

———. "*Jinghua Yuan* de Yinlun" (An introduction to *The Flowers in the Mirror*). In *Hu Shi Wencun* (Works of Hu Shi), Vol. 3, Book 2, 400–433. Taibei: Yuandong Tushu, 1965.

Huckle, Patricia. "Women in Utopias." In *The Utopian Vision: Seven Essays on the Quincentennial of Sir Thomas More,* edited by E. D. S. Sullivan, 115–36. San Diego: San Diego State Univ. Press, 1983.

Hunter, Dianne. "Hysteria, Psychoanalysis, and Feminism: The Case of Anna O." In *The (M)other Tongue,* edited by Shirley Nelson Garner, Claire Kahane, and Madelon Sprengnether, 89–115. Ithaca: Cornell Univ. Press, 1985.

Jackson, Rosemary. *Fantasy: The Literature of Subversion.* New York: Methuen, 1981.

Jacobs, Naomi. "Beyond Stasis and Symmetry: Lessing, Le Guin, and the Remodeling of Utopia." *Extrapolation* 19, no. 1 (1988): 34–45.

Jacoby, Henry. "China as Utopia," *Schweizer Monatshefte* (Switzerland) 54, no. 2 (1974): 90–94.

Jameson, Fredric. "Of Islands and Trenches: Neutralization and the Production of Utopian Discourse." *Diacritics* 7, no. 2 (1977): 2–22.

———. "Progress Versus Utopia; Or, Can We Imagine the Future?" *Science-Fiction Studies* 27 (1982): 147–59.

———. "World Reduction in Le Guin: The Emergence of Utopian Narrative. *Science-Fiction Studies* 7 (1975): 221–31.

Ji Mulin. "Xinban Xu" (Preface to the new edition). In *Sanbao Taijian Xiyang Ji Tongsu Yanyi* (Sanbao's expedition to the western ocean), by Luo Maodeng, 1–5. Shanghai: Guji, 1982.

Jones, Libby Falk, and Sarah Webster Goodwin, eds. *Feminism, Utopia, and Narrative.* Knoxville: Univ. of Tennessee Press, 1990.

Jordan, Richard Douglas. "Una Among the Satyres: *The Faerie Queene,* 1.6." *Modern Language Quarterly* 38, no. 2 (1977): 123–31.

Kang Youwei (Kang Yuwei). *The One-World Philosophy of Kang Yu Wei* (Datong Shu). Translated by L. G. Thompson. London: George Allen & Unwin, 1958.

Kao, Hsinsheng C. *Li Ju-chen.* Boston: Twayne, 1981.

Keinhorst, Annette. "Emancipatory Projection: An Introduction to Women's Critical Utopias." *Women's Studies* 14 (1987): 91–99.

Kelso, Ruth. *Doctrine for the Lady of the Renaissance.* 1956. Reprint. Urbana: Univ. of Illinois Press, 1978.

Kendrick, Water. "Earth of Flesh, Flesh of Earth: Mother Earth in *The Faerie Queene.*" *Renaissance Quarterly* 27 (1974): 533–48.

Kessler, Carol Farley, ed. *Daring to Dream.* Boston: Pandora, 1984.

Keyser, Elizabeth. "Looking Backward: from Herland to Gulliver's Travels." *Studies in American Fiction* 11, no. 1 (1983): 31–46.

Kingston, Maxine Hong. *The Woman Warrior.* New York: Knopf, 1976.

Kleinbaum, Abby Wettan. *The War Against the Amazons.* New York: McGraw-Hill, 1983.

Knoll, S. B. "Form or Content? Reflections and the Concept of Utopia in Asian and West European Thought." *Alternative Futures* 3, no. 3 (1980): 3–14.

Knox, John. *The First Blast of the Trumpet Against the Monstrous Regiment of Women.* 1558. Reprint. London: Arber, 1878.

Kolodny, Annette. "Dancing Between Left and Right: Feminism and the Academic Minefield in the 1980s." *Feminist Studies* 14, no.3 (1988): 453–66.

Kristeva, Julia. *About Chinese Women.* New York: Urizen, 1974.

———. "Woman's Time." *Signs* 7, no. 1 (1981): 13–35.

Ku Yen. "Chiang Ch'ing's Wolfish Ambition in Publicizing 'Matriarchal Society.' " *Chinese Studies in History* 12, no. 3 (1979): 75–79.

Kumar, Krishan. *Utopia and Anti-Utopia in Modern Times.* New York: Basil Blackwell, 1987.

Lane, Ann J. "Introduction." *The Charlotte Perkins Gilman Reader.* New York: Pantheon, 1980.

Lane, Mary E. Bradley. *Mizora: A Prophecy.* 1889. Reprint. Boston: Gregg, 1975.

Lanser, Susan S. "Feminist Criticism, 'The Yellow Wallpaper,' and the Politics of Color in America." *Feminist Studies* 15, no. 3 (1989): 415–42.

Lao Zi (Lao Tzu). *The Tao of Power* (Dao De Jing). Translated by R. L. Wing. New York: Dolphin, 1986.

Lefanu, Sarah. *In the Chinks of the World Machine: Feminism and Science Fiction.* London: Women's Press, 1988.

Le Guin, Ursula K. *Always Coming Home.* New York: Harper & Row, 1985.

——. *Dancing at the Edge of the World: Thoughts of Words, Women, Places.* New York: Grove, 1989.

——. "The Day Before the Revolution." In *The Wind's Twelve Quarters,* 261-77. New York: Harper & Row, 1975.

——. *The Dispossessed: An Ambiguous Utopia.* New York: Avon, 1974.

——. "Is Gender Necessary?" In *Aurora: Beyond Equality,* edited by Vonda N. McIntyre and Susan Janice Anderson, 131-39. Greenwich: Fawcett, 1976.

——. *The Language of the Night.* Revised edition. New York: Harper Collins, 1992.

——. *The Left Hand of Darkness.* New York: Walker, 1969.

——. *The Wind's Twelve Quarters.* New York: Harper & Row, 1975.

Leith, Linda. "Women and Science Fiction." *Science-Fiction Studies* 10 (1983): 247–50.

Lerner, Gerda. *The Creation of Patriarchy.* Oxford: Oxford Univ. Press, 1986.

Levin, Harry. *The Myth of the Golden Age in the Renaissance.* Bloomington: Indiana Univ. Press, 1969.

Levy, Dore J. "Female Reigns: *The Faerie Queene* and *The Journey to the West.*" *Comparative Literature* 39, no. 3 (1987): 218–35.

Levy, Howard S. *Chinese Footbinding: The History of a Curious Erotic Custom.* London: Neville Spearman, 1966.

Lewis, C. S. *English Literature in the Sixteenth Century Excluding Drama.* Oxford: Clarendon, 1954.

Li Changzhi. "*Jinghua Yuan* Shilun" (A tentative appraisal of *Jing Hua Yuan.*" *Xinjianshe* 86 (1955): 52–58.

Li Ruzhen. *Jinghua Yuan* (The flowers in the mirror). Beijing: Renmin Wenxue, 1955.

Li Xiaofeng. "Nüxing Wenxue Tengqi Hou de Shiluo" (The pitfalls after the rise of feminist literature). *Wenxue Pinglunjia* (Jinan) 3 (1990): 49–53.

Li Youning and Zhang Yufa, eds. *Jindai Zhongguo Nüquan Yundong Shiliao 1842-1911* (Documents on the Feminist Movements in Modern China: 1842–1911). Taibei: Zhuanji Wenxue, 1976.

Liang Qichao. *Xin Zhongguo Weilai Ji* (The future of new China). 1902. Reprint. 1–86. Taiwan: Guangya, 1984.

Lin, Forest. "Utopias East and West: The Relationship Between Ancient and Modern Chinese Ideals." *Alternative Futures* 3, no. 3 (1980): 15–24.

Lin Tai-yi, trans. *The Flowers in the Mirror*. By Li Juchen (Li Ruzhen). Berkeley: Univ. of California Press, 1965.

Lin Yutang. "Feminist Thought in Ancient China." *Tien Hsia Monthly* 1, no. 2 (1935): 127–50.

———. *Looking Beyond*. New York: Prentice-Hall, 1955.

Liu Dajie. *Zhongguo Wenxue Fada Shi* (The Developing history of Chinese literature). Taibei: Zhonghua shuju, 1967.

Liu Chongyi. "Youxu" (Introduction). In *Zaisheng Yuan* (The destiny of the next life), by Chen Duansheng, 5–22. Henan: Zhongzhou Shuhua, 1982.

Liu, James J. Y. *Chinese Theories of Literature*. Chicago: Univ. of Chicago Press, 1975.

Liu Zaifu and Lin Gang. *Chuantong yu Zhongguoren*. (Tradition and the Chinese). Hong Kong: Sanlian, 1988.

Liu Zhi'e. *Zheng He*. Jiangsu: Guji, 1984.

Loris, Michelle Carbone. "Images of Women in Books III and IV of Spenser's *Faerie Queene*." *Mid-Hudson Language Studies* 8 (1985): 9–19.

Lu Gong, ed. *Liang Shanbai he Zhu Yingtai Yanchang Gushi Ji* (A collection of Liang Shanbai and Zhu Yingtai's tales in ballard form). Shanghai: Guji, 1985.

Lu Shulun and Zhu Shaohua. "Qianyan" (Foreword). In *Sanbao Taijian Xiyang Ji Tongsu Yanyi* (Sanbao's expedition to the western ocean), by Luo Maodeng, 6–18. Shanghai: Guji, 1982.

Lu Xun. *A Brief History of Chinese Fiction*. Peking: Foreign Languages, 1976.

———. " Chu Guan" (Passing the pass) and "Qi Si" (The rising dead). In *Lu Xun Sanshi Nian Ji* (A collection of Lu Xun: thirty years' works) Vol. 4, 117–31, 149–64. Beijing: Xinyi, 1971.

———. *Gushi Xinbian* (Retold Stories) Beijing: Renmin Wenxue, 1978.

Lucas, R. Valerie. "*Hic Mulier:* The Female Transvestite in Early Modern England." *Renaissance and Reformation* 12, no.1 (1988): 65–84.

Luo Maodeng. *Sanbao Taijian Xiyang Ji Tongsu Yanyi* (Sanbao's expedition to the western ocean). Shanghai: Guji, 1982.

Manuel, Frank. E., ed. *Utopias and Utopian Thought*. Boston: Beacon, 1965.

Manuel, Frank. E, and Manuel, F. P. *Utopian Thought in the Western World*. Cambridge, Mass.: Belknap, 1979.

Marcuse, Herbert. *An Essay on Liberation*. Boston: Beacon, 1969.

———. *Five Lectures*. Boston: Beacon, 1970.

Marinelli, Peter V. *Pastoral*. London: Methuen, 1971.

Marx, Karl, and Frederick Engels. *The Communist Manifesto*. London: Penguin, 1988.

Maynard, Mary. "Privilege and Patriarchy: Feminist Thought in the Nineteenth Century." In *Sexuality and Subordination: Interdisciplinary Studies of Gender in the Nineteenth Century*, edited by Susan Mendus and Jane Rendall. London: Routledge, 1989. 221–47.

McCormack, Win, and Anne Mendel. "Creating Realistic Utopias: The Obvious Trouble with Anarchism Is Neighbors." *Seven Days,* 11 April 1977: 39–40.

McMahon, Keith. *Causality and Containment in Seventeenth-Century Chinese Fiction.* New York: E. J. Brill, 1988.

Mears, Amelia Garland. *Mercia, the Astronomer Royal; A Romance.* London: Simpkin, Marshall, Hamilton Kent, 1895.

Meisner, Maurice. "Maoist Utopianism and the Future of Chinese Society." *International Journal* (Canada) 26, no. 3 (1971): 535–55.

———. *Marxism, Maoism and Utopianism:* Madison: Univ. of Wisconsin Press, 1982.

Mellor, Anne K. "On Feminist Utopias." *Women's Studies* 9 (1982): 241–62.

Mill, John Stuart. *The Subjection of Women.* London, 1869.

Miller, Margaret. "The Ideal Woman in Two Feminist Science-Fiction Utopias." *Science-Fiction Studies* 10 (1983): 191–98.

Minnet, Cora. *The Day After Tomorrow.* London: F. V. White, 1911.

Modern Review, The, 1890.

Modleski, Tania. *Feminism Without Women: Culture and Criticism in a "Postfeminist" Age.* New York: Routledge, 1991.

Moi, Toril. *Sexual/Textual Politics: Feminist Literary Theory.* New York: Routledge, 1985.

Montrose, Louis Adrian. "The Elizabethan Subject and the Spenserian Text." In *Literary Theory/Renaissance Texts,* edited by Patricia Parker and David Quit, 303–40. Baltimore: Johns Hopkins Univ. Press, 1986.

———. " 'Shaping Fantasies': Figurations of Gender and Poet in Elizabethan Culture." *Representations* 1, no. 2 (1983): 61–94.

More, Thomas. *Utopia. The Complete Works of St. Thomas More.* New Haven: Yale Univ. Press, 1965.

Moylan, Tom. *Demand the Impossible: Science Fiction and the Utopian Imagination.* New York: Methuen, 1986.

Needham, Joseph. *Science and Civilization in China.* Cambridge: Cambridge Univ. Press, 1956.

Neely, Carol Thomas. "Constructing the Subject: Feminist Practice and the New Renaissance Discourses." *English Literary Renaissance* 18 (1988): 5–18.

Niu, Zhiping. "Wu Zetian yu Tangdai Funü" (Wu Zetian and the Tang women." In *Wu Zetian yu Qianling* (Wu Zetian and Qianling tombs), edited by Zhang Yuliang and Hu Ji, 38–47. Shanxi: Sanqin, n.d.

Nudelman, Rafail. "An Approach to the Structure of Le Guin's SF." *Science-Fiction Studies* 2 (1975): 210–20.

Nye, Andrea. *Feminist Theory and the Philosophies of Man.* London: Croom Helm, 1988.

Ono Kazuko. *Chinese Women in a Century of Revolution, 1850–1950.* Edited by Joshua A. Fogel. Stanford: Stanford Univ. Press, 1989.

Orwell, George. *Nineteen Eighty-four.* New York: New American Library, 1971.

Osenberg, Frederick Charles. "The Idea of the Golden Age and the Decay of the World in the English Renaissance." Ph.D. diss., Univ. of Illinois, 1939.

Patai, Daphne. "Beyond Defensiveness: Feminist Research Strategies." In *Women and Utopia*. edited by Marleen S. Baar and Nicholas D. Smith, 148–69. Lanham, Md., Univ. Press of America, 1983.

Pearson, Carol S. "Beyond Governance: Anarchist Feminism in the Utopian Novels of Dorothy Bryant, Marge Piercy and Mary Staton." *Alternative Futures* 4, no. 1 (1981): 126–35.

———. "Coming Home: Four Feminist Utopias and Patriarchal Experience." In *Future Females: A Critical Anthology*, edited by Marleen S. Barr, 63–70. Bowling Green: Bowling Green State Univ. Popular Press, 1981.

———. "Women's Fantasies and Feminist Utopias." *Frontiers* 1, no. 3 (1977): 50–61.

Pepper, Suzanne. "Review Articles: Liberation and Understanding: New Books on the Uncertain Status of Women in the Chinese Revolution." *China Quarterly* 108 (1986): 704–18.

Personal Rights Journal, June 1890: 61.

Pfaelzer, Jean. *The Utopian Novel in America 1886–1896: The Politics of Form*. Pittsburgh: Univ. of Pittsburgh Press, 1984.

Phillips, James E., Jr. "The Background of Spenser's Attitude Toward Women Rulers." *Huntington Library Quarterly* 5 (1942): 5–32.

———. "The Woman Ruler in Spenser's *Faerie Queene*." *Huntington Library Quarterly* 5 (1942): 211–34.

Phillis, Andors. *The Unfinished Revolution of Chinese Women, 1949–1980*. Bloomington: Indiana Univ. Press, 1983.

Piercy, Marge. *Woman on the Edge of Time*. New York: Fawcett Crest, 1976.

Pisan, Christine de. *The Book of the City of Ladies*. New York: Persea, 1982.

Plato. *Plato's Republic*. Translated by Desmond Lee. Baltimore: Penguin, 1974.

Pomeroy, Sarah B. *Goddesses, Whores, Wives, and Slaves: Women in Classical Antiquity*. New York: Schocken, 1975.

Qi Ming. "Nüren de Jiazhi: Gongguan zai Zhongguo" (The value of women: ladies of public relations in China). *Zhongguo Zuojia* 44, no. 2 (1992): 39–63.

Qiu Jin. *Jingwei Shi* (Pebbles that fill up the sea). In *Qiu Jin Ji* (Works of Qiu Jin), 117–60. Hong Kong: Changfeng Tushu, 1974.

Qiu Xinru. *Bi Shenghua* (Flowers from the brush). Henan: Zhongzhou Guji, 1984.

Quilligan, Maureen. "The Comedy of Female Authority in *The Faerie Queene*." *English Literary Renaissance* 17 (1987): 156–71.

Ramazanoglu, Caroline. *Feminism and the Contradictions of Oppression*. London: Routledge, 1989.

Rankin, Mary Backus. "The Emergence of Women at the End of the Ch'ing: The Case of Ch'iu Jin." In *Women in Chinese Society*, edited by Margery Wolf and Roxane Witke, 39–66. Stanford: Stanford Univ. Press, 1975.

Reeve, Clara. *Plans of Education; with Remarks on the System of Other Writers*. London: 1792.

Relf, Jan. "Women in Retreat: The Politics of Separatism in Women's Literary Utopias." *Utopian Studies* 2, no. 1 & 2 (1991): 131–46.

Rhodes, Jewell Parker. "Ursula Le Guin's *The Left Hand of Darkness*: Androgyny and the Feminist Utopia." In *Women and Utopia* edited by Marleen S. Barr and Nicholas D. Smith, 108–120. Lanham, Md.: Univ. Press of America, 1983.

Ricci, N. P. "The Ends of Woman." *Canadian Journal of Political and Social Theory* 11, no. 3 (1987): 11–27.

Roberts, Brian. *Ladies in the Veld*. London: John Murray, 1965.

———. *The Mad Bad Line*. London: Hamish Hamilton, 1981.

Robinson, Lillian S. *Monstrous Regiment: The Lady Knight in Sixteenth-Century Epic*. New York: Garland, 1985.

Roche, Thomas P., Jr. *The Kindly Flame: A Study of the "Faerie Queene" III and IV*. Princeton: Princeton Univ. Press, 1964.

Roemer, Kenneth, ed. *America as Utopia*. New York: Burt, Franklin, 1981.

Rohrlich, Ruby, and Elaine Hoffman Baruch, eds. *Women in Search of Utopia: Mavericks and Mythmakers*. New York: New York Press, 1984.

Ropp, Paul S. *Dissent in Early Modern China: Ju-lin wai-shih and Ch'ing Social Criticism*. Ann Arbor: Univ. of Michigan Press, 1981.

Russ, Joanna. "Amor Vincit Foeminam: The Battle of the Sexes in Science Fiction." *Science-Fiction Studies* 7 (1980): 2–15.

———. *The Female Man*. New York: Bantam, 1975.

———. "Recent Feminist Utopias." In *Future Females: A Critical Anthology*, edited by Marleen S. Barr, 71-85. Bowling Green: Bowling Green State Univ. Popular Press, 1981.

Salmonson, Jessica Amanda, ed. *Amazons*. New York: Daw, 1979.

———. *Amazons II*. New York: Daw, 1982.

Sanday, Peggy Reeves. *Female Power and Male Dominance: On the Origins of Sexual Inequality*. Cambridge: Cambridge Univ. Press, 1981.

Sargent, Lyman Tower. "English and American Utopias: Similarities and Differences." *Journal of General Education* 28, no. 1 (1976): 16-22.

———. "A New Anarchism: Social and Political Ideas in Some Recent Feminist Eutopias." In *Women and Utopia*, edited by Marleen S. Barr and Nicholas D. Smith, 3–33. Lanham, Md.: Univ. Press of America, 1983.

———. "Featured Discussion of Ursula K. Le Guin's 'Omelas.' " *Utopian Studies* 2, no. 1–2 (1991): 1–62.

Scharnhorst, Gary. *Charlotte Perkins Gilman*. Boston: Twayne, 1985.

Schleiner, Winfried. "*Divina virago*: Queen Elizabeth as an Amazon." *Studies in Philology* 75 (1978): 164–79.

Schnorrenberg, Barbara Brandon. "A Paradise Like Eve's: Three Eighteenth Century English Female Utopias." *Women's Studies* 9 (1982): 263–73.

Scholes, Robert. "A Footnote to Russ's Recent Feminist Utopias." In *Future Females: A Critical Anthology*, edited by Marleen S. Barr, 86–87. Bowling Green: Bowling Green State Univ. Popular Press, 1981.

Schram, Stuart R. "To Utopia and Back: A Cycle in the History of the Chinese Communist Party." *China Quarterly* 87 (1981): 404–39.

Scott, Sarah Robinson. *A Description of Millenium Hall, and the Country Adjacent*. 1762. Reprint. New York: Bookman Associates, 1955.

Shatin, N. T. "In and Out of Utopia: K'ang Yu-wei's Social Thought, 2: Road to Utopia." *The Chung Chi Journal* 7 (Hong Kong, 1968): 101–49.

Sheldon, Alice (James Tiptree, Jr.). "Houston, Houston, Do you Read?" In *Star Songs of an Old Primate*, 164–226. New York: Ballantine, 1978.

Silberman, Lauren. "The Hermaphrodite and the Metamorphosis of Spenserian Allegory." *English Literary Renaissance* 17 (1987): 207–23.

———. "Singing Unsung Heroines: Androgynous Discourse in Book 3 of *The Faerie Queene*." In *Rewriting the Renaissance: The Discourses of Sexual Differences in Early Modern Europe*, edited by Margaret W. Ferguson, Maureen Quilligan, and Nancy J. Vickers, 259–71. Chicago: Univ. of Chicago Press, 1986.

Silvani, Giovanna. "Woman in Utopia From More to Huxley." *Requiem pour l'utopie? Tendances autodestructives du paradigme utopique*. Paris: Nizet, 1986.

Sima Guang. *Zizhi Tongjian* (Comprehensive mirror for aid in government). 1084. Reprint. Shanghai: Feiying Guan, 1888.

Smith, Marsha A. "The Disoriented Male Narrator and Social Conversion: Charlotte Perkins Gilman's Feminist Utopian Vision." *ATQ* (1989): 123–33.

Song Zhaolin. *Gongfu Zhi yu Gongqi Zhi* (Polyandry and polygyny). Shanghai: Sanlian Shudian, 1990.

Spenser, Edmund. *The Faerie Queene*. Edited by A. C. Hamilton. New York: Longman, 1977.

———. "Letter to Raleigh." In Spenser, 737–38.

Spivack, Charlotte. *Ursula Le Guin*. Boston: Twayne, 1984.

Stacey, Judith. *Patriarchy and Socialist Revolution in China*. Berkeley: Univ. of California Press, 1983.

Staton, Mary. *From the Legend of Biel*. New York: Ace, 1975.

Staton, Shirley F. "Reading Spenser's *Faerie Queene*—in a Different Voice." In *Ambiguous Realities: Women in the Middle Ages and Renaissance*, edited by Carole Levin and Jeanie Watson, 145–62. Detroit: Wayne State Univ. Press, 1987.

Sterling, Eric. "Spenser's *Faerie Queene*." *Explicator* 46, no. 3 (1988): 9–11.

Su Zhecong, ed. *Zhongguo Lidai Funü Zuopin Xuan* (Selected writings of Chinese women in history). Shanghai: Guji, 1987.

Sun Jiaxun. *Jinghua Yuan Gong'an Bianyi* (Controversies on *The Flowers in the Mirror*). Jinan: Qilu Shushe, 1984.

Sung, Marina Hsiu-wen. "The Chinese Lieh-nü Tradition." In *Women in China*, edited by Richard W. Guisso and Stanley Johannesen, 63–74. Youngstown, N.Y.: Philo, 1981.

———. "The Narrative Art of 'Tsai-sheng-yuan': A Feminist Vision in Traditional Confucian Society." Ph.D. diss., Univ. of Wisconsin, 1988.

Suzuki, Mihoko. *Metamorphoses of Helen: Authority, Difference, and the Epic.* Ithaca: Cornell Univ. Press, 1990.

Swift, Jonathan. *Gulliver's Travels.* New York: Oxford Univ. Press, 1977.

Tan Zhengbi. *Tanci Xulu* (Plots of *Tanci*). Shanghai: Guji, 1981.

————. *Zhongguo Nüxing Wenxue Shihua* (History of Chinese women's literature). Tianjin: Baihua Wenyi, 1984.

————, and Tan Xun, comps. *Pingtan Tongkao* (Historical Comments on *Pingtan*). Beijing: Zhongguo Quyi, 1985.

Tang Xianzu. *The Peony Pavilion.* Translated by Cyril Birch. Bloomington: Indiana Univ. Press, 1980.

Thompson, William. *Appeal of one half the human race, women, against the pretensions of the other half, men, to retain them in political, and thence in civil and domestic slavery, in reply to a paragraph of Mr. Mill's celebrated "article on government."* London, 1825.

Thomsen, Christen Kold. "Le Guin's Science Fiction Fantasies Defended." In *Inventing the Future: Science Fiction in the Context of Cultural History and Literary Theory,* edited by Ib Johansen and Peter Ronnov-Jessen, 59–72. Aarhus, Denmark: Univ. of Aarhus, 1985.

Tonkin, Humphrey. "Spenser's Garden of Adonis and Britomart's Quest." *PMLA* 88 (1973): 408–17.

Urbanowicz, Victor. "Personal and Political in *The Dispossessed.*" In *Ursula Le Guin,* edited by Herald Bloom, 145–54. New York: Chelsea House, 1986.

Waley, Arthur. *Three Ways of Thought in Ancient China.* Garden City: Doubleday, 1956.

Walsh, Correa Moylan. *Feminism.* New York: Harper & Row, 1962.

Wang, Pi-twan H. "Utopian Imagination in Traditional Chinese Fiction." Ph.D. diss., University of Wisconsin, 1981.

Wang Jianhui and Yi Xuejin, eds. *Zhongguo Wenhua Zhishi Jinghua* (The essentials of Chinese culture). Hubei: Renmin, 1989.

Wang Zhangling. *Bai Hua de Lu* (The "path" of Bai Hua). Taibei: Liming Wenhua, 1982.

Welch, Holmes. *Taoism: The Parting of the Way.* Boston: Beacon, 1966.

Wells, Robin Headlam. *Spenser's Faerie Queene and the Cult of Elizabeth.* London and Canberra: Croom Helm, 1983.

Whyte-Melville, George J. *Sarchedon: A Legend of the Great Queen.* London: W. Thacker, 1875.

Widmer, Ellen. *The Margins to Utopia: Shui-hu hou-chuan and the Literature of Ming Loyalism.* Cambridge: Harvard Univ. Press, 1987.

Widmer, Kingsley. "The Dialectics of Utopianism: Le Guin's *The Dispossessed.*" *Liberal and Fine Arts Review* 3, no. 1–2 (1983): 1–11.

Wiesner, Mary E. "Spinsters and Seamstresses: Women in Cloth and Clothing Production." In *Rewriting the Renaissance: The Discourses of Sexual Differences in Early Modern Europe,* edited by Margaret W. Ferguson, Maureen Quilligan, and Nancy J. Vickers, 190–205. Chicago: Univ. of Chicago Press, 1986.

Wilhelm, Richard. *A Short History of Chinese Civilization*. New York: Kenni-kat, 1970.

Williams, Kathleen. "Venus and Diana: Some Uses of Myth in *The Faerie Queene*." *Journal of English Literary History* 28 (1961): 101–21.

Williams, Lynn F. "Everyone Belongs to Everyone Else: Marriage and the Family in Recent American Utopias 1965–1985." *Utopian Studies* vol. 1, edited by Arthur O. Lewis. University Park: Pennsylvania State Univ. Press, 1987.

Willig, Rosette F., trans. *The Changelings: A Classical Court Tale*. Stanford: Stanford Univ. Press, 1983.

Wilson, Christopher P. "Charlotte Perkins Gilman's Steady Burgers: The Ter-rain of Herland." *Women's Studies* 12 (1986): 271–92.

Wilson, Jesse. *When the Women Reign*. London: Arthur H. Stockwell, 1909.

Wollstonecraft, Mary. *A Vindication of the Rights of Woman*. 1791. Reprint. New York: Norton, 1975.

Woman's Herald, The, 1890.

Woodbridge, Linda. *Women and the English Renaissance: Literature and the Nature of Womankind, 1540–1620*. Chicago: Univ. of Illinois Press, 1984.

Woods, Susanne. "Spenser and the Problem of Women's Rule." *Huntington Library Quarterly* 48 (1985): 141–58.

———. "Amazonia Tyranny: Spenser's Radigund and Diachronic Mimesis." In *Playing with Gender: A Renaissance Pursuit*, edited by Allison P. Coudert and Maryanne C. Horowitz, 52–61. Urbana: Univ. of Illinois Press, 1991.

Woolf, Virginia. *Orlando*. New York: Harcourt Brace Jovanovich, 1956.

———. *A Room of One's Own*. 1929. Reprint. London: Hogarth, 1967.

Wright, Celeste Turne. "The Amazons in Elizabeth Literature." *Studies in Philology* 37 (1940): 433–56.

Wu, Qingyun. "Feminist Potentialities and Dilemmas: *The Changelings* and *The Destiny of the Next Life*." In *Proceedings of the Thirteenth Interna-tional Symposium on Asian Studies*, 211–21. Hong Kong: Asian Research Service, 1991.

———. "Validity of Western Feminist Theories in Interpreting Chinese Texts." A paper presented at the Second Conference of the American Association of Chinese Comparative Literature. Los Angeles: Univ. of California, 1992.

Xiang Da (Xiang Jueming). "Lun Luo Maodeng Zhu *Sanbao Taijian Xiyang Ji Tongsu Yanyi*" (On Luo Maodeng's *San Bao's Expedition to the West-ern Ocean*). In *Sanbao Taijian Xiyang Ji Tongsu Yanyi* (Sanbao's expe-dition to the western ocean), by Luo Maodeng, 1291–97. Shanghai: Guji, 1982.

———. "Guanyu *Sanbao Taijian Xia Xiyang* de Jizhong Ziliao" (Sources for *Sanbao's Expedition to the Western Ocean*). *Xiaoshuo Yuebao* 20, no. 1 (Jan. 1929).

Xinhua Cidian (New Chinese dictionary). Beijing: Shangwu, 1985.

Xu Tianxiao. *New History of Chinese Women*. Shanghai: Shen Zhou, 1913.

Xu Wei. *Nü Zhuangyuan* (The female number one scholar). In *Sisheng Yuan*, edited by Zhou Zhongming, 62–106. 1588. Reprint. Shanghai: Guji, 1984.

Xu Yingshi. *Chen Yinke Wannian Shiwen Shizheng* (On the poems and essays of Chen Yinke in his late years). Taibei: Shibao Wenhua, 1984.

Yan Ruxian, and Song Zhaolin. *Yongning Naxi Zu de Muxi Zhi* (Yongning Naxi's matrilineality). Yunnan: Renmin, 1983.

Yang Xiao. "From SF world to World SF in China." *LOCUS* 28, no. 1 (1992): 43.

Yang Yi. *Zhongguo Xiandai Xiaoshuo Shi* (History of modern Chinese fiction). Beijing: Renmin Wenxue, 1986.

Yao, Esther S. Lee. *Chinese Women: Past and Present*. Mesquite, Tex.: Ide House, 1983.

You Xinxiong, ed. *Jing Hua Yuan* (The flowers in the mirror). By Li Ruzhen. Taiwan: Sanmin Shuju, 1983.

Yu, Anthony C., trans. *The Journey to the West*. 2 vols. Chicago: Univ. of Chicago Press, 1977–1983.

Yu, Wang-luen, and Ho, Peng-yoke. "Knowledge of Mathematics and Science in Ching-hua-yuan." *Orieus Extremus* 21, no. 2 (1974): 217–36.

Yuan Ke, comp. *Gu Shenhua Xuanshi* (Ancient myths of China). Beijing: Renmin wenxue, 1979.

———, ed. *Shan Hai Jing* (The wonders of the mountains and rivers). Shanghai: Guji, 1985.

Zaki, Hoda M. "Utopia and Ideology in *Daughters of a Coral Dawn* and Contemporary Feminist Utopias." *Women's Studies* 14, no. 2 (1987): 119–33.

Zamyatin, Eugene. *We*. Translated by Gregory Zilboorg. Boston: Gregg, 1975.

Zhan Chengxu, Wang Chengquan, Li Jinchun, and Liu Longchu. *Yongning Naxi Zu de Azhu Hunyin he Muxi Jiating* (Yongning Naxi's Azhu marriage and matrilineal family). Shanghai: Renmin, 1980.

Zhang Dejun. "Chenduan Sheng de Muqin Dui Ta Zai Wenxue Shang de Yingxiang" (The influence of Chen Duansheng's mother on her literary career) *Guangming Ribao*, 25 July 1961.

Zhang Yuliang and Hu Ji, ed. *Wu Zetian yu Qianling* (Wu Zetian and Qianling tombs). Shanxi: Sanqin, n.d.

Zhang Zhenli. *Zhongyuan Gudian Shenhua Liubian Lunkao* (On the transformations of ancient myths in the Central Plains). Shanghai: Wenyi, 1991.

Zhao Jingshen. "Sanbao Taijian Xiyang Ji" (On Sanbao's expedition to the western ocean), 1935. Reprint. In *Sanbao Taijian Xiyang Ji Tongsu Yanyi* (Sanbao's expedition to the western ocean), by Luo Maodeng, 1298–1328. Shanghai: Guji, 1982.

———. "Zhongguo Gudian Jiangchang Wenxue Congshu Xu" (Preface: the classical telling and singing literature in China). In *Zaisheng Yuan* (The destiny of the next life), by Chen Duansheng, 1–4. Henan: Zhongzhou Shuhua, 1982.

Zheng Wenguang. "Speech by Zheng Wenguang." *LOCUS* 28, no. 1 (1992): 43.

Zheng Zhenduo. *Zhongguo Suwenxue Shi* (History of Chinese popular literature) Shanghai: Shanghai Shudian, 1984.

Zhuang Zi. *Zhuang Zi*. Taibei: Taiwan Shangwu, 1968.

Zimmerman, Bonnie. "What Has Never Been: An Overview of Lesbian Feminist Criticism." In *Making a Difference: Feminist Literary Criticism*, edited by Gayle Greene and Coppélia Kahn, 177–210. New York: Methuen, 1985.

Zipes, Jack. *Breaking the Magic Spell: Radical Theories of Folk and Fairy Tales*. London: Heinemann, 1979.

Index